CW00515455

POLITICAL ISLAM OBSERVED

FRÉDÉRIC VOLPI

POLITICAL ISLAM
OBSERVED

HURST AND COMPANY, LONDON

First published in the United Kingdom in 2010 by
C. Hurst & Co. (Publishers) Ltd.,
41 Great Russell Street, London, WC1B 3PL
© Frédéric Volpi 2010
All rights reserved.
Printed in India

The right of Frédéric Volpi to be identified as the author
of this publication is asserted by him in accordance with
the Copyright, Designs and Patents Act, 1988.

A Cataloguing-in-Publication data record for this book
is available from the British Library.

ISBN: 978-1-84904-060-0 *hardback*
      978-1-84904-061-7 *paperback*

www.hurstpub.co.uk

This book is printed using paper from registered, sustainable
and managed sources.

à Jean et Janine
à Louis-Marie et Marie-Ange

CONTENTS

ACKNOWLEDGEMENTS

This book is the product of several years of reflection on the topic of political Islam. It is also the result of a fair amount of frustration with academic and policy debates that purport to address the issue of Islamism. The last ten years have been particularly fertile for the research on political Islam. Yet, as is often the case when a topic becomes particularly fashionable and/or policy relevant, the quantity of research produced was not always matched by quality. In 2001, as I was finishing my book on the Islamist revolt in Algeria, the literature on political Islam was relatively well-bounded, as befitted a topic of marginal relevance to world politics at the time. A mere nine years later, Islamism has become a phenomena so widely investigated that hardly a branch of the social sciences lacks its cohort of experts with definite views on the matter. In some cases, this reflects a genuine renewal of interest and of research on the topic; in many other instances, the notion of Islamism is simply used for interested motives. All in all, however, this multiplication of narratives about political Islam created more confusion than it generated understanding of the phenomenon. This book, then, is an attempt at introducing a modicum of order among the many disciplinary views on political Islam that have gained recognition in contemporary social science debates.

Over the last few years I have most benefited from the discussions that I have had on this topic with many colleagues working on similar themes. The views that I have formed regarding political Islam and its representation in academic and policy discourses owe much to them. For the past five years, I have been fortunate enough to enjoy the collegial and stimulating intellectual atmosphere of the School of International Relations at St Andrews University. There, I have particularly benefited from my involvement in the Institute for Middle Eastern and Central Asian

Studies. For the last three years, it has also been a privilege to lead the research network of the British Society for Middle Eastern Studies on 'domination, expression and liberation'. This network provided a wealth of opportunities to engage with very different views and scholars of the Middle East. An earlier version of a section of this manuscript was published as the following journal article: 'Political Islam in the Mediterranean: the view from democratization studies', *Democratization* 16 (1) 2009, pp. 20–38.

I simply have had too many interlocutors in the last few years to individually list all those who contributed to shaping my current views on Islamism. I would like to thank my colleagues at St Andrews, for all the interesting debates we have had on this topic, and most particularly Sally Cummings and Ray Hinnebusch at the Institute for Middle Eastern and Central Asian Studies. I would also like to thank all the contributors to the British Society for Middle Eastern Studies network. In this context, I am particularly appreciative of extended discussions that I have had with Salwa Ismail, Peter Mandaville, Emma Murphy, Armando Salvatore and Salman Sayyid. More generally, I have also benefited over the years from the insights of colleagues whose views on Islamism have constructively challenged my own. In this respect, thanks are due to Francesco Cavatorta, Robert Gleave, John Horgan, Luis Martinez, Andrea Teti, Ben Thirkell-White, Bryan Turner and Sami Zemni. Finally, I am very grateful to Francesco Cavatorta, Ray Hinnebusch, Peter Mandaville, Jeffrey Murer and Salman Sayyid for reading and commenting on various chapters of this book. These friends and colleagues have had a direct impact on the writing of this book. The misunderstandings and misrepresentations that the book may contain are of course entirely my own.

1

INTRODUCTION

'WE HAVE FACTS AND DATA'

In his thought-provoking *Globalized Islam*, Olivier Roy points out that there are serious methodological difficulties in analyzing an Islamic phenomenon taking place on a global scale. He ponders on how researchers can 'isolate and categorise the complex and multilevel practices of more than one billion Muslims living in so many different social, cultural and geographical conditions.' Roy finds comfort in the fact that as long as the political dimension of this phenomenon can be analyzed separately from the other processes, there is hope for such a global investigation. He suggests that if the analysts remain in the field of political sciences, they can head off criticism that this topic is simply too large and diverse to be analysed with a single conceptual framework. For Roy:

Islamist movements are organised; they have an official ideology and program, and official publications; they participate in political life; their leaders (who write and speak) are known public figures. There are sometimes elections, opinion polls, demonstrations, arrests (more often) and trials. We can use statistical data, biographies, texts and interviews. In other words, we have facts and data.[1]

The present book challenges this apparently straightforward suggestion about political Islam. It does so not by querying the validity of the 'facts and data' that academic scholarship can yield. Instead, it is asking: who is

[1] Olivier Roy, *Globalized Islam: The Search for a New Ummah* (London: Hurst & Co, 2004), pp. 6–7.

this 'we' that 'has' all this information? While most of the research focusing on this phenomenon, in the narrow sense of 'politicized' Islamic activities, is keen nowadays to emphasize the heterogeneity of the field and of the dynamics that animate it, little is being said about the heterogeneity of those academics, analysts, policy makers, and other opinionated participants who form the 'observing community'. Commonly, when querying the political activities of the Islamists, very little is said about the very notion of 'Politics'. There is a resounding silence regarding how various disciplines in the social sciences define the 'political' that Islamic actors are, rightly or wrongly, supposed to be engaging with.

In many ways, this is not a very novel predicament. Repeatedly it is useful to consider the role of the theoretical frameworks that structure contemporary debates. Making a distinction between problem-solving approaches and critical ones, Robert Cox reminded international relations specialists in the final years of the Cold War that 'theory is always *for* someone and *for* some purpose'[2] This reminder is clearly highly relevant for all the debates surrounding political Islam. In part, as Roxanne Euben stresses, 'current scholarship on fundamentalism is an exercise in power: the power to construct and control a subject that has little opportunity to contest either the interpretation or the terms of the discourse; the power to dictate the parameters of the field, from which experts regularly pronounce the identity, meaning and function of a movement without reference to the adherents' own understanding of the connection between action and meaning'.[3] Any quest for a holistic account of Islamism is itself taking a particular perspective on the issue, and merely recognizing that the phenomenon is multifaceted, no matter how adroitly one presents it, does not amount to overcoming this perspectival stance. Rather than attempting to brush perspectivism under the carpet, it may be more sensible to address it frontally. Hence, in social anthropology Talal Asad proposed an investigation of the 'secular' that could be launched from a religious tradition. In this fashion, he proposed to construct a more com-

---

[2] Robert C Cox, 'Social forces, states and world orders: beyond international relations theory', *Millennium: Journal of International Studies* 10 (2) 1981, pp. 126–55.

[3] Roxanne L. Euben, *Enemy within the Mirror: Islamic Fundamentalism and the Limits of Modern Rationalism: A Work of Comparative Political Theory* (Princeton: Princeton University Press, 1999), p. 43.

prehensive picture of the societal interactions that are involved in religious and secular understandings of one another.[4]

The title of the present book is also a wink to another well-known work of social anthropology by Clifford Geertz; whom Asad precisely criticised for proposing his own all-encompassing account of religion and Islam.[5] In *Islam Observed*, Geertz introduced some of the key themes that would constitute the foundations of his argument in his seminal *The Interpretation of Culture*.[6] He stressed that the study of religious activity—Islam in this case—was itself a social construct, relying as much on its explicit codes, implicit practices and shared understanding as those of the anthropologists studying it. He argued that Islamic culture, like all cultural constructs, was interpreted through and through, and was not most meaningfully described in terms of the logical outcomes of various hard 'facts'. The 'observation' of political Islam then, taking the cue from Geertz, is a two-sided process: a 'political' evolution is been observed from a (western) social science perspective, while at the same time social and political theory itself changes in the light of its own critical self-examination. In their turn, Muslims are observing—i.e. following—a more or less 'political' version of Islam in relation to both an evolving theological doctrine, and the gaze of Muslim and non-Muslim observers.[7] The two processes are shaping each other over time, producing a never-ending debate about what is internal and external to contemporary Islam.

Reflecting on the changes that occurred in social anthropology in the last fifty years, Geertz subsequently noted that the object of study and

---

[4] Talal Asad, *Formations of the Secular: Christianity, Islam, Modernity* (Stanford: Stanford University Press, 2003).

[5] In particular, Asad criticises the static nature of Geertz' explanations; a point of particular relevance for political Islam, as Geertz ultimately presented it as an irruption of the 'ideological' into the ordinary form of the 'religious'.

[6] Clifford Geertz, *Islam Observed: Religious Development in Morocco and. Indonesia* (Chicago: University of Chicago Press, 1968); *The Interpretation of Culture* (New York: Basic Books, 1973).

[7] Asef Bayat notes that whilst for most of the nineteenth century social scientists were busy erasing the analytical boundaries between studies of religious and non-religious communities, at the end of the twentieth century they are concerned with differentiating between the religious and the 'more religious'. Asef Bayat, *Making Islam Democratic: Social Movements and the Post-Islamist Turn* (Stanford: Stanford University Press, 2007).

type of explanation that the study of religion was looking for, changed quite dramatically. Turning away from a primary concern with uncovering the shared myths that were meant to underpin all religious traditions, the discipline began to address religions directly in their contemporary forms in order to replace them within the social and historical contexts in which they operated. Researchers began to address the question of how and how much did 'religion' matter in contemporary social processes.[8] For Geertz, this change in focus immediately introduced new difficulties for the discipline. First and foremost, the move away from ancient religious meta-narratives to the contemporary imbrications of religious beliefs and practices brought to the fore definitional difficulties. Scholars taking part in this new approach pondered on how best to identify religion in modern settings and queried about what was to be included in this category, where its boundaries lied, and how to encapsulate notions like 'belief', 'observance', or 'faith'. Geertz remarked that to a degree this was a familiar conundrum in anthropological studies concerned with naming and classifying 'cultural formations in other societies that are at once broadly similar to ones in our own and oddly *sui generis*, strange and different'. In this situation, he noted that 'the usual tack is to begin with our own, more or less unexamined, everyday sense of what 'the family', 'the state', or, in the case at hand, 'religion' comes to, what counts for us as kinship, or government, or faith, and what, family-resemblance style, looks... well... resemblant, amongst those whose life-ways we are trying to portray'.[9]

For Asad, this kind of approximation is precisely the reason why modern western social sciences fail to adequately understand the religious and more particularly Islam, Christianity's religious 'Other'.[10] Hence, Asad set out to outline an anthropology of the secular that would do to secularized thinking what the positive social sciences do to religious culture, thereby exposing these mutually constitutive processes in reverse. The purpose of his study was to provide an alternative to analyses of the contemporary Islamist phenomenon that invoked common western political

---

[8] Clifford Geertz, 'Shifting aims, moving targets: on the anthropology of religion', *Journal of the Royal Anthropological Institute*, no. 15, 2005, pp. 1–15, at p. 2.

[9] Geertz, 'Shifting aims, moving targets', p. 5.

[10] Talal Asad, *Genealogies of Religion: Discipline and Reasons of Power in Christianity and Islam* (Baltimore: Johns Hopkins University Press, 1993).

notions like the 'state' or 'democracy' in order to understand and explain the trajectory of Islamic movements addressing issues that were well ... resemblant.[11] The difficulty of performing such a reversal of perspective is stressed by Mohammed Arkoun at the beginning of *Rethinking Islam* when he asks his (putatively) secular and western readers: 'can one speak of a scientific understanding of Islam in the west or must one rather talk about a western way of imagining Islam?' Arkoun's own analysis illustrates that the second option may well be the only real option available today, as western social science approaches can be as lacking in critical self-examination as the fundamentalist discourses that they are investigating. Regarding political Islam in particular, he notes that 'the media in the West seize upon this monolithic, fundamentalist view of Islam that dominates the contemporary Muslim imaginary and transpose it into a discourse suitable to the social imaginary of western countries without any intermediate critique from the social sciences'.[12]

The view from political sciences

From a political sciences perspective, it would be of the utmost importance to start such an investigation into political Islam with some definitional clarity. It would be common sense to suggest, as Mohammed Ayoob does, that 'before beginning a discussion of issues related to political Islam, one must provide an adequate definition of the terms *political Islam* or *Islamism*—that is, Islam as political ideology rather than religion or theology'.[13] Such a proposition seems to be both logical and unproblematic since such a disciplinary approach has to explain and understand processes involving slippery 'religious' and 'theological' dimensions. As

---

[11] I will return in chapter four to this notion of family resemblances which remains quite central in comparative sociological approaches to religious 'fundamentalism'. See for example Gabriel A. Almond, Emmanuel Sivan and R. Scott Appleby, 'Fundamentalism: genus and species', pp. 339–424, and 'Explaining fundamentalisms', pp. 425–44, in M.E. Marty and R.S. Appleby (eds.), *Fundamentalisms Comprehended* (Chicago: Chicago University Press, 1995).

[12] Mohammed Arkoun, *Rethinking Islam: Common Questions, Uncommon Answers*, trans. R.D. Lee (Boulder: Westview Press, 1994), pp. 6–7.

[13] Mohammed Ayoob, *The Many Faces of Political Islam: Religion and Politics in the Muslim World* (Ann Arbor: The University of Michigan Press, 2007), p. 2.

such, the inquiry is best articulated with refferences to well-known concepts like 'political ideology'. The didactic purpose of this type of positioning is also evident in Roy's definition of Islamism, which he uses as
a synonym of political Islam. For Roy Islamism is:

the brand of modern political Islamic fundamentalism that claims to re-create a
true Islamic society, not simply by imposing *sharia*, but by establishing first an
Islamic state through political action. Islamists see Islam not as a mere religion,
but as a political ideology that should reshape all aspects of society (politics, law,
economy, social justice, foreign policy, and so on). The traditional idea of Islam
as an all-encompassing religion is extended to the complexity of modern society
and recast in terms of modern social sciences.[14]

As a starting point, this definition helpfully accounts for the fact that
unlike other trends in Islamic movements, Islamists seem to prioritize
politics over religiosity and political action over theological reflection.
However, in the light of Asad's critique of Geertz, it makes sense to question how long one can retain 'everyday sense' definitions of the state,
society, politics, ideology and so on. If these western political categories
are fixed and taken for granted, the analysis is likely to underestimate the
ambiguities inherent to these power-laden notions of social interactions;
and then to 'discover' these tensions anew in the Islamic communities
under investigation. To insist on the political character of Islamist activities may be a useful corrective in a context where observers may perceive
them to be driven primarily by an ill-defined spiritual or theological
quest. Yet, an undue reliance on common sense notions of politics may
easily deflect the light that one is trying to shed on Islamic activism.

In such analyses there is a slippery slope from the descriptive to the
normative. At first glance, an account contrasting the characteristics of
fundamentalism (an essentially 'religious' activity) with those of Islamism
(a notoriously 'political' one) such as the one presented by Guilain
Denoeux appears highly reasonable. His narrative stresses that:

Politics lies at the heart of Islamism, which ultimately has far more to do with
power than with religion. To Islamists, Islam is more a political blueprint than a
faith, and the Islamist discourse is to a large extent a political discourse in religious garb. Thus, while fundamentalists are typically concerned primarily with

[14] Roy, *Globalized Islam*, p. 58.

ideas and religious exegesis, Islamists are action-oriented; they are preoccupied first and foremost with changing their world.[15]

By turning these analytical distinctions—power-hungry, this-worldly Islamists versus individual-focused, inward-looking fundamentalists—into a defining feature of Islamism that explains the internal dynamics of these movements, Denoeux is led to the conclusion that Islamism is 'a form of instrumentalization of Islam by individuals, groups and organizations that pursue political objectives'.[16] Here, the 'thin rationality' (means-end) framework of the political sciences is fully imposed upon the activities of the subject. These groups and individuals are meant to use rationally and instrumentally a set of conceptual and practical resources 'x'—in this case Islam—in order to achieve a political objective 'y', in this case an institutional framework called an Islamic state.

As the bulk of the contemporary literature on Islamism illustrates, there is considerable scope for further reifying these distinctions along the lines of Geertz' dichotomy between Islam as religion and as ideology. For an idiosyncratic Islamic specialist like Basam Tibi it is clear that 'the religion of Islam and Islamism are two different issues'. Turning analytical distinctions into substantive claims, Tibi argues that:

to understand political Islam, one should focus, not on the religion of Islam and its beliefs, but rather on the political concepts developed on the grounds of the politicisation of Islam. It is not the substance of religion that is of interest for the exponents of political Islam; not spirituality, but religious symbolism employed in the pursuit of political ends is their concern.[17]

In a similar vein, though in a more nuanced fashion, political analyst Fawaz Gerges suggests that 'both Islamists and jihadists use religion as a means to a political end, not as an end in itself'. Hence Gerges can conclude that 'Islamists and jihadists are not born-again democrats and will never be', in the sense that their political project is totalitarian and not primarily based on popular choice.[18] If the task of social and political

---

[15] Guilain Denoeux, 'The forgotten swamp: navigating political Islam', *Middle East Policy* 9 (2) 2002, pp. 56–81, at p. 63.

[16] Denoeux, 'The forgotten swamp', p. 61.

[17] Bassam Tibi, 'Post-bipolar order in crisis: the challenge of politicised Islam', *Millennium: Journal of International Studies*, 29 (3) 2000, pp. 843–59, at p. 847.

[18] Fawaz Gerges, *Journey of the Jihadist: Inside Muslim Militancy* (Orlando: Hartcourt, 2006), pp. 14, 16.

scientists consists primarily in analysing the dynamics that Islamism sets in motion and then explaining their success or failure by relating a means to an end, then it is indeed crucial to assess such (putative) instrumental goals accurately. Not uncommonly, however, there are criticisms directed at specialists of political Islam suggesting that scholars themselves may instrumentally invoke particular Islamist movements or ideologues in order to be able sustain their prefered explanation (and/or prediction) for political Islam as a whole. These tensions are well encapsulated in the French context in the exchanges between Olivier Roy, Francois Burgat and Alain Roussillon on the question of whether specialists of political Islam 'invented' the notion of Islamism; much in the same way as orientalist scholars framed the idea of the Orient.[19]

Instrumentally, to the question 'why do Islamists engage in politics'?, there is a straightforward answer of the type: ...well, because they want power, they need power to change society, and state power is this ultimate form of power. Since revolution is the shortest path to state power (democratization being second best), a sound account of political Islam may be best structured according to the political standards used to measure the capture of the institutions of the state. This institutionalist narrative about political Islam, which can also be voiced by Islamic activists themselves, leads to a characterization of Islamism that is somewhat tautological. It is premised on a western notion of the political as the natural framework for social activism; activism that is best depicted in connection to the institutions of the modern nation-state. The grand narratives developed in the 1990s by Islamist specialists like Roy or Kepel trace precisely the emergence of contemporary forms of political Islam in relation to power politics.[20] Using a model for Islamism centred on a sudden capture of state power in order to establish an Islamic state, Roy could argue that since the 1979 Iranian revolution, a recognisable template of political Islam never succeeded in achieving this crucial feat of power and, there-

---

[19] See Francois Burgat, 'De l'islamisme au postislamisme, vie et mort d'un concept', pp. 82–92, Alain Roussillon, 'Les islamologues dans l'impasse', pp. 93–115, and Olivier Roy, 'Les islamologues ont-ils inventé l'islamisme?', pp. 116–38, in *Esprit*, August 2001.

[20] Olivier Roy, *The Failure of Political Islam*, trans. C. Volk (Cambridge: Harvard University Press, 1996); Gilles Kepel, *Jihad: The Trail of Political Islam*, trans. A. Roberts (London: I B Tauris, 2002).

fore, that Islamism was on the wane. The use of 'unexamined' notions of state power and revolutionary politics to map out the rise and fall of political Islam over the last half-century or so is evidently problematic as it leads to the reification of both the object of the struggle (state power), and the means used to obtain it (armed militancy). In addition, from this perspective, since political Islam 'failed' in the 1990s, there is now a need to identify and account for 'new' forms of Islamic activism.

Islamism and the State

What is noticeable in the abovementioned approaches is the close connection that is made between political Islam and the modern state. These analyses view the interaction between the two as central to a proper appreciation of the Islamist phenomenon. In particular, the creation of an Islamic state is commonly presented at once as a defining feature of political Islam, and at the same time as an intensely problematic (if not altogether unrealistic) aspect of Islamism. Typically, the root of the problem is deemed to be a lack of concrete historical antecedents for this system. Ayoob suggests that 'the reappropriation of the past, the "invention of tradition" in terms of a romanticized notion of a largely mythical golden age, lies at the heart of this instrumentalization of Islam. It is the invention of tradition that provides the tools for de-historicizing Islam and separating it from the various contexts in which it has flourished over the past fourteen hundred years.'[21] He therefore concludes that 'modern Islamist political thinkers devised the term "Islamic state" in order to reconcile their romanticized vision of the Islamic polity with the existence of sovereign states on the European model'.[22] In themselves, observations of this kind have value, as they contextualize the possible sources of institutional legitimacy. Unfortunately such perspectives often lead the analysis astray by implying that there is something unusually problematic about political Islam in this respect. To a degree, they are useful reminders of the difficulty of establishing with precision what constitutes a meaninful embodiment of Islamic institutions today—a topic of much debate within Islamist circles. Yet, at the same time, they are very mundane remarks

[21] Mohammed Ayoob, 'Political Islam: image and reality', *World Policy Journal* 21 (3) 2004, p. 1.
[22] Ayoob, 'Political Islam', p. 2.

about social and political identity that are not specific to political Islam or the Muslim community.

The very notion of a Democratic state which looms large in western political thought and practice since the end of the eighteenth century, is itself an imaginative re-appropriation of the past. It is an invented tradition based on a romanticized notion of classical Greek democracy, which served to de-centre and de-historicize the local political cultures that existed at the time in Europe and North America.[23] In the context of democratic political thought, however, this muddied genealogy and the often unreflective appropriation of this myth does not in itself constitute a lethal flaw in the activities of the individuals and polities now drawing inspiration from this tradition. Democratic thinkers, policy makers, and citizens alike keep fantasizing about an ideal democratic order—be it modelled on perceptions of past achievements or futuristic utopian constructions—and keep trying to give shape to their ideas without too much concern for historical accuracy. It could even be suggested that what might be identified as a delusional streak in democratic thinking—i.e. the notion of a *meaningful* political voice for all—may be one of the feature that ensure the enduring appeal of democracy as we know it in the face of its many flaws.[24]

Because these notions and practices of democratic, revolutionary or religious politics are fluid and evolving in both liberal-democratic and Islamic traditions, the attempt to fix them momentarily in order to map out the specific trajectory of political Islam against this background is only meaningful with very specific caveats. It may yield useful analytical insights, but used without due caution it may also obscure the issue. In *The Failure of Political Islam*, Roy stresses that 'it is intellectually imprudent and historically misguided to discuss the relationships between Islam and politics as if there were one Islam, timeless and eternal'.[25] Coming from the perspective of a specialist on Islamism, this advice is both sound and much needed in the contemporary context. Yet, it is obvious that it should be accompanied by a self-reflective note of caution regarding west-

---

[23] See for example John Dunn, *Setting the People Free: The Story of Democracy* (London: Atlantic Books, 2005).

[24] See, Raymond Geuss, *History and Illusions in Politics* (Cambridge: Cambridge University Press, 2001).

[25] Roy, *The Failure of Political Islam*, p.vii.

ern political science as well. One should therefore quickly add that it is equally intellectually imprudent and historically misguided to discuss the relationships between Islam and politics as if there were one notion of Politics, timeless and eternal. Roy's analysis of the failure of revolutionist brand of political Islam in the 1980s, provides interesting insights into the modus operandi and evolution of this particular form of Islamic activism. At the same time, it is not at all obvious that one should concentrate on evaluating the successes and failures of this particular strand of Islamism in relation to the state to produce a generic account of political Islam. Other strands of activism have profoundly and durably influenced the organization of Muslim societies without necessarily taking control of state institutions—indeed one might argue that failure to capture state power was instrumental in ensuring the ongoing appeal of Islamist themes.[26]

Turning on their head the above-mentioned views regarding the Islamists' engagement with state politics, one could suggest that many western political science perspectives seem commonsensical only when a society has gone through a process of nationalization of the political, which is then presented as the norm. Asad argues that 'Islamism's preoccupation with state power is the result not of its commitment to nationalist ideas but of the modern nation-state's enforced claim to constitute legitimate social identities and arenas'. He suggests that given the structures of authority in contemporary societies, religious activists of any kind have little choice but to engage the state since 'no movement that aspires to more than mere belief or inconsequential talk in public can remain indifferent to state power in a secular world'.[27] From a grassroots perspective, Saba Mahmood concurs that, 'it is not that the pietists have "politicized" the spiritual domain of Islam (as some scholars of Islamism claim) but that conditions of secular liberal modernity are such

---

[26] It has been a recurrent observation in recent years that the lack of genuine democratic opening in most of the countries of the Muslim world was instrumental in allowing the Islamists to cast themselves as a virtuous opposition to corrupt and autocratic regimes without having to prove their actual worth in government. See for example, Graham Fuller, *The Future of Political Islam* (London: Palgrave Macmillan, 2003).

[27] Talal Asad, 'Religion, ation-state, secularism', in P. van der Veer and H. Lehmann (eds.), *Nation and Religion: Perspectives on Europe and Asia* (Princeton: Princeton University Press, 1999), p. 191.

that for any world-making project (spiritual or otherwise) to succeed and be effective, it must engage with the all-encompassing institutions and structures of modern governance, whether it aspires to state power or not.'[28]

In the main, the 'political' character of political Islam cannot simply be attributed to a strategy by various Islamist movements to capture state power. It must also be seen as a re-interpretation of various social activities that were previously not considered to be political, by the state authorities and by those analyzing social life from a statist perspective. As Charles Hirschkind notes, the relationship between 'traditional' Islamic authority and 'modern' national politics has to be seen for most of the last century in the context of an increasing encroachment of the latter on the former. He emphasizes that if we oppose modern political objectives to traditional religious ones, then the term 'political Islam' cannot address the issue adequately since it arbitrarily poses what are normal and abnormal religious practices. In this perspective, Hirschkind comments, 'the intrusive disruptions or outward destruction enacted upon society by the modernizing state never even figures in the analysis'.[29]

Religiosity as political activism

If not its engagement with state politics, then what can primarily define Islamism? Could it be that conventional political science approaches fail to understand and explain meaningfully political Islam because they are not taking into consideration enough of the relevant criteria? If so, what would better criteria look like? It cannot be the case that political Islam is presented purely on its own terms, as the discourse of the Islamists on its own would not necessarily be meaningful to western analysts or institutions. Islamic scholars and activists do indeed hotly debate notions that often appear relatively similar to the ones western social sciences categorize as state, democracy, human rights, etc. However, simply highlighting these internal Islamic debates would not ensure that they become comprehensible. More than a translation, what is required is some recontext-

---

[28] Saba Mahmood, *Politics of Piety: The Islamic Revival and the Feminist Subject* (Princeton: Princeton University Press, 2004), pp. 193–4.

[29] Charles Hirschkind, 'What is political Islam?', *Middle East Report*, No. 205, 1997, pp. 12–14, at p. 14.

ualization using adequate hermeneutic devices.[30] There is a particular difficulty from a western social sciences perspective to make sense of Islamist narratives that superficially may look the same, but that beyond terminological similitudes take different approaches to social and political issues. (Reciprocally for those schooled in the Islamic tradition there remain serious obstacles to overcome to make sense of the historicity of the views proposed in western political philosophy.) In this situation, there is a very real danger of missing the relevant dimensions of the debate. Indeed, in what remains a pioneering study of political Islam, Nazih Ayubi suggested that 'apart from a moral code and a few 'fixations' related to dress, penalties, and halal/haram foods, drinks and social practices, there is no well defined comprehensive social-political-economic programme that can be described as "Islamic".[31]

But what other ways are there to understand and evaluate systematically the activities of the Islamists beside rating them against common notions of politics, institutionalization, democracy, human rights, and so on? Islamism is certainly not best presented purely as a debate over the ultimate ends of religion, or an articulation of the functional role of religion. It cannot remain the first type of analysis because there is an increasingly significant process of objectification of religion in contemporary settings.[32] It cannot fully become solely the second type of inquiry because there remains those 'high values', as Jurgen Habermas suggests—or conversation stoppers, as Richard Rorty would have it—that individuals chose as primary markers of their social condition.[33] Importantly, as soon as religion ceases to be associated primarily with ultimate values (salvation, good and evil, etc.) and starts to be conceived as a practical process of social organization, a debate over the basic tenets of religious doxa may not be particularly illuminating way of approaching

---

[30] For some sophisticated propositions see, Arkoun, *Rethinking Islam*; Euben, *Enemy within the Mirror*.

[31] Nazih N. Ayubi, *Political Islam: Religion and Politics in the Arab World* (New York: Routledge, 1992), p. 230.

[32] See in particular, Dale Eickelman and James Piscatori, *Muslim Politics* (Princeton: Princeton University Press, 1996).

[33] Jurgen Habermas, 'Equal treatment of cultures and the limits of postmodern liberalism', *The Journal of Political Philosophy* 13 (1) 2005, pp. 1–28; Richard Rorty, Gianni Vattimo, and Santiago Zabala, *The Future of Religion* (New York: Columbia University Press, 2005).

religious activism.[34] Once religiosity is also seen in a significant way as this-wordly, we cannot escape analyzing the nature of the relation between religious knowledge and political agency. This includes going down well-trodden paths to query what constitutes the status of this religious knowledge; why should a believer seek this knowledge; what should s/he do with it, etc.?

From a social and political sciences perspective, a pragmatic starting point would commonly be to posit that Islam grounds its practical claims to authority on its ability to provide the community and the individual with some sense of order and a place in the world through its normative guidelines. In this perspective, Graham Fuller suggests that at heart, 'an Islamist is one who believes that Islam as a body of faith has something important to say about how politics and society should be ordered in the contemporary Muslim world and who seeks to implement this idea in some fashion'.[35] It may be useful to modify this proposition to emphasize that an Islamist is one who believes that Islam as a body of faith has something *crucial* to say about how politics and society should be ordered in the contemporary *ummah* and who seeks to implement this idea in some fashion *as a matter of priority*. To characterize the Muslim community as the loci for political Islam, is to stress that the Muslim world is not best conceived as a geographical entity composed of Muslim-majority countries, but rather as a composite of polities where Islamist movements are a main transformative force.[36] Dale Eickelman and James Piscatori thus stress the contextual emergence of 'Muslim politics' as regimes that depend on Islam in a variety of ways for their legitimation, get involved in 'the competition and contest over both the interpretation of symbols and the control of the institutions, both formal and informal, that produce and sustain them'.[37]

---

[34] In this instance, I am referring to a pragmatic notion of the religious defined in terms of its usefulness to the analysis. I am not seeking to define the religious as a formal category of political analysis distinct from other variables and ideologies (such as nationalism) due to the specificity of its belief and practices. For an attempt at the latter see Eric O. Hanson, *Religion and Politics in the International System Today* (Cambridge: Cambridge University Press 2006).

[35] Fuller, *The Future of Political Islam*, p. xi.

[36] See Frédéric Volpi, 'Pseudo-democracy in the Muslim world', *Third World Quarterly* 25 (6) 2004, pp. 1061–78.

[37] Eickelman and Piscatori, *Muslim Politics*, p. 5.

Such definitional frameworks still leave the analyst with a wide variety of ways in which propositions about political Islam could be expressed and implemented. At one end of the spectrum, as Peter Mandaville notes vis-à-vis some of the new Islamists based in western polities, 'Islam exists first and foremost to provide certainty and order in a turbulent world where individual identities—and particularly those with multiple affiliations viewed as (potentially) mutually exclusive—are apt to get lost in the maelstrom of competing cultural and political discourses vying for allegiance and consumption'. Pointing to the example of al-Muhajiroun in the UK, he highlights how 'when confronted with a given situation, this Islam provides a set of analytical tools that permit the adherent to diagnose the prevailing circumstances and behave accordingly, secure in the knowledge that their actions fit the requirements of an authoritative model based on the example of the earliest companions of the Prophet Muhammad'.[38] Roy defines this mode of interpretation of the relationship between religion and social order as 'neofundamentalism', and suggests that it is fast becoming a dominant trend in the globalized ummah. Assessing that neofundamentalism promotes the decontextualization of religious practices, he estimates that 'it is perfectly adapted to a basic dimension of contemporary globalization: that of turning human behaviour into codes, and patterns of consumption and communication, delinked from any specific culture'.[39]

At the other end of the spectrum, we are witnessing a process of functional pluralization of Islamic knowledge, and the social and political implications of this pluralism. For Mandaville this corresponds to 'a move away from the idea that religion is the primary source from which one gains knowledge about what to do in the world when faced with a given set of circumstances', and towards a view of Islam that 'cuts across and infuses a number of disparate orientations towards knowledge without

---

[38] Peter Mandaville, 'Globalization and the politics of religious knowledge: pluralizing authority in the Muslim world', *Theory, Culture and Society* 24 (2) 2007, p. 101–15, at p. 107. See also passim Peter Mandaville, *Transnational Muslim Politics: Reimagining the Umma* (London: Routledge, 2001).

[39] Roy, *Globalized Islam*, p. 263. In particular, Roy notes how in western settings, 'traditional fundamentalists are at a loss how to deal with deculturation, while neofundamentalists consider this deculturation as an almost positive factor that permits the decontextualisation of Islam'. Ibid, p. 258.

necessarily becoming the organizing principle of authoritative discourse'.[40] The functional pluralization of authority is not an argument about religion being confined to the private or spiritual realm. Instead it is a revision of traditional views of secularization in order to better consider how new forms of religiosity are intersecting with modernity. In this context, Islamist specialists have noted how notions of public or common good (*maslaha*) become more central as organizing principle of Islamism.[41] This is evidently not a process that is unique to Islam in this period of globalization, nor is it a process that is without parallels in history. However, such dynamics of pluralization are shaped by the particular configuration of the current encounter between western secular power and the reconfiguration of Islamic religiosity (by Muslims and non-Muslims).[42]

Significantly, the current strength of the 'neo-fundamentalist' trend, creates an ebullient type of Islamic activism as its proponents reflexively try to translate all aspects of modern life into a reconstructed religious template for 'good' behaviour. Their impact can be highly political, when movements estimate that state politics are a crucial factor in the success of their project. It can be far more elusive, as in the case of the activities of the Tablighi Jamaat, when institutionalized politics are not perceived to be a distinct category that require the immediate application of specifically Islamic rules. Yet, it remains remarkable how far the political visibility/invisibility of Islamist actors is more determined by their topic of discussion than by their actual societal project. Commonly, so-called 'Islamic liberals', linking up liberal political precepts with Islamic principles are not deemed by western social scientists and policy-makers to be mixing religion with politics, but merely to express how Islam can be integrated into existing liberal-democratic frameworks.[43] Of course, this assessment would be resisted and presented as misleading by 'Islamic

---

[40] Mandaville, 'Globalization and the politics of religious knowledge', p. 107.

[41] See for example the contributors to A. Salvatore and D. F. Eickelman (eds.), *Public Islam and the Common Good* (Leiden: Brill, 2004); and to A. Salvatore and M. LeVine (eds.), *Religion, Social Practice, and Contested Hegemonies: Reconstructing the Public Sphere in Muslim Majority Societies* (London: Palgrave, 2005).

[42] See, Armando Salvatore, *Islam and the Political Discourse of Modernity* (Reading: Ithaca Press, 1997).

[43] See for example the contributors to O. Safi (ed.), *Progressive Muslims: On Justice, Gender, and Pluralism* (Oxford: Oneworld Publications, 2003).

liberals' genuinely holding their religious knowledge above or on a par par with the positive sciences. By the same token, those identified as 'radical Islamists', though they may selectively connect religious and scientific knowledge on the same basis as the 'liberals', are deemed to constitute a different kind of activism, primarily because their conclusions on the proper relation between the two types of knowledge on particular issues of contemporary relevance goes against current liberal thinking.[44] These classifications are evidently quite arbitrary; hence the ease with which some thinkers and activists can speedily be moved from one category to the next. These categories do not reflect the internal dynamics of the epistemic communities that create these discourses, but are framed in relation to debates internal to various academic disciplines and policy-making communities.

What does analysing political Islam mean today?

The present book aims to provide a narrative that connects different social science approaches to political Islam. It does not seek to offer a comprehensive account of the growth and significance of political Islam 'out there'. It is not meant to be a self-standing narrative of this phenomenon or an empirical analysis of the putative causes and effects of Islamism today. In particular, it is not yet another explanation of the 'revival' of an Islamic worldview, and of its impact on western views of the Muslim world. Rather, it is an approach that details how a western political subjectivity mediated by the social sciences frames what it perceives to be mainly an exception to the natural 'order of things'. Functionally and historically 'political Islam' plays specific roles in academic disciplines. These roles are primarily structured not according to the mechanisms or dynamics of Islamism itself, but by the discursive and theoretical opportunities that emerge in preexisting scholarly debates.

Since the present account is designed to build bridges between different disciplinary perspectives, it is to be expected that no single definition of political Islam will satisfy every one of them. Within each discipline, competing characterizations of this phenomenon have merits in connec-

---

[44] Clearly, there may also be more generally a possibility of consciously preserving some theocratic enclaves even in liberal systems. See Lucas A. Swaine, 'Institutions of conscience: politics and principle in a world of religious pluralism', *Ethical Theory and Moral Practice* 6 (1) 2003, pp. 93–118.

tion to their particular field of expertise, as well as drawbacks in relation to other disciplinary perpectives. Hence, in relational terms, the relevant question to ask is: what is such a definition needed for? Typically, it could be used primarily to ensure that political Islam is an analytically useful term to explain and understand—and more boldly, predict—the evolution of a particular dimension of Islamic reconfiguration. Alternatively, it could be required to make sense of the discrepancies that exist between different observations about political Islam. Finally, and most ambitiously, it could be proposed as a means to connect the insights gained from studying this process to other key concepts in the social sciences. In the following account, I am proposing a modular definition of political Islam that begins with the first aspect mentioned above and progresses toward the second type of definition within each discipline. The book proposes to shift the definitional focus from the first to the second characterization of political Islam, with the final propositions aiming to introduce a degree of synthetic assessment. This modular approach has two key components: (i) how scholars define their subject matter to make sense of what they consider to be the main building blocks of the phenomenon and, (ii) how they use these key features to explain the phenomenon in relation to the paradigms of their discipline. In relational terms, therefore, political Islam is the recognition of the Islamic tradition in social processes described in the paradigmatic terms of secular-scientific narratives from relevant social sciences disciplines.

Throughout the book, the usefulness of the term political Islam will reside principally in its ability to remind the reader of inherent tensions contained in the explanations used by different types of scholarship to account for rather similar processes. Religion and politics are two totalizing entities, and using these terms in concert to define a phenomenon such as political Islam is to highlight less a paradox than a creative tension. From an external perspective Islam is necessarily objectified in relation to pre-existing analytical distinctions between religion and politics, sacred and secular, etc. Political Islam is therefore a re-created category that merges previously segregated mechanisms of political and religious practice and thought. Here, the term will serve to highlight specific aspects of the relationship between religion and politics that appear to be crucial today, in seven disciplinary fields. The objective of the book is to highlight how discourses and patterns of explanation within different academic disciplines construct many of the 'facts' about political Islam that scholars are attempting to uncover. These processes are highlighted here in fields which can be named following a social science nomenclature as: (1) postcolonial studies, (2) international studies, (3) sociology of religion, (4) democratization studies, (5) multicultural studies, (6) security studies and, (7) globalization studies.

In western social sciences descriptions, political Islam is brought under the general framework of political causality, with religion being a residual category of explanation. From the perspective of the Islamic tradition(s), there is likewise an attempt to contextualize these processes within a religious worldview, with politics being a residual category. This situation generates a dialogical interaction between these two views. Social sciences accounts impact on the development of an Islam that is deemed to be more or less political, whilst also contributing to the revision of their own perspectives on politics in the process. Islamists too have a direct impact on 'western' notions of the political, as well as redefine their own modes of religiosity in the process. From an insider's perspective, the practice of one's faith in all the relevant public and private dimensions, from social justice to personal spirituality, is structured in relation to the referent 'Islam' without strict predefinition of the (secular) boundaries between notions of the political and the religious. In the abstract, faithful observance of Islam is structured looking inward towards the Islamic tradition not outwards towards other religious or secular traditions. In practice, evidently, external inferences also contribute to the formation of contemporary Islamic thought and practice. Islamists are considering their own grand narratives and rules of conduct in the light of these external perceptions of, and at times impositions on the Islamic tradition(s). Religion and Politics remain two open-ended and interlocked interpretative fields that are consistently redefined in order to meet the explicit or implicit needs of their users. As social sciences try to come to grip with political Islam, each disciplinary approach evaluates and engages with this phenomenon partly on its own terms. Political Islam is thus a contextual construct that refers to what individuals in a particular socio-historical context think about the political and the religious.

In the next seven chapters, the notion of political Islam will be critically examined in relation to seven disciplinary fields of expertise in the social sciences that are the primary contributors to today's dominant narratives and associated counter-discourses on Islamism. In chapter two, I look into the historical construction of a political Islam marked by colonialism and the subsequent emergence of postcolonial studies, which becomes a building block in contemporary notions of (good) civilization and (bad) imperialism. In chapter three, I address the international representation of the Muslim world as a distinct geopolitical entity permeated by Islamism, especially since the collapse of the Communist Threat, and its role in narratives about the post-Cold War (dis)order. In chapter four, I turn to the more sociological explanations of the religiosity associated with political Islam, and their presentation of the predicament of Muslim individuals and communities in modern, then postmodern social settings. In chapter five, I investigate the impact of the 'wave' of democratizations that slowly reached through Muslim countries in the postcolonial period, and the insights produced by the democratization literature concerning the relationship between democratic politics and political Islam. In chapter six, I analyze the imbrication of political Islam into the contemporary brand of liberal multiculturalism that increasingly shapes the domestic social and political institutions of western democracies where Muslims are a significant minority. In chapter seven, I focus on the security issues that have been particularly associated with political Islam since organizations like al-Qaeda made their mark on the international stage, and particularly after 9/11 during the period of the 'War on Terror'. In chapter eight, I locate the reconfiguration of political Islam in the context of generic narratives about globalization that have become increasingly pervasive since the turn of the century. In chapter nine, the conclusion will bring together these different strands of analysis, though not in an attempt to produce a unitary concept of political Islam that would subsume all these approaches in a single framework. Rather, it proposes a narrative that indicates the respective contribution of each interpretative strand to the dominant 'western' readings of Islamism today.

2

FROM CRITICIZING ORIENTALISM
TO FRAMING ISLAMISM

At the beginning there was the 'Orient'; then came orientalism, the field of systematic study of all things oriental. Islam was part and parcel of this naturalistic 'Orient' that began to be studied systematically by western social sciences from Napoleon's brief foray into Egypt onward. All too naturally, Islam in the 'Orient' became a central subject of inquiry for this new academic discipline. As a relatively new form of scholarship, orientalism had a very useful property: it was additive. The prospect of producing an incremental system of knowledge was for a long time the holy grail of scientific inquiries. Over time, albeit reluctantly, the philosophy of science chipped away little by little at the prospects for such linear progress, especially as paradigm shifts came to be understood as part of its intrinsic workings. In the social sciences, orientalist scholarship long resisted abandoning this quest for a comprehensive knowledge of really existing oriental objects and subjects. Reading Bernard Lewis at the beginning of the twenty-first century and reading the works of Ernest Renan produced at the end of the nineteenth century; the continuities in their approaches to Islam are as striking as their divergences. For didactic purposes, it is instructive to approach first the issue of political Islam from an orientalist perspective. By orientalism I mean an approach to Islam that tries to build a comprehensive and systematic picture of an Islamic civilization, with its own logic and system of values. Admittedly, this Islamic world is being analysed and explained with western concepts and methodology. Yet, as long as these concepts and methods are presented as rational universals, orientalist accounts have no particular difficulty in making their case.

21

They are firmly in the lineage of the positive social sciences and have an unmistakable positivist epistemology. From this perspective, there is an object out there called Islam or the Muslim world that can be the topic of systematic study. And the task of academic scholarship is precisely to contribute little by little to providing the grand picture of the internal workings of this phenomenon and society.[1]

The 'fact of the matter', at once obvious and problematic, about an orientalist field of expertise is that it exists as an intellectual discipline with distinct practical benefits. It is the practical political embedding of this scholarship that most critical approaches to areas studies, as well as all those postcolonial studies influenced by Edward Said, are still in the process of challenging in the contemporary neo-orientalist readings of the Muslim world that permeate the policy-making community.[2] The seemingly ubiquitous presence of orientalist scholarship, and for a long time its unquestioned dominance, kept at bay the calls for a serious consideration of the circumstances in which such views of the Orient were generated. In particular, the perception of a 'natural' expertise facilitated the continuous acceptance of a scholarship, particularly in Islamic studies, that was primarily an experiment in scientific inquiry from the nineteenth century. Perhaps one can point to Napoleon's Egyptian venture in 1798 as the earliest and clearest indication of this mode of scientific and policy formulation.[3] Napoleon's scientific mission to Egypt is pertinent in the

---

[1] See for example Hamilton A.R. Gibb, *Modern Trends in Islam* (Chicago: University of Chicago Press, 1947). Both critics and proponents of this type of scholarship agree that traditional orientalists had a detailed knowledge of many aspects of the object of their study. What remains more contentious, however, is how this expertise was put to use to construct grand explanations of Islam and of Muslim societies.

[2] See Zachary Lockman, *Contending Visions of the Middle East: The history and Politics of Orientalism* (Cambridge: Cambridge University Press, 2004); Daniel M. Varisco, *Reading Orientalism: Said and the Unsaid* (Seattle: University of Washington Press, 2007); E. Burke III and D. Prochaska (eds.), *Genealogies of Orientalism: History, Theory, Politics* (Lincoln: University of Nebraska Press, 2008).

[3] The French sent to Egypt of a whole cohort of scientists entrusted with the mission of elucidating the mysteries of the Egyptian and Muslim civilizations. On this process of invasion and discovery see Juan Cole, *Napoleon's Egypt: Invading the Middle East* (London: Macmillan, 2007).

genesis of a new field of knowledge because it was part of a grand scheme for the sciences which the new French empire and its 'enlightened' dictator were bent on creating. Diderot may have given the Enlightenment the Encyclopaedia, but Napoleon was keen to devise for it an 'Ideology', that is the science of the systematic studies of ideas. The enthusiasm for classification of nineteenth century thinkers and scientists is well known, and here is not the place to debate why various schemes were more successful than others, or for longer periods of time (e.g. racial studies). What is relevant in these early French experiments is that while the science of Ideology was quickly torn apart by the many centrifugal forces that made up the world of ideas, the field of orientalism went from strength to strength as a cohesive field of studies (with regional variations). This was particularly remarkable in the late nineteenth century and early twentieth century, as Oriental and Islamic studies increasingly faced competition from other emerging disciplines, from sociology to anthropology, which attempted to cut social reality at different junctures.

Anyone schooled in the orientalist tradition might rejoice at this point and argue that this specialised field of knowledge survived and prospered because there is indeed a specific object of study—oriental cultures and religions—that hold all these analyses together in a structured whole. Such an argument would have been perfectly plausible up to the middle of the twentieth century since scientific arguments did not make until then, a strong distinction between 'Truth' and appropriateness.[4] Yet, whatever the 'truth of the matter' might be, simply voicing some truth claims is not sufficient to ensure that a specific scientific methodology will prosper. And conversely, some rather hazy scientific schemes might be able to provide appropriate explanations in specific historical circumstances and thrive regardless of their conceptual incoherence—again racial studies may come to mind, nationalism too perhaps. For nineteenth century and early twentieth century orientalists and Islamologists, simply to uncover the facts and present them 'objectively' could be genuinely seen as the best reason why their discipline became recognized. Unmistakably, this recognition was not only scientific but also political, due to the potential of such works to inform models of colonial governance. As Edward Said, and many others in his footsteps, indicated however, ingenuity was not

---

[4] See Richard Rorty, *Philosophy and the Mirror of Nature* (Princeton: Princeton University Press, 1979).

always a main feature of these discourses, especially for those analyses firmly harnessed to colonial and imperial features of domination.[5] For orientalist-inspired scholarship in the second half of the twentieth century, therefore, this naturalistic objectivism became increasingly harder to sustain in the context of the generalized linguistic turn that progressively affected the whole of the social sciences. Ernest Gellner's later works probably illustrate best an ambitious but ultimately flawed attempt at retaining this traditional scientific high ground, free from political influences.[6]

Initially, the swift rise to prominence of oriental and Islamic studies in the nineteenth century made perfect sense. They promised a true and useful account of those societies that western colonial powers were increasingly trying to rule directly. They were therefore highly appropriate at the time; a situation not unlike that of terrorism studies at the beginning of the twenty-first century, as will be discussed in chapter seven. They were also rigorous in relation to the positivist methodology that was dominant at the time, and could therefore claim to provide a sound account of the oriental societies that they studied. The continuing success of this scholarship as the twentieth century progressed is less evident to account for. (The mounting challenges to orientalist views are as much a sign of its increasing discredit as one of its continuing resilience.) In particular, it is harder to frame in instrumental terms, since the European grip over their colonies loosened despite the superior knowledge of the 'Orient' that they were supposed to have acquired. (Neo-orientalist scholars could of course defend the discipline by arguing that policy-makers did not in fact listen properly.) It is also difficult to understand conceptually in view of the breaking down of the positivist epistemology that underpinned this field of knowledge. In this respect, one of the principal factors that appears to be responsible for the resilience of the discipline is the constitution of orientalism as a distinct and cohesive field of studies.[7]

For twentieth century orientalism, the best defence against any criticism has been to emphasize unity in diversity. Yes, it is said, there are

---

[5] Edward Said, *Orientalism: Western Conceptions of the Orient* (London: Penguin Classics, 2003).

[6] See Ernest Gellner, *Postmodernism, Reason and Religion* (London: Routledge, 1992).

[7] These features remain salient in the debate about 'civilizations' re-sparked by Huntington. See Samuel P. Huntington, *The Clash of Civilizations and the Remaking of World Order* (New York: Simon & Schuster, 1998).

many versions of Islam, but there is one Muslim mind, always lurking in the background and shaping the evolution of Muslim societies. The workings of this Muslim mind can be derived from an understanding of Islamic theology, interpreted through the lenses of Islamic history, and then be invoked to explain both the unity and the diversity of contemporary experiences. This argument, it seems, has littled evolved despite an increasing sophistication between the time when Ernest Renan wrote his essay on 'Islam and Science' and the present-day views detailed in Bernard Lewis' *What Went Wrong*.[8] Unity in diversity means that one consistently reattaches specific features of Muslim societies, in specific historical contexts, to some essential characteristics of Islam. Thinkers from various disciplines with a passing interest in the Orient—Marx and Weber among others—adopted such an orientalist *explanan* to help in explaining regional differences in their own schemes (e.g. the Asiatic mode of production for Marx, the 'sultanistic' model of patrimonial rule for Weber).[9] In their turn, Marxist notions of an Asiatic mode of production and the Weberian notion of patrimonialism contributed to the construction of an Oriental system best explained by western social sciences, yet unique in its otherness. As Talal Asad noted, 'since the orientalist is concerned by definition with "a society" of much complexity, he must stress what may be called a form of horizontal integration: the fact that Muslims as Muslims seemed bound together, despite their subjection to different secular rulers, by their common loyalty to Islam as a religious system'.[10] This 'Islamic' foundation is then contrasted to a vertical political struggle that may be explained by Weberian or Marxian models, but that remains shackled to the purportedly 'Islamic' nature of this social order. Marshall Hogson's later works propose an interesting and sophisticated example of late orientalist writings that stress an enduring core common to the religious traditions—piety in this case—at the expense of transient

---

[8] Bernard Lewis, *What Went Wrong? Approaches to the Modern History of the Middle East* (New York: Oxford University Press, 2002); Ernest Renan, *L'islam et la science* (Apt: L'Archange Minotaure, 2005 [1883]).

[9] For critical analyses of these trends see Bryan S. Turner, *Weber and Islam: A Critical Study* (London: Routledge and Keegan Paul, 1973*)*; *Marx and the End of Orientalism* (London: Allen and Unwin, 1978).

[10] Talal Asad, 'Two European images of non-European rule', *Economy and Society* 2 (3) 1973, pp. 263–77, at p. 271. See also T. Asad (ed.), *Anthropology and the Colonial Encounter* (London: Ithaca Press, 1973).

socio-economic factors.[11] More often than not in these accounts, however, this Islamic bond is emphasized at the expense of other, 'missing' social characteristics like rationalism and materialism, which are attributed mainly to western societies.

The gist of these orientalist accounts applied to Islamic objects/subjects is to demonstrate that their specialist knowledge provides a rational account of the historical evolution of these societies in relation to a relatively unchanging Islamic theological core. They seek to explain 'rationally' the interaction between an immoveable theological creed, and various ideological and material developments in Muslim societies. As Mahmood Mamdani put it succinctly, orientalist scholars 'assume that every culture has a tangible essence which defines it, and then explain politics as a consequence of that essence'.[12] A key endeavour of Islamology has been precisely to provide this hermeneutic connection between past and living tradition. There are evidently many different ways of emphasizing the coherence of the Islamic tradition in opposition to other traditions—usually Christian ones—though over time the invocation of the public-private distinction has proved to be particularly handy at performing this task. Thus in the contemporary context, Lewis can argue that one of the key distinctions between the Western and the Middle Eastern context is that 'in Islam religion is not, as it is in Christendom, one sector or segment of life regulating some matters and excluding others; it is concerned with the whole of life, not a limited but a total jurisdiction'.[13]

From an orientalist perspective, the rationalism underpinning western scientific inquiries was for a long time deemed to be value-free. Objective scientific knowledge was meant to be uninfluenced by societal power relations; it was genuinely 'objective'. The power of this objective knowledge resided in it being a manifestation of 'Truth' itself—and should one fail to recognise this, then the laws of nature (as previously those of God) would ensure that any enterprise not based on such knowledge would

---

[11] See Marshall Hodgson, *The Venture of Islam: Conscience and History in a World Civilisation* (Chicago: University of Chicago Press, 1974).

[12] Mahmood Mamdani, *Good Muslim, Bad Muslim* (New York: Three Leaves Press, 2004), p. 17.

[13] Bernard Lewis, *Islam and the West* (Oxford: Oxford University Press, 1994), p. 136.

unavoidably fail. Natural and religious laws, like universal laws of physics, had a power of their own, and scientific inquiry was simply meant to uncover those regularities of power. It is questionable how far this debate may still be going on in the 'hard' sciences today, but in the social sciences it has increasingly become untenable in the last couple of decades. Michel Foucault's analysis of power-knowledge and Richard Rorty's analysis of objectivism are good illustrations of this reconfiguration of the field of social inquiry. Foucault suggested in particular that 'there is no power relation without the correlative constitution of a field of knowledge, nor any knowledge that does not presuppose and constitute at the same time power relations'.[14] It is by using Foucault's analyses as his point of departure that Said in his turn challenged the traditional view of the 'Orient' and of its subjects in orientalist scholarship in his insightful book, *Orientalism*.

In these new perspectives, truth does not have a power of its own which endows its knower with specific abilities to master the world. Rather truth is a component of a pre-existing and always changing system of power relations, which is only recognized as the truth because it is able to mobilize these power relations in ways which are found useful. As Foucault highlighted in his work, there are no such natural categories as 'criminality', 'madness' or 'deviancy' about which an objective knowledge can be gained and used; rather these categories are made up as new systems of institutionalised power—in this case the state system—expand their remit and classify the social phenomena that they encounter in ways that they find useful for their purposes (penitentiary, mental asylum, clinic). New social norms and views are thus moulded and deviances from these norms become the subject matter of specific disciplinary fields and institutions that provide 'objective' authoritative discourses on each of these phenomena. In this context, power relations shift from being located mainly in subjective interactions between individuals and are recomposed via governmentality in institutional and discursive apparatuses that shape everyday social relations.[15]

[14] Michel Foucault, *Discipline and Punish: The Birth of the Prison* (London: Tavistock, 1977), p. 27.

[15] For the relevance of these Foucauldian approaches to the post-colonial and the post-9/11 context see, J.X. Inda (ed.), *Anthropologies of Modernity: Foucault, Governmentality, and Life Politics* (Oxford: Blackwell, 2005); S. Morton and S.

In this new intellectual climate, a key factor that contributed to the resilience of orientalist scholarship is, counter-intuitively, the lack of social science training of many leading orientalist scholars. From the beginning, orientalist scholarship was dominated by scholars with mainly a philological training. That linguists should be deeply involved in the study of social and political traditions transmitted in foreign languages is not in itself a problem, far from it. That direct access to texts written in an oriental language should become the main criterion for understanding a living social and political tradition is far more problematic. Yet, this is what happened in the orientalist tradition, particularly in the field of Islamic studies due to the strong linkages established between the Arabic language and Islamic law and dogma.[16] When political science clearly became a significant sub-discipline in the social sciences in the middle of the twentieth century, the scholars producing some of the pioneering works in comparative politics in the Muslim world could not see a way past orientalism, and attempted instead to build on it. In the early 1960s, Manfred Halpern noted that in his view, 'it would be quite impossible for students of political modernization to do any sensible work without, for example, drawing upon the works of H. A. R. Gibb, Gustave von Grunebaum, or Wilfred Cantwell Smith'.[17] He recognized nonetheless that there were some serious problems with the way in which these traditional orientalists approached the issue of contemporary politics. In particular, Halpern, noted that with many orientalists, 'so great is their philological contribution to documentation that Middle Eastern actions are neglected, especially contemporary events that are accompanied by silence or demagogy, since these do not demand a high philological skill for interpretation'.[18]

From the 1960s onwards, the more direct criticisms of the essentialism promoted by traditional orientalist scholarship came from the Marxian tradition. The ideological context prevalent at the time also meant that

---

Bygrave (eds.), *Foucault in an Age of Terror: Essays on Biopolitics and the Defence of Society* (Basingstoke: Palgrave Macmillan, 2008).

[16] See for example Gustave E Von Grunebaum, *Islam: Essays in the Nature and Growth of a Cultural Tradition* (London: Routledge, 1961).

[17] Manfred Halpern, 'Middle Eastern studies: a review of the state of the field with a few examples', *World Politics* 15 (1) 1962, pp. 108–22, at p. 111.

[18] Halpern, 'Middle Eastern studies', p. 116.

they often had a limited impact on mainstream political science debates. From Anouar Abdel-Malek to Abdallah Laroui there were well-articulated challenges particularly on the alleged distinctiveness and meaning of Islam as a 'culture' creating a specific set of socio-economic and political dilemmas.[19] As Maxime Rodinson, another Marxist scholar, neatly summarized, the overflow of orientalist thinking into political theorizing led to 'theologocentrism', namely the assumption that 'almost all observable phenomena can be explained by reference to Islam, in societies where Muslims are the majority or where Islam in the official religion'.[20] Yet, even those critical leftist approaches that constituted the most sustained challenge to traditional orientalism until the late 1970s could only cast aside Islam as the main category of analysis at the cost of introducing a Marxist view of socio-economic structures that was not itself without problems. When it came to attacking orientalism, Bryan Turner noted pointedly at the time, 'modern Marxism is fully equipped to do this work of destruction, but in this very activity Marxism displays its own internal theoretical problems and uncovers those analytical cords which tie it to Hegelianism, to nineteenth-century political economy and to Weberian sociology. The end of Orientalism, therefore, also requires the end of certain forms of Marxist thought and the creation of a new type of analysis.'[21]

Old versus new orientalism in contemporary readings of political Islam

In recent decades, and particularly since the end of the Cold War, orientalist scholarship has been revitalized in the political field. In this respect, we can identify today three main tendencies. The first type of scholarship, which is now fast disappearing, is constituted by the traditional orientalists. The most emblematic figure in the field today is probably Bernard Lewis, who began to write on this topic in the 1950s and who has hardly deviated from his initial political analysis of a civilizational struggle ever

[19] Anouar Abdel-Malek, 'Orientalism in crisis', *Diogenes* 11 (44) 1963, pp. 102–40; Abdallah Laroui *The Crisis of the Arab Intellectual: Traditionalism or Historicism?*, trans. D. Cammell (Berkeley: University of California Press, 1976).
[20] Maxime Rodinson, *Europe and the Mystique of Islam*, trans. R. Veinus (London: I.B Tauris, 1988), p. 102.
[21] Tuner, *Marx and the End of Orientalism*, p. 85.

since. Until recently, Elie Kedourie was also an influential figure in this trend.[22] The second category comprises those neo-orientalist authors whose writings clearly post-date the linguistic turn and the beginning of the critique of orientalist methodology. Some of the most vocal advocates of this approach, like Daniel Pipes, remains on the margins of the academic field, though their influence in the policy-making community made up for a limited academic visibility. More standard scholarship is also produced in this field, from that of Martin Kramer, a former student of Lewis, to that of Ephraim Karsh, whose work is in the line of Kedourie.[23] One can also mention in this category the contribution of regional authors like Fouad Ajami, who started from the intellectual perspective of Arab nationalism but who recast himself in the orientalist mould to analyse Islamism (particularly post-9/11), as well as, from a secularized Muslim perspective, that of Bassam Tibi.[24] The third category is that of the critical neo-orientalists. Unlike the other neo-orientalists who simply reject most of the criticism directed at this field of study, these authors take stock of these criticisms but estimate that on the whole, for both conceptual and practical reasons, this approach to the Orient and Islam is still the best available in the circumstances. Ernest Gellner was probably the most articulate proponent of this constructive engagement with orientalism. While the analyses belonging to the first two categories display the same qualities and flaws than the older orientalist scholarship, those in the third group are more productive in their internal problematization of Islam and of its relationship with the social sciences.[25] In particular, Gellner's argument addresses frontally one of the main difficulties of the postmodern critique of orientalism, namely that for all its effective-

---

[22] See Elie Kedourie, *Islam in the Modern World and Other* Studies (London: Mansell, 1980).

[23] Ephraim Karsh, *Islamic Imperialism: A History* (New Haven: Yale University Press, 2006). See also the critical analysis of Pipes' and Kramer's approaches and impact proposed in Lockman, *Contending Visions of the Middle East.*

[24] See Fouad Ajami, *The Foreigner's Gift: The Americans, the Arabs, and the Iraqis in Iraq* (New York: Free Press, 2006); R. Bassam Tibi, *The Challenge of Fundamentalism: Political Islam and the New World Disorder* (Berkeley: University of California Press, 1998).

[25] For recent overviews of these themes see Alexander Lyon Macfie, *Orientalism: A Reader* (New York: New York University Press, 2001); Lockman, *Contending Visions of the Middle East.*

ness in deconstructing the problem, it only offers tentative means of reconstructing what might resemble a solution.

Since the end of the Cold War, the lack of visible reconstructive power of post-modernist and post-orientalist scholarship has been problematic for those seeking to have an impact on policy making. Akbar Ahmed's preface to the 2004 edition of his book, *Postmodernism and Islam*, highlights that while intellectually the argument about a postmodernist approach to Islamic studies might already have won the day when his book was first published some twelve years earlier, the policy choices that were devised after 9/11 very much reflected the views of Islam put forward by old and new orientalists.[26] The collapse of the 'Grand Narrative', typical of the postmodern approaches that became common in western academia from the 1980s onwards began to reach political consciousness by the early 1990s, as the collapse of the communist bloc induced a search for new paradigms in international politics.[27] Yet, in Islamic studies, there was clearly a strong resistance to the death of this 'Grand Narrative' by orientalists—an exercise that often turned to demonology against Said among the neo-orientalists. Importantly, there was also resistance by scholars and commentators in other disciplines who sought to propose new over-arching paradigms and who found comfort in the stability that orientalists proposed in their cultural paradigms. Clearly, Huntington's notion of clash of civilizations is directly connected to Lewis' argument on the same topic. Benjamin Barber's explanatory scheme in *Jihad vs. MacWorld* is also organized on some grand binary division of tradition and modernity.[28] While such arguments were alive and well throughout the 1990s, they often gave the impression of fighting a rearguard battle against post-orientalist perspectives. Yet, at the beginning of the twenty-first century, in policy circles, they were repositioned at the forefront of

[26] As for the Muslim community, Ahmed already observed in the early 1990s that the turn to postmodernism there was at best a sparkle in the eyes of some young thinkers. Akbar S. Ahmed, *Postmodernism and Islam: Predicament and Promise*, revised edition (London: Routledge, 2004).

[27] See Jean-Francois Lyotard, *The Post-Modern Condition: A Report on Knowledge*, trans. G. Bennington and B. Massumi (Minneapolis: University of Minnesota Press, 1984); and compare, Q. Skinner (ed.), *The Return of Grand Theory in the Human Sciences* (Cambridge: Cambridge University Press, 1985).

[28] Benjamin Barber, *Jihad vs. McWorld: How Globalism and Tribalism are Reshaping the World* (New York: Ballantine Books, 1996).

the intellectual debate due to the propitious circumstances created for them by 9/11.

Throughout the 1990s, there were also inadvertent supporters of a return to a Grand Narrative for Islam from unexpected quarters, such as feminist scholarship. In that context, the brand of western feminism that targeted new audiences in the countries of the developing world inadvertently recreated artificial totalities like the oppressed 'Women' versus the oppressive 'Tradition'. Thus, blanket statements about Islam, as a single cohesive entity, being inimical to the emancipation of 'Women' (another unitary category), permeated the literature and the policy-making community.[29] In these perspectives it was not only the 'Orient' and particularly the Muslim world that were problematic, but also those Muslim communities living in the 'West' and the intellectual and policy views informed by strong notions of multiculturalism.[30] One central orientalist bias reproduced in those debates was the binary opposition between Islam and the West—with the 'West' representing an advanced stage of women's emancipation and empowerment, while the Muslim world and its traditions were synonymous with sustained incivility toward women. The other important bias that was introduced was the representation of Muslim women as passive agents and victims of socio-political transformations and not as productive agents of change. Eventually, these over-deterministic views from orientalist-influenced feminist analyses began increasingly to be challenged in the second half of the 1990s by field-work-informed research by feminist scholars in the region.[31]

---

[29] For critiques of these tendencies see, U. Narayan and S. Harding (eds.), *Philosophy for a Multicultural, Postcolonial and Feminist World* (Bloomington: Indiana University Press, 2000); Lila Abu-Lughod 'Orientalism and Middle East feminist studies', *Feminist Studies*, 27 (1) 2001, pp. 101–13.

[30] See the tense debates on this issue among the contributors to Susan Moller Okin, *Is Multiculturalism Bad for Women?* (Princeton: Princeton University Press, 1999).

[31] See particularly, Parvin Paidar, *Women and the Political Process in Twentieth Century Iran* (Cambridge: Cambridge University Press, 1995); Nilüfer Göle, *The Forbidden Modern: Civilization and Veiling* (Ann Arbor: University of Michigan Press, 1996). More recent analyses in the same vein also emphasize the active and transformative role of women in Islamic mobilization. See Jenny White, *Islamist Mobilization in Turkey: A Study in Vernacular Politics* (Seattle: University of Washington Press, 2002); Saba Mahmood, *Politics of Piety: The*

Perhaps more than the internal strength of orientalist scholarship, this resilience of orientalist narratives in analyses of political Islam pointed to the relative weakness of non-essentialist alternatives—especially those with clear policy options. Turner stressed that, 'it is difficult for critics of orientalism to confront the issue of the "real Orient", particularly if they adopt an anti-foundationalist position of discourse. Postmodern episte-mologies do not promise an alternative orthodoxy'.[32] In addition, there is the extra difficulty introduced by various forms of orientalism 'in reverse' and self-orientalization—i.e. local attempts at indigenizing one's own culture to make it look more 'genuine'.[33] Importantly, however, the field of post-orientalist approaches to Islamism does not constitute by any degree of imagination a homogeneous disciplinary domain. Concep-tually, these approaches are less likely to produce such homogeneity since they are not based on the premises of a grand narrative that would char-acterize Islam and Muslim societies. Practically, their heterogeneity is underpinned by a situation in which, as Zackary Longman suggested, 'the "revolt" against Orientalism took the form of an assertion of the superiority of discipline-based approaches and methods over the civili-zational paradigm and philological methods now increasingly perceived as the hallmarks of Orientalism'.[34] To a degree, the contemporary frag-mentation and the lack of interconnected narratives in post-orientalism is a structural consequence of the over-homogenization of the field of Islamic studies generated by preceding orientalist approaches.

Mapping out post-orientalist readings of Islamism

Three main approaches have been consistently developed from the 1980s onwards in order to move past orientalism. First, in the aftermath of

---

Islamic Revival and the Feminist Subject (Princeton: Princeton University Press, 2004).

[32] Bryan S. Turner, *Orientalism, Postmodernism and Globalism* (London: Routledge, 1994), p. 101.

[33] See Sadiq Jalal Al-'Azm, 'Orientalism and Orientalism in reverse' in J. Roth-schild (ed.), *Forbidden Agendas: Intolerance and Defiance in the Middle East* (London: Al-Saqi Books, 1984); Mona Abaza and Georg Stauth, 'Occidental reason, Orientalism, Islamic fundamentalism: a critique', *International Sociol-ogy* 3 (4) 1988, pp. 343–64.

[34] Lockman, *Contending Visions of the Middle East*, pp. 165–6.

Said's pioneering work, there has been a keen interest in Islamism as a postcolonial discourse in the field of postcolonial studies. Second, merging earlier political economy approaches and post-structuralist perspectives, there have been attempts in the field of historical sociology and anthropology at detailing the micro-politics of power and knowledge, particularly in the Middle East. Third, there has been a political science and area-studies drive towards analyzing Islamism as a distinctly modern/post-modern set of processes and practices.

From the perspective of what could be loosely termed postcolonial studies, analysts are attempting to understand and explain better the dynamics of change by stressing the need to give a 'voice' to the 'subaltern'. In our context, this means presenting the views of the local actors without prejudging on the basis of epistemic superiority what are valid and invalid statements regarding Islam and Muslim society. The basic advantages and the dilemmas of this approach are well articulated in Gayatri Spivak's analysis of the relation between European intellectuals and the representatives of non-European traditions.[35] She emphasizes how the weight of the epistemic structures that are pressed upon the 'subaltern knowledges', renders them unable to present meaningfully their perspectives unless it is articulated in the terminology of 'western' social (or scientific) theory. In such postcolonial studies, the task of academic research is not to trivialize or invalidate local views but rather to enable them to have an impact on the debate by widening the parameters of what counts as valid discourse. This is no easy task, and at times postcolonial theorists have questioned the ingenuity of this de-centring of the western social sciences by scholars wanting to engage with outsiders/subalterns. Arjun Appadurai contrasts the 'weak internationalization' of knowledge, which amounts to the hegemony and institutionalization of Euro-American scholarly views and methods in the contemporary social sciences, to what would be a 'strong internationalization' of knowledge in which subaltern perspectives would also be included in an expended conceptual horizon.[36] The conceptual difficulties of a genuine engagement

---

[35] Gayatri C. Spivak, 'Can the subaltern speak?', in C. Nelson and L. Grossberg (eds.), *Marxism and the Interpretation of Culture* (Chicago: Chicago University Press, 1988); *A Critique of Postcolonial Reason: Toward a History of the Vanishing Present* (Cambridge: Harvard University Press, 1999).

[36] Arjun Appadurai, 'Grassroots globalization and the research imagination', *Public Culture* 12 (1) 2000, pp. 1–19.

with non-'western' knowledges have to do with the complexity of a putative fusion of perspectives; while the practical difficulties are due to the
resistance offered by some sections of the western social sciences that are
primarily interested in talking to themselves. Additionally, there is a risk
that essentialism returns in disguise if one was to take the notion of 'western' versus 'Islamic' science too far. Homi Bhabha notes that both in general conceptual terms and vis-à-vis specific cases, eurocentrism and
orientalism have clear practical manifestation. At the same time, however,
they should not be viewed as fully hegemonic systems. Bhabha stresses
how these structuring discourses can never remove all forms ambivalence
and hybridity; be it in official public narratives or in the everyday practices of people producing and consuming these views.[37]

In relation to political Islam, these conceptual and practical difficulties
are clearly mutually reinforcing. Conceptually, a postcolonial approach to
knowledge would require an inbuilt uncertainty regarding the outcome
of the engagement with the 'Other'. Crucially, as Aziz Al-Azmeh stresses
from a non-essentialist position, Islam (and Islamism) do not refer to an
immutable set of beliefs and practices, but are what Muslims make of it,
and any sense of cohesiveness is based on repeated iteration and implementation of specific aspects of the doctrine.[38] Talal Asad concurs that
from such a perspective, Islam is most readily understood as 'a discursive
tradition that connects variously with the formation of moral selves, the
manipulation of populations (or resistance to it), and the production of
appropriate knowledge'.[39] Islam can thus be seen as a 'master signifier',
as Salman Sayyid suggested; that is to say, something that every Muslim
can agree upon without having to or being able to attribute to it a specific
meaning.[40] In this process, not only Muslims are involved but also all
those non-Muslim actors interacting with them and trying to influence
the way in which they conceive and implement Islamic practice. In this
sense, the very battle to claim a unified structure of meaning is what
defines political Islam.

[37] Homi K. Bhabha, *The Location of Culture* (London: Routledge, 1994).

[38] Aziz Al-Azmeh, *Islams and Modernities* (London: Verso, 1993).

[39] Talal Asad, 'The idea of an anthropology of Islam', Center for Contemporary
Arab Studies Occasional Paper Series, Georgetown University, 1996, p. 7.

[40] Salman Sayyid, *A Fundamental Fear: Eurocentrism and the Emergence of Islamism*, revised edition (London: Zed Books, 2003).

The tensions between subaltern heterogeneity and hegemonic knowledge are well articulated in Sayyid's study of Eurocentrism and Islamism. His account of pre and post-colonial discourses on political Islam addresses the gaps in Said's work concerning the substantive aspects of an Islamic entity that are not captured by the generalities of orientalists narratives. Conceptually, Sayyid is defending a 'strong' version of anti-orientalism, grounded on anti-foundationalism, that places on an equal footing the forceful imposition of western political models during the colonial period and the lengthier intellectual hegemony of the western philosophical tradition(s) on the worldviews of the Muslim communities. From this perspective, the challenge is to specify how one can move away from essentialist accounts of Islam without ending up merely saying that there are different 'Islams'.[41] In the contemporary context, Sayyid proposes that Islam as a unitary (power-laden) idea has been inadvertently constructed by failing Kemalist regimes, at a time when the ideological retreat of what is perceived as the 'West' facilitated the renewal of non-western centric modes of societal organization. In this context, the models of privatization of religion, rise of individualism, scientific materialism and so on contributed to the decentring of the 'West'; which responded by promoting even more its ideals as 'universals'. Thus, for Sayyid, Islamists can very well challenge the intellectual supremacy of the western tradition without knowing exactly what it is they attacking. Yet, he insist that this not a mere reversal of roles, as Islamist discourse has its own potential to generate meaning and practices that are not simply a mirror image of the dominant western structures.[42]

The open-ended interaction with the 'West' is mirrored by a similar process vis-à-vis those resources which are deemed to be 'Islamic'. Asad stresses that a reconstructed Islamic discursive tradition 'addresses itself to conceptions of the Islamic past and future, with reference to a particular Islamic practice in the present'.[43] Such social-anthropology approaches

---

[41] Regarding the difficulties of identifying the nature and relevance of differences in Islam see Al-Azmeh, *Islams and Modernities*, particularly the prologue.

[42] Sayyid, *A Fundamental Fear*. See also Roxanne L. Euben, *Enemy within the Mirror: Islamic Fundamentalism and the Limits of Modern Rationalism: A Work of Comparative Political Theory* (Princeton: Princeton University Press, 1999).

[43] Asad, 'The idea of an anthropology of Islam', p. 14.

emphasize in particular that one should not essentialize these internal 'Islamic' processes, as not everything Muslims say today belongs to an Islamic discursive tradition; nor is this Islamic tradition necessarily imitative of what was done in the past. By their very nature, those analyses of the internal complexities of Islamist constructs offer only limited recommendations that the policy community can directly put to use, considering the blunt tools of policy making at its disposal. They show how important it is to listen and engage with what is happening in these local debates; but even then, the focus is on processes and not outcomes—a process similar to that envisioned by deliberative democracy, but with a different epistemic framework. There is clearly no guarantee that the mere reversal of the existing power-laden systems will not in practice be the outcome of such deliberative processes.[44] Mere duplication remains a possibility; but it is only that, a possibility, not an inevitability. This uncertainty is evidently not something western policy makers or ruling autocrats in the Muslim world are particularly keen to contemplate. In policy contexts, there is a proclaimed willingness to engage only with those 'moderate' Islamists who can duplicate the liberal political discourse. At the same time, those scholars who try to expand the boundaries of the dialogue can be accused of 'going native' and to jettison their moral and intellectual position for an Islamic worldview.

Islamism as (post)modernity: micro-analyses of practical knowledge

A common policy criticism of analyses informed by post-colonial theory is that they remain far too textual and abstract to be used to understand how social and political processes unfold on the ground. As Christine Sylvester noted, when considering the interconnections between postcolonial scholarship and developmental expertise, 'development studies does not tend to listen to subalterns and postcolonial studies does not tend to concern itself with whether the subaltern is eating'.[45] John Briggs and

---

[44] Undoubtedly, Islamist-inspired structures of governance can also be a simple reversal of the order instituted by colonial powers and/or their nationalist successors. For an argument that stresses this aspect of the dynamics of political Islam in the contemporary Middle East, see Nicola Pratt, *Democracy and Authoritarianism in the Arab World* (Boulder: Lynne Rienner, 2007).

[45] Christine Sylvester, 'Development studies and postcolonial studies: disparate

Joanne Sharp similarly stressed that 'many postcolonial theorists consider development studies still to be mired in modernist, or even colonialist, mindsets; to many involved with development work, postcolonialism is seen to offer overly complex theories ignorant of the real problems characterizing everyday life in the majority world.[46] They further note a lack of cross-referencing between the different types of literature, which undermines the strength of 'postdevelopmental' approaches. This post-developmental drive, as Arturo Escobar suggested, would combine postmodern/postcolonial critiques of a full reliance on western phrased expertise/rationality with a better integration of grassroots knowledges and alternative socio-economic experiences.[47] It would involve a marked break with the assumption that 'developing' communities are in need of 'development' because they deviate from the norms produced and measured from a western perspective. In this sense, to understand better the local dynamics of Islamism it may be extremely useful to stop 'seeing like a state', as James Scoot suggested.[48] Evidently, however, empowering local knowledges should not mean believing in the necessary superiority of local discourses.

The accounts of the micro-constructions of power and of truth in the Middle Eastern context using Foucauldian methods of analysis have been well elaborated by Timothy Mitchell in his influential *Colonizing Egypt*.[49] Mitchell's emphasis is not so much on the theoretical opposition between a scientific and a local knowledge but rather on the practical and unmedi-

---

tales of the Third World', *Third World Quarterly* 20 (4) 1999, pp. 703–21, at p. 703.

[46] John Briggs and Joanne Sharp, 'Indigenous knowledges and development: a postcolonial caution', *Third World Quarterly* 25 (4) 2004, pp. 661–76, at p. 663.

[47] Arturo Escobar, *Encountering Development: The Making and Unmaking of the Third World* (Princeton: Princeton University Press, 1995).

[48] Scott's suggestion does not apply specifically to Islamism but to all local knowledges. James C Scott, *Seeing like a State: How Certain Schemes to Improve the Human Condition Have Failed* (New Haven: Yale University Press, 1999).

[49] Timothy Mitchell, *Colonising Egypt* (Berkeley: University of California Press, 1991). See also the more recent assessment contained in Timothy Mitchell, *Rule of Experts: Egypt, Techno-Politics, Modernity* (Berkeley: University of California Press, 2002).

ated interpenetration of 'East' and 'West'. It is not a case of the colonial powers imposing a blueprint for development on their conquered lands, but more a case of an uncoordinated internal colonization of a traditional worldview, by a series of scientific-technical-bureaucratic measures designed to 'help' the (relevant) people to help themselves. As Khaled Fahmy highlighted from a similar perspective, not only colonial powers, but also the would-be new Egyptian elite contributed to this process.[50] This occurred less out of political calculation than through a pragmatic reorganization of their own knowledge and access to expanding Europeanized power networks. Although these works are mostly concerned with the diffusion of Europeanized models of governance in a Muslim polity, similar studies of the capillaries of power have been proposed regarding the process of 'colonization' of the institutions of the modern state by political Islam.[51]

Considering the case of women's pietist organizations in the Egyptian context, Saba Mahmood stresses that it is not the case that the pietists have 'politicized' the spiritual domain but that circumstances are such that for any social project to be effective, it must engage with the all-encompassing institutions of the modern state.[52] The emergence of a recognizably political form of Islam is less the outcome of the reaffirmation of 'old' models of social order in the face of 'new' imported models, than the reorganization of interpenetrated systems of social ordering. As Salwa Ismail suggests in opposition to orientalist arguments about theological structures forcing Islamists to make no distinction between the religious and the political, Islamism evolves as a bottom up local tradition alongside other pre-existing modes of social organisation that are also re-inserted into the new networks of governance created by the modern state.[53] The insights gained from such micro-analyses of power can remain nonetheless difficult to generalize using the standard positivist epistemology

---

[50] Khaled Fahmy, *All the Pasha's Men: Mehmed Ali, His Army and the Making of Modern Egypt* (Cambridge: Cambridge University Press, 1997).

[51] Clearly, Islamist actors are only one of the many actors involved in the everyday practices of government that shape the micro-political and micro-social formation and circulation of power in the Egyptian polity. Compare Salwa Ismail, *Political Life in Cairo's New Quarters: Encountering the Everyday State* (Minneapolis: University of Minnesota Press, 2006), with Salwa Ismail, *Rethinking Islamist Politics: Culture, the State and Islamism* (London: I. B. Tauris, 2003).

[52] Mahmood, *Politics of Piety*, pp. 193–4.

[53] Ismail, *Rethinking Islamist Politics*.

that dominates the policy field. In particular they cannot easily compete with the grand narratives about political Islam proposed by neo-orientalism, as what may be useful to know about suburban Cairo may appear less relevant to policy makers than what is proposed in those accounts purportedly describing Islamism in its entirety.

Those post-orientalist scholars concerned with policy making who do not operate primarily on the basis of micro-analyses separate themselves from the orientalist tradition by proposing that political Islam is best understood as a break between past and present, and primarily as a contemporary phenomenon. In the 1980s, Middle Eastern specialists ranging from Nazih Ayubi to Sami Zubaida began to produce sophisticated analyses of what was then called the 'Islamic revival' that avoided many of the pitfalls of orientalism. Ayubi suggested that political Islam was 'not an old doctrine that is currently being resurrected, but rather a new doctrine that is in the process now of being invented'. In historical terms, he estimated that the Islamist phenomenon 'emerged as a moralist/culturalist response to a severe developmental crisis that engulfs many Arab societies'.[54] Nonetheless, Ayubi recognized that there was no straightforward connection between the concrete problems of this crisis and the ideological responses offered by Islamist movements. Zubaida too stressed the view that, 'current Islamic movements and ideas are not the product of some essential continuity with the past, but are basically "modern"'. He argued that 'the Islamic phenomenon in politics is the product of particular political and socio-economic conjunctures, and that the success of the Islamic revolution in Iran is a major (if not *the* major) factor in these conjunctures'. Yet, Zubaida also recognized that economic and political problems did not in themselves determine an Islamic response.[55]

In these early post-orientalist accounts of Islamism, analysts commonly over-emphasized the causal connections between a given economic or political situation and the specific articulation of political Islam. Many of the 'political economy' accounts of Islamism in the 1980s tended to reduce the phenomenon largely to the revolt of marginalized male constituencies

---

[54] Nazih N. Ayubi, *Political Islam: Religion and Politics in the Arab World* (London: Routledge, 1992), pp. 119, 230.

[55] Sami Zubaida, *Islam, the People and the State: Political Ideas and Movements in the Middle East* (London: I. B. Tauris, 1993), pp.ix, xviii.

in specific socio-economic circumstances.[56] Undoubtedly, this relation may be very relevant at times, but it does not encapsulate the entire dynamics of the contemporary articulation of political Islam. For many scholars, it soon became evident that there was a need for more precise interpretations that distinguished between the material and ideational elements of the process. Materially, it remained questionable how far Islamism represented primarily a reaction to the perceived failures of the secular developmentalist ideologies of the postcolonial regimes.[57] Ideo-logically it was also unclear how far it amounted to what Fred Halliday presented as 'a general rejection of the secular modernity associated with radical nationalist politics and with the modernizing state'.[58] Sayyid warned that unless one reverted to traditional orientalist stereotypes there was no straightforward and necessary connection between failing nation-alist regimes and the emergence of a specifically Islamic alternative to westernized modernity.[59] John Esposito concurred that these failures strengthened alternative discourses proposing Islamic types of devel-opment and modernity, but noted that this was not an unavoidable or natural outcome.[60] What was highly relevant for these post-orientalist analyses, as Zubaida emphasized, was that Islam was becoming 'estab-lished as dominant idiom of political expression'.[61] This did not mean that political Islam was an uncontested (or incontestable) model for political engagement in the late twentieth century, but it was one that had to be taken seriously for practical political purposes.

This last point has been mostly developed throughout the 1990s by scholars who engaged critically with the views proposed by contemporary Islamist movements and ideologues. This represented an effort to free up the scholarship in Islamic studies from the rigid analytical framework

[56] See for example, Bruce Lawrence, *Defenders of God The Fundamentalist Revolt Against the Modern Age* (San Francisco: Harper & Row, 1989).

[57] For an account of their successes and failures see, Roger Owen, *State, Power and Politics in the Making of the Modern Middle East*, 3rd edition (London: Routledge, 2004).

[58] Fred Halliday, *The Middle East in International Relations: Power, Politics and Ideology* (Cambridge: Cambridge University Press, 2005), p. 122.

[59] Sayyid, *A Fundamental Fear*.

[60] John L. Esposito, *Political Islam: Revolution, Radicalism, or Reform?* (Boulder: Lynne Rienner, 1997).

[61] Zubaida, *Islam, the People and the State*, p.xxi.

derived from traditional orientalist approaches, and from their tendency towards textual and historical over-determination. In this context, two main perspectives have been particularly useful for subsequent research on Islamism. First, they highlighted the hermeneutic character of the Islamic tradition(s) and the openness of the contemporary politico-theological debates. They stressed that contemporary interpretive efforts amounted to making sense of modern developments in the light of the past but not predetermined by the past. Second, they emphasized the complexities and diversity of the socio-historical context of Muslim (rather than primarily 'Islamic') societies; thereby providing a more open-ended account of the non-textual traditions influencing the formation of contemporary Islamism.[62] Regarding the relationship between the failure of nationalist models and the rise of Islamism, the influence of what could be loosely termed the French school (Olivier Roy, Gilles Kepel, and their colleagues) is also noticeable. What characterizes these approaches is a progression of the theorizing of the emergence of Islamism from the local to the global. Developing their research on the basis of their area studies specialism—Afghanistan (Roy), Egypt (Kepel)—these scholars proposed more sophisticated narratives to explain the variable process of social construction of Islamism that avoided essentialist constructions of Islam.[63] As Roy put it succinctly in his case against modern versions of orientalism, 'historical and cultural paradigms are misleading to the extent that they do not help us to understand what is new'.[64] Their alternative explanations of the contemporary strength of Islamism emphasize instead the mechanisms of path-dependency.

As the controversies generated by Roy's *The Failure of Political Islam* illustrated, there are drawbacks to path-dependency approaches that display some of the flaws of the orientalist narratives. By taking a specific form of Islamic political activism—in this case the militant and revolutionist strand—, to be representative of political Islam as a whole, Roy

---

[62] See particularly, Dale F. Eickelman and James Piscatori, *Muslim Politics* (Princeton: Princeton University Press, 1996).

[63] Olivier Roy, *The Failure of Political Islam*, trans. C. Volk (Cambridge: Harvard University Press, 1994); Gilles Kepel, *Jihad: The Trail of Political Islam*, trans. A.F. Roberts (London: I.B. Tauris, 2002).

[64] Olivier Roy, *Globalized Islam: The Search for a New Ummah* (London: Hurst & Co., 2004), p. 15.

contributed to the recreation of a grand narrative. As many critics pointed out, however, it required an effort of imagination (or a lack of attention to details) to see all the developments of political Islam in the twentieth century as spin-off of this type of armed militancy.[65] Many other forms of Islamism not directly linked to these movements—Wahabbi rigourism, Tablighi pietism, etc.—grew in strength quite independently of these militant political movements. What could be said to have failed, then, was more modestly a particular strand of Islamic political militancy, not the entire Islamist phenomenon. It was suggested earlier that one of the key dimensions of orientalist scholarship that ensured its resilience over-time was its centrifugal character. Every aspect of this expertise was locked into a symbiotic relation with a master interpretation of the Islamic tradition. Every contemporary trend could be understood better by linking it to an historical and textual reading of Islam; every local reading of Islam, past and present, could be understood better in the light of western intellectual and scientific advances. Internally and externally there has been a buttressing of the position that an adequate understanding of Muslim society could not be gained without these insights into the 'Muslim mind' provided by such an appreciation of history and the Scriptures. In doing so, traditional Islamic studies stressed two types of continuities at the expense of all others. First they emphasized the semantic continuity provided by the Islamic legal and theological texts (usually written in Arabic). Second, they emphasized the historical continuity between past—often the very distant past—and present. Because of these choices regarding what counts at 'proper' data for analyzing the Islamic/Islamist phenomenon the possibilities of invalidating or challenging these 'findings' were extremely limited. Turner's observation that 'orientalism is a self-validating and closed tradition which is highly resistant to internal and external criticism' remains highly relevant to this day.[66] Indeed, in 1990, Lewis had asserted that what was at the heart of the process of 'clash of civilizations' was 'the perhaps irrational but surely historic reaction of an ancient rival against our Judeo-Christian heritage, our secular

---

[65] See François Burgat, 'De l'islamisme au postislamisme, vie et mort d'un concept', pp. 82–92; Alain Roussillon, 'Les islamologues dans l'impasse', pp. 93–115; as well as the reply by Olivier Roy, 'Les islamologues ont-ils inventé l'islamisme?', pp. 116–38, in *Esprit*, August 2001.

[66] Turner, *Orientalism, Postmodernism and Globalism*, p. 31.

present, and the worldwide expansion of both'.[67] The enduring attractive-ness of these views is unmistakable today, especially in policy circles and the mass media. Yet, the purported rationale for this 'irrational' but 'his-toric' reaction is as wanting as it ever was. What remains abundantly clear is how the reutilization of orientalist clichés on a piecemeal basis in neighbouring disciplines—as with Huntington's revised version of civi-lizational *realpolitik*—helps perpetuate these narratives.

[67] Bernard Lewis, 'The Roots of Muslim Rage', *The Atlantic Monthly* 266 (3) 1990, pp. 47–60, at p. 60.

3

INVOKING ISLAMISM
IN INTERNATIONAL STUDIES

Challenging return of the religious or mere accommodation?

Across the board, political Islam appears very little in mainstream international studies literature. Recently, however, it is repeatedly mentioned in those readings of International Relations (IR) influenced by Samuel Huntington's idiosyncratic 'clash of civilizations'. Yet, few if any serious IR specialists have rallied behind Huntington's theoretical propositions. To casual observers of the discipline, it may seem that the situation has changed very little from the one prevailing fifty years ago when Arnold Toynbee's ambitious scheme regarding the rise and fall of civilizations was completely dismissed by a leading IR writer like E.H Carr. For Carr, the explanation of western expansion was to be narrated in terms of the increasing power of the nation-state, and not through civilization or religion.[1] And as with Huntington, by volume seven of Toynbee's massive work it is increasingly clear that civilization becomes a byword for religion in this explanatory scheme. Though the notion of religion *cum* civilization dovetails neatly with the views of orientalist scholarship mentioned in the previous chapter, such a convergence appeared to have little practical relevance in the face of state-centric views or notions of *realpolitik*. In western international studies circles, representations of pan-

---

[1] Compare Arnold J. Toynbee, *A Study of History, Vol. VII-X* (Oxford: Oxford University Press, 1988), with Edward H. Carr, *The Twenty Years Crisis 1919–1939* (London: Palgrave 2001).

Islamism from the end of the Ottoman Empire to the end of World War II are little theorised and remain mainly a side issue.[2] In those debates, religion is indeed mentioned, and political Islam is repeatedly being invoked as an odd occurrence—in much the same way as it would be used after the Iranian Revolution of 1979. Religious factors, then like now, remain in the background, as a set of interesting but idiosyncratic dependent variables that few self-respecting IR theorists would use as the foundations of a serious explanation of international relations.[3]

In the margins of the IR debates there have been repeated calls for including religion in international studies.[4] It is being suggested that the international community is changing, and that religion is a main engine of change—as opposed to the traditional view that religion is conservative, otherworldly, and legitimates the status quo. Hence religion has to be included in IR theorising because it has a tangible relevance to contemporary IR. In the 1980s there were calls for a change, in the way IR viewed and explained the world from well-established scholars in the discipline. Hedley Bull viewed this transformation as an outcome of the maturation of IR in the developing world.[5] At the time, such calls were given a tangible urgency by the Islamic revolution in Iran.[6] Later in the 1990s, similar arguments were supported by the apparent rise of ethno-religious conflict. The ethno-religious and 'civilizational' factors were popularized by Huntington's 'clash' theory, though Huntington him-

[2] Dwight E. Lee, 'The origins of pan-Islamism', *The American Historical Review* 47 (2) 1942, pp. 278–87.

[3] See Terry Nardin, 'Epilogue', in F. Petito and P. Hatzopolous (eds.), *Religion in International Relations: The Return from Exile* (New York: Palgrave Macmillan, 2003), pp. 271–82; Nicholas Rengger, '*Eternal return? Modes of encountering religion in international relations*', Millennium 32 (2) 2003, pp. 327–36.

[4] See Scott M. Thomas, *The Global Resurgence of Religion and the Transformation of International Relations: the Struggle for the Soul of the Twenty-first Century* (London: Palgrave, 2005).

[5] H. Bull and A. Watson (eds.), *The Expansion of International Society* (Oxford: Oxford University Press, 1985).

[6] See A.E.H. Dessouki (ed.), *Islamic Resurgence in the Arab World* (New York: Praeger 1982); Leonard Binder, 'Failure, defeat, debacle: US policy in the Middle East', *World Politics* 36 (3) 1984, pp. 437–60; Ali A. Mazrui, 'Changing the guards from Hindu to Muslims: collective Third World security in a cultural perspective', *International Affairs* 57 (1) 1980–81, pp. 1–20.

self did not really propose anything else than a regional-based form of neo-realism. His 'civilizations' correspond to a traditional typology of Great Powers and their zones of influence. Although the 'Islamic' zone does not have a real Great Power at its core, Huntington interprets political Islam as having a Wahhabi (Saudi) and Khomeinist (Iranian) core. Beyond such a simple re-modelling, however, some analysts argued for a more thorough re-conceptualisation of the way IR was being explained and understood in the post-Cold War context. Scott Thomas suggested that:

> the Western culture of modernity and the institutions of international society embedded in it are being challenged by the global resurgence of religion and cultural pluralism in international relations. As a result of this large-scale religious change, international society is becoming a genuinely multicultural international society for the very first time.[7]

The invocation of an international society in opposition to a Westphalian state system driven by anarchy and national interest is again not new.[8] The key issue remains to appreciate fully how far religion is, or can be, a main factor in such a reconfiguration of world order.

The dramatic events of 9/11 lent more ammunition to those scholars calling for a genuinely new framework to study international politics. In the wake of the al-Qaeda attacks, many international studies specialists began to speculate that this new form of transnational Islamic radicalism constituted a novel and significant challenge to the world order and to conventional views of international relations.[9] One such grand statement about the demise of the Westphalian synthesis is depicted, with the

[7] Scott M. Thomas, 'Taking religious and cultural pluralism seriously: the global resurgence of religion and the transformation of international society', *Millennium* 29 (3) 2000, pp. 815–41, at p. 815. See also Scott M. Thomas, *The Global Resurgence of Religion*.

[8] See for example, Timothy Dunne, *Inventing International Society: A History of the English School* (London: MacMillan 1998); Mathias Brock, Lothar Wolf and Klaus Dieter Albert, *Civilizing World Politics: Society and Community Beyond the State* (Lanham: Rowman & Littlefield, 2000).

[9] See for example, Jonathan Fox and Shmuel Sandler, *Bringing Religion into International Relations* (New York: Palgrave, 2004); Eric O. Hanson, *Religion and Politics in the International System Today* (Cambridge: Cambridge University Press 2006).

appropriate lyrical overtones, in the pages of *World Politics* by Daniel Philpott:

On September 11 the synthesis was shaken by the fitful rumblings of a Rip Van Winkle awakening from long centuries of slumber, a figure whose identity is public religion—religion that is not privatized within the cocoon of the individual or the family but that dares to refashion secular politics and culture. Of all the fits and starts in the arousal of public religion over the past generation, the most radical and volatile is a political theology—radical Islamic revivalism, it can be called—that directly challenges the authority structure of the international system.[10]

With surprising rapidity after 9/11, a new consensus emerged stressing that, yes, some things had changed, but by and large the era of the 'War on Terror' was very similar to earlier periods in international relations. Political Islam, for all the 'radical' religiosity that accompanies it, did not appear to be providing enough of an impulse to change the dominant world order (and the dominant interpretations of it).[11] It seemed that the demands for taking religion seriously could be accommodated within pre-existing paradigms, or that they could even remain safely unanswered at the level of theory. Fred Halliday's works in IR theory and on the Middle East and political Islam provide a good illustration of such a deflationary approach. In the 1980s, when he produced his *Rethinking International Relations*, it was clear that of all the concepts that needed to be rethought, religion was not one of them. A decade later, in *Islam and the Myth of Confrontation*, he quite persuasively argued that beyond the Middle East, the case for commonalities that supposedly characterise Islamic politics rested on rather flimsy premises. In the aftermath of 9/11, Halliday concluded that a better understanding of socio-economic transformations, from a neo-Marxist perspective, allied to a more constructivist approach to power politics in international relations, would provide a much better understanding of the evolution of politics in the Middle East and of the growth of political Islam.[12]

---

[10] Daniel Philpott, 'The challenges of September 11 to secularism in international relations', *World Politics* 55 (1) 2002, pp. 66–95, at p. 67.

[11] See the contributors to K. Booth and T. Dunne (eds.), *Worlds in Collision: Terror and the Future of Global Order* (London Palgrave-Macmillan, 2002).

[12] Fred Halliday, *Rethinking International Relations; Islam and the Myth of Confrontation: Religion and Politics in the Middle East*, revised edition (London: I.B

In many ways, the calls for rethinking IR after 9/11 resemble the concerns that were expressed after the Iranian Revolution, as do the answers provided. After the initial surprise and the flurry of activities concerning the potential challenges to world order posed by the Islamic Republic of Iran, the bulk of IR theory simply took Iran in its stride. From the mid 1980s onward, the consensus which emerged was distinctly that the Islamic Republic was very much behaving like any other nation-state around it.[13] Undoubtedly, its foreign policy had some idiosyncratic elements—the attempts at winning over the Shi'a population of Iraq, the support for Hizbollah in Lebanon, or even Khomeini's death sentence for the British-based author Salman Rushdie. By and large, IR specialists argued, these idiosyncrasies were no more of a challenge to the international system and the conventional understanding of its workings than that of other troublesome nation-states. This normalization of Iranian exceptionalism became even more marked after the death of Khomeini. Then, the new leadership turned away from a policy of making Iran the centre of an expanding Islamic revolution and tried to ensure instead that the country became once more the dominant regional player in the Gulf.[14]

These insights suggest that there may be few good reasons to invest time and energy trying to understand the specific impact of political Islam, since it appears that it can be subsumed under traditional (neo) realist or (neo)liberal-institutionalist frames of reference. In this perspective, the controversies surrounding political Islam are primarily a matter confined to the behaviour of militarily, politically, and economically emergent states that are at best regional powers—Iran, Saudi Arabia, Pakistan, etc. Thus it makes sense to look past the theoretical debates about religion, since at policy level much of the effort of the main international actors during the period of the 'War on Terror' consisted in co-opting such regional powers. Following Kenneth Waltz' lead that a 'general

---

Tauris, 2003); *The Middle East in International Relations: Power, Politics and Ideology* (Cambridge: Cambridge University Press, 2005).

[13] For a pragmatic reading of Iranian foreign policy see, Rouhollah K. Ramazani, *Revolutionary Iran: Challenge and Response in the Middle East* (Baltimore: John Hopkins University Press, 1987).

[14] See Anoushiravan Ehteshami, *After Khomeini: The Iranian Second Republic* (London: Routledge, 1995).

theory of international politics is necessarily based on the great powers', many neo-realist analysts simply do not see any reason or cause for change in their views of IR in this context.[15] Even for more constructivist-minded scholars, the risk that international relations may just amount to a Eurocentric framework, focusing primarily on what interests western policy-makers, is not deemed to be an insurmountable problem. Clearly there are times at which the behaviour of peripheral state and non-state actors is quite troublesome or unexpected, but by and large, the dominant western understandings of IR have proven to be quite resilient in the face of these rather limited material and conceptual challenges.[16]

Disciplinarity in IR and orientalism

The theoretical perspectives outlined in the abovementioned debates point to an affinity between the self-referential construction of orientalism, as a specific corpus of knowledge, and that of IR theory, at least until very recently. For critical analysts these views constitute a dominant discourse in support of the exercise of power in the international system. Richard Ashley suggested that such a situation generates in particular, 'silence regarding the historicity of the boundaries it produces, the space it historically clears and the subjects it historically constitutes'.[17] By trying to uncover the 'iron laws' of the international system, several strands of the realist tradition constructed idealized historical narratives that illustrated the 'timeless truths' of power politics, as expressed in scholarly works going back to Thucydides or Hobbes. Unsurprisingly, such textual historical approaches heightened the relevance of the narratives produced by orientalist scholars.

[15] Kenneth Waltz, *Theory of International Politics* (New York: McGraw-Hill, 1979), p. 73.

[16] See the overview provided in Barry Buzan and Richard Little, *International Systems in World History: Remaking the Study of International Relations* (Oxford: Oxford University Press, 2000). And compare the more critical assessment contained in Tarak Barkawi and Mark Laffey, 'The postcolonial moment in security studies', *Review of International Studies* 32 (2) 2006, pp. 329–32.

[17] Richard K. Ashley, 'The geopolitics of geopolitical space: toward a critical social theory of international politics', *Alternatives* 12 (4) 1987, pp. 403–34.

Beside such similarities regarding the centrality of historical texts and events in the construction of theory, there are particular affinities between foreign policy analysis and the notion of an Islamic/Muslim mindset developed through orientalism. The 'political culture' debates that became fashionable in the 1960s, alongside the behaviouralist and rational choice trends in comparative politics, rapidly colonized the field of IR.[18] These arguments inserted themselves into pre-existing specialism such as the older corpus of literature on military cultures in security studies and on diplomatic culture in international relations—a corpus with clear links to the orientalist tradition. In such a context, it is unsurprising that if mainstream IR theory can leave some room for manoeuvre to the 'cultural' aspect of the international, it is only at the margins. As David Elkins and Richard Simeon argued at the time of the Iranian revolution, political culture becomes the explanation of last resort when everything else has failed.[19] More recent culturalist efforts, particularly in security studies, have tried to strengthen their methodological approach to ensure that they are not providing merely a stop-gap theory when various rational choice models fail to provide useful explanations. Commonly, however, such reworking is viewed as supplementing (neo)realism/(neo)institutionalism rather than replacing these paradigms.[20] Noticeably, although no other theoretical approaches in IR may provide a better set of conceptual premises for thinking about these issues, few constructivist accounts have thus far addressed frontally the religious issue.

Culturalist perspectives in foreign policy analysis repeatedly show that they are prone to revert to the kind of essentialism that characterizes ori-

---

[18] See for example, Leonard Binder, *The Ideological Revolution in the Middle East* (New York: John Wiley and Sons, 1964); Gabriel Ben-Dor, 'Political culture approach to Middle East politics', *International Journal of Middle East Studies* 8 (1) 1977, pp. 43–63. See also the more recent reappraisal in S.P. Huntington and L.E. Harrison (eds.), *Culture Matters: How Values Shape Human Progress* (New York: Basic Books, 2001).

[19] David J. Elkins and Richard E.B. Simeon, 'A cause in search of its effect, or what does political culture explain?', *Comparative Politics* 11 (2) 1979, pp. 127–45.

[20] See Michael C. Desch, 'Culture clash: assessing the importance of ideas in security studies', *International Security* 23 (1) 1998, pp. 141–70; Jonathan Fox, 'Religion as an overlooked element of international relations', *International Studies Review* 3 (3) 2001, pp. 53–73.

entalism. This essentialist tendency is well represented in the analyses of the Islamic revolution in Iran. In this context, a very common explanation remains that the two main interpretative trends in the Islamic tradition, Sunnism and Shi'ism, are distinct and self-contained phenomena that can be analysed independently in international relations. Revising orientalist propositions, international studies in the late twentieth century presented the Sunni populations as being passive and fatalist, while the Shi'a were deemed to be moved by fanaticism. Mavtin Zonis suggested, a few years after the Iranian revolution, that for Shi'a leaders 'the principal themes of clerical rule include: grandiosity, an insistence on unity, ascription of hostile motives to the actions of other states, a preference for military solutions to political problems, and a belief in ultimate victory'.[21] Even cautious foreign policy assessments of contemporary Shia politics are not impervious into relapsing into clichés, especially after the 2003 invasion of Iraq and the rise of Shi'a activism there. Recently, Vali Nasr commented that 'Shiism since its inception has been defined by the [martyrdom] spirit of Karbala and the passionate rituals whose performance kept the intensity of that searing experience alive and burning bright. While Shias take the notion of Islamic law seriously, their faith is not primarily a law-bound or law-ruled phenomenon'.[22] The tendency toward cultural essentialism is not solely noticeable in relation to Shi'ism. Noting that valuing the example set by the Prophet is an important common denominator between contemporary trends in political Islam, James Bill and Carl Leiden suggested that 'it is not surprising, therefore, that twentieth-century Muslim political leaders often have styles and use strategies that are very similar to those instituted by the Prophet Muhammad in Arabia some 1,400 years ago'.[23]

Conceptually, such invocations of cultural exceptionalism reduce the intellectual challenge posed by political Islam to IR theory since only a fraction of the Islamic world is non-conformist e.g. (the Shi'a, al-Qaeda

---

[21] Marvin Zonis, 'The rule of the clerics in the Islamic Republic of Iran', *ANNALS of the American Academy of Political and Social Science*, vol. 482, 1985, pp. 85–108.

[22] Vali Nasr, *The Shia Revival: How Conflict within Islam will Shape the Future* (New York: Norton & Co, 2006), pp. 134–5.

[23] James Bill and Carl Leiden, *Politics in the Middle East*, 2nd ed. (Boston: Little, Brown & Co., 1984), p. 133.

and its likes). In their turn, the behavioural characteristics of these elements could be assessed using rational choice models and various forms of psycho-pathological analyses. There is a long tradition in comparative politics of cultural analysis; a tradition which has distinctive offshoots in foreign policy analysis, and in security and diplomatic studies. These analyses describe how the cultural specificities of individual nation-states lead them to 'deviate' from the usual 'rational' behaviour in the international domain. In this perspective, 'political Islam' may blend into an Arab culture approach and the Muslim world may be presented as the Middle East writ large. In practice, these cultural approximations enabled foreign policy scholars and practitioners to use traditional realist calculations of balance of power. As Fawaz Gerges illustrated, while Iran might have been beyond the pale in the 1980s, American proxy wars could still go on in Afghanistan where the United States supported a neo-traditionalist rebel movement in collaboration with regional Muslims allies, Pakistan and Saudi Arabia.[24]

Recent perspectives on regionalism portray regions as sub-units of the international system characterized by agents—commonly but not exclusively states—displaying some particular patterns of behaviour. This may be a self-reflective phenomenon akin to a regional 'imagined community' whose common identities and practices may become institutionalized, as in Emanuel Adler's framework.[25] There is a growing influence of globalization theory in this literature emphasising that regions should be conceived less in geographical/physical terms and more in terms of functional entities characterized by flows of ideas and practices, as well as commodities.[26] Commonly the less ambitious (i.e. more statist) notions of regionalism are usually the ones preferred in most of the IR literature.[27] In any

[24] Fawaz A. Gerges, *America and Political Islam: Clash of Cultures or Clash of Interests?* (Cambridge: Cambridge University Press, 1999). See also Fawaz A. Gerges, 'The study of Middle East international relations: a critique', *British Journal of Middle Eastern Studies* 18 (2) 1991, pp. 208–20.

[25] E. Adler and M. Barnett (eds.), *Security Communities* (Cambridge: Cambridge University Press, 1998).

[26] For a useful analogy between physical and functional regions, and Manuel Castells' idea of a space of places and a space of flows see, Raimo Väyrynen, 'Regionalism: old and new', *International Studies Review* 5 (1) 2003, pp. 25–51.

[27] See the contributors to L. Fawcett and A. Hurrell (eds.), *Regionalism in World Politics* (Oxford: Oxford University Press, 1995).

case, there is renewed interest in how regional processes produce specific international outcomes, particularly after the end of the Cold War when accounts of power politics are deemed to be less relevant to the localised behaviour of states and non-state actors.[28] Neo-liberal and neo-institutionalist views as well as constructivist perspectives have used these developments, particularly in connection to models of cooperation in highly integrated regions such as Europe (and increasingly also in the regional contexts of East and South-East Asia). In these debates, the important distinction that is made is between 'universalist' notions of cooperation and the contextual ideas and perspectives of the agents involved.[29] As Andrew Hurrell suggests, context is crucial to understand specific regional dynamics but this does not mean that an entire 'Culture' should be invoked as an explanation.[30] A regional political culture of cooperation may or may not be specifically grounded in the Islamic tradition, but it cannot be assumed that it is the case simply because the agents involved are nominally Muslims.

From these debates it appears that a regionalist model for International Relations is caught between a rock and a hard place. On the one hand, if the focus is on large cultural entities (e.g. 'civilizations') then in superseding the frameworks of other IR paradigms, regional culturalism loses a specific agency for order and change.[31] On the other hand, if it focuses on particular political cultures (e.g. Islamism), this ability to identify the precise loci of agency comes at the price of remaining subservient to the overall statist framework of earlier paradigms. To date, as Raymond Hinnebusch has indicated, to produce a working synthesis of the more

---

[28] See Barry Buzan and Ole Waever, *Regions as Powers: The Structure of International Security* (Cambridge: Cambridge University Press, 2003).

[29] Compare Daniel Philpott, *Revolutions in Sovereignty: How Ideas Shaped Modern International Relations* (Princeton University Press 2001), with Amitav Acharya, *Constructing a Security Community in Southeast Asia: ASEAN and the Problem of Regional Order* (London: Routledge, 2001), and Amitav Acharya, 'How ideas spread: whose norms matter? Norm localization and institutional change in Asian regionalism', *International Organization* 58 (2) 2004, pp. 239–75.

[30] Andrew Hurrell, 'One world? Many worlds? The place of regions in the study of international society', *International Affairs* 83 (1) 2007, pp. 127–46.

[31] See Philip Sutton and Stephen Vertigans, *Resurgent Islam: A Sociological Approach* (Cambridge: Polity Press, 2005).

constructivist-minded and the more realist-minded insights into the contemporary Middle East remains an elusive task.[32] Whatever regional cohesion may have emerged elsewhere in the last few decades, in the Middle East the political dynamics are still characterized by unilateralism and a tangible lack of regionalism.[33] Hence, there remains a dilemma in the sense that, as Louise Fawcett notes, 'identity—as Arabism or Islam— explains important aspects of alliance behaviour, even if there remains a striking disjuncture between shared ideas and institutions'.[34] Critics of the 'cultural' approach, like Halliday, would argue that this dilemma is generated by the too great emphasis placed on the unity of both the Muslim world and the Middle East, and that heterogeneity is more relevant than putative homogenizing forces.[35] From a post-orientalist perspective, Roy concurs that there is no such thing as the 'geopolitics of Islam'.[36] Still, it is quite common for foreign policy analyses to start from very loose premises about the historical and geographical cohesion of the Middle East as a culturally and/or structurally coherent entity.[37] And when the regional dimension of the analysis can no longer hold in the face of evidence, it triggers a retreat into the traditional culturalist views of orientalism. Far too rarely is there an in-depth effort at uncovering some systemic elements of regional politics that can create specific sets of regional opportunities or dilemmas—such as the one that Michael Barnett proposed in relation to Arabism.[38] Similarly, detailed analyses of Islamism

[32] See Raymond Hinnebusch, 'Explaining international politics in the Middle East: the struggle of regional identity and systemic structure', in G. Nonneman (ed.), *Analyzing Middle East Foreign Policies and the Relationship with Europe* (London: Frank Cass, 2005), pp. 243–56. See also Andrea Teti, 'Bridging the gap: IR, Middle East studies and the disciplinary politics of the area studies controversy', *European Journal of International Relations* 13 (1) 2007, pp. 117–45.

[33] Paul Aarts, 'The Middle East: a region without regionalism or the end of exceptionalism?' *Third World Quarterly* 20 (5) 1999, pp. 911–25.

[34] Louise Fawcett, 'Exploring regional domains: a comparative history of regionalism', *International Affairs* 80 (3) 2004, pp. 429–46, at p. 442.

[35] Halliday, *Islam and the Myth of Confrontation*.

[36] Olivier Roy, *The Politics of Chaos in the Middle East* (London: Hurst & Co., 2008).

[37] See L. Carl Brown, *Religion and State: The Muslim Approach to Politics* (New York: Columbia University Press, 2000).

[38] Michael N. Barnett, *Dialogues in Arab Politics: Negotiations in Regional Order*

via the notion of 'Muslim politics', such as the one outlined by Eickelman and Piscatori, remain the exception rather than the rule among the orientalist-leaning trends that commonly shape these IR debates.

Political Islam as shari'a and Islamic state

In neo-liberal and neo-realist approaches looking at the constitution and role of norms in the international system, the role played by culture in a Muslim/Islamic system remains generally under-theorised.[39] The textual emphasis on an 'Islamic' essence over-determines the representation of Islamic normativity in the international community. Such interpretations, which attempt to reintroduce a religious factor in IR theorising, commonly re-articulate descriptions of 'Islamic revival' underpinned by orientalist clichés. After describing with sophistication the way in which the construction of a Wespthalian system became a process of intellectual and practical separation of political and religious rules in European countries, Philpott introduces a crude portrait of contemporary Islamism as an unproblematic and straightforward programme aiming to bring 'Islamic societies under the authority of divine law, *sharia*.'[40] These arguments resonate with common orientalist (and Islamist) discourses, which insist that the development of the modern state is going hand in hand with the secularization of social and political life. Yet, from a more critical perspective, it is readily noticeable that earlier orientalist attempts to present an organic Muslim society divided up by mundane political rivalries have in effect elevated the notion of the shari'a to that of an ubiquitous Islamic cement. Asad stresses that traditionally, 'this contrast between an integrated Islamic society and a fragmented Islamic polity has encour-

---

(New York: Columbia University Press, 1998); Michael Barnett, 'Identity and alliances in the Middle East', in P. Katzenstein (ed.), *The Culture of National Security* (New York: Columbia University Press, 1996), pp. 400–47.

[39] Overall, realism largely downplayed norms, or saw them as instrumental intervening variables between material forces and outcomes. I do not wish to re-open the debate about the role that norms plays in various IR approaches. Rather, I am stressing that even for those approaches concerned with the normative dimension of international interactions, Islamic normativity remains largely a black box.

[40] Philpott, 'The Challenge of September 11', at p. 85.

aged orientalists to oppose the supposedly universal authority of the shari'a (Islamic law), to the changing constellation of political regimes and practices, often accompanied by violence.'[41] In the contemporary context too, neo-liberal and neo-realist accounts, like orientalist ones, are keen to emphasize a chasm between Westphalian notions of secular international order grounded on sovereign states and an 'Islamic' notion of universal order grounded on God's rule. Ultimately, as scholars from Elie Kedourie to Bertrand Badie have argued, this amounts to a categorical incompatibility between Islamic political thought and the concept of sovereign state.[42]

From a critical perspective, by contrast, Sami Zubaida shows how much convergence of views there is between western analysts and Islamist ideologues on the purported place of the shari'a in the political system. He suggests in particular that:

there is a common view that the shari'a is fixed and clearly discernible from its sacred sources. For Muslim ideologists this fixity and clarity are functions of its divine origin. For many Western observers they are functions of the fixity of 'Muslim society', totally other from 'the West', with religion as its essence.[43]

Yet, to take the norms of the shari'a seriously in the production of an international order does not imply interpreting it as a rigid structural whole. As Zubaida emphasizes, one of the key players in the re-positioning of the shari'a in the international system, the Islamic Republic of Iran under Khomeini, was also a main actor in the conceptual and practical overstretching of its role. He notes that because 'the public-law provisions of the shari'a have remained largely theoretical, to do, for instance, with the laws of war and the division of the spoils (…) the task of the Islamic Republic, then, was to derive public law and policy within the framework and vocabulary of legal discourses developed and applied primarily in private contexts'.[44] Soon Khomeini found himself too constrained by tra-

[41] Talal Asad, 'Two European images of non-European rule', *Economy and Society*, 2 (3) 1973, pp. 263–77, at p. 271.

[42] Elie Kedourie, 'The nation-state in the Middle East', *The Jerusalem Journal of International Relations*, 9 (3) 1987, pp. 1–9; Bertrand Badie, *Les Deux Etats: Pouvoirs et société en Occident et en terre d'Islam* (Paris: Fayard, 1986).

[43] Sami Zubaida, *Law and Power in the Islamic World* (London: I.B. Tauris, 2005), p. 1.

[44] Zubaida, *Law and Power in the Islamic World*, p. 2.

ditional readings of the shari'a—for example those endorsing private property when his government wanted to legislate in favour of land redistribution—and argued that the Islamic Republic could abrogate some basic provisions of Islamic law if it was in the public interest (*maslaha*). Increasingly in recent decades, this emphasis on the public interest in Islamist discourse has been repeatedly invoked as an exemption clause in policy discourse. In a constructivist perspective, one could suggest that the role that God's constitution must play in the international system, to paraphrase a well-know argument about anarchy, is what people make of it.

Problematically, those constitutionalist approaches invoking the framework of the shari'a as possible foundation for an institutional order, commonly refer to already well-established (and usually conservative) institutional players.[45] The issue is not so much whether Muslims around the world would entertain the notion of a domestic and international system governed by an ideal shari'a, but what this means in practice for individuals and communities. The question, as An-Naim puts it, 'is not whether a Muslim is committed to the fundamentals of Islam because this is a sentiment shared by the vast majority of Muslims but rather how to implement that commitment in concrete policy and legal terms today'. An-Naim suggests that Muslim communities are better represented by a system of classification that corresponds to 'their commitment to the implementation of the totality of the Shar'ia, including its public law, or their willingness to accept the need for significant revisions and reformulations of some aspects of that law'.[46] One does not need to fully endorse An-Naim's holistic attempt at capturing the practical meaning of the

---

[45] See S.A. Arjomand (ed.), *Constitutional Politics in the Middle East: With Special Reference to Turkey, Iraq, Iran and Afghanistan* (London: Hart Publishers, 2008). This is not a problem specific to political Islam but one that affects most challengers to existing sovereign powers and forms of sovereignty. See from a neo-marxist perspective, Stephen Gill, 'Constitutionalizing inequality and the clash of globalizations', *International Studies Review* 4 (2) 2002, pp. 47–65.

[46] Abdullahi Ahmed An-Naim, *Toward an Islamic Reformation: Civil Liberties, Human Rights, and International Law* (Syracuse: Syracuse University Press, 1990), p. 3. See also more concretely, Abdullahi Ahmed An-Naim, *African Constitutionalism and the Role of Islam* (Philadelphia: University of Pennsylvania Press, 2006).

shari'a and categorizing of states and communities in relation to this, in order to appreciate the level of detail needed to obtain a meaningful analysis of the interaction between Islamist and international practices.[47] In many domestic contexts today there are vigorous debates assessing the depth and breath of the articulation of Islamic jurisprudence in judicial systems grounded in positive law, with clear international implications for human rights.[48] At the constitutional level there are also consequences of seriously considering the shari'a for the institutional structure of the state.[49] However, these two sets of debates do not necessarily shed much light on political Islam itself, simply because they have the term shari'a woven into their narratives.

The other key issue that is commonly deemed to be crucial in IR debates is the notion of state sovereignty. Two observations usually delimit the boundaries of these arguments. On the one hand, as Ayubi remarks, it is argued that 'Islam has no specific theory of the State or of Economics'.[50]. On the other hand, it is said that sovereignty in Islam is not vested in the people but in God. As Gudrun Krämer stresses, however, what is commonly unnoticed in these discussions is that in the Islamic tradition, the notion of sovereignty is more legal and moral than it is political.[51] In this perspective, what is crucial for the Islamic community is to have a specific set of political institutions through which the Law can be implemented and social order maintained. In this respect, Krämer notes that 'while the state is considered to be central to having Islamic law enforced, its form and organization are declared to be secondary, a matter not of

---

[47] See for example Steven C. Roach, 'Arab states and the role of Islam in the International Criminal Court', *Political Studies* 53 (1) 2005, pp. 143–61; Katerina Dalacoura, *Islam, Liberalism and Human Rights: Implications for International Relations* (London: I. B. Tauris, 2003).

[48] See B. Dupret (ed.), *Standing Trial: Law and People in the Modern Middle East* (London: I.B. Tauris, 2004).

[49] Arjomand, *Constitutional Politics in the Middle East*; Nathan J. Brown, *Constitutions in a Nonconstitutional World: Arab Basic Laws and the Prospects for Accountable Government* (New York: State University of New York Press, 2001), particularly chapter six.

[50] Nazih N. Ayubi, *Political Islam: Religion and Politics in the Arab World* (New York: Routledge, 1992), p. 230.

[51] Gudrun Krämer, 'La politique morale ou bien gouverner à l'islamique', *Vingtième Siècle* 82 (2) 2004, pp. 131–144.

substance but of technique'.[52] Hence, it is not entirely surprising that contemporary debates among Islamic ideologues provide very few specifics regarding the actual form of the system, especially in relation to institutional and constitutional design. Instead, the focus of state governance is on the moral quality of the individuals who are meant to be in charge of this system for the public interest.[53] Because the actual political structure that would be compatible with Islamic norms and practice is not thought to be of great importance, references to the state in the Islamic literature fall into two mains categories. First, those which are actual designations of the standard model of sovereign nation-state. Second, those which are aspirational state-like structures that would govern a self-designated Islamic community. In the current international and domestic contexts dominated by regimes unsympathetic to political Islam, the flaws identified in the first type of state are far better debated and identified than the merits of the alternative 'ideal type'. Ultimately, these aspirational Islamic models of governance are appropriate to frame local and transnational forms of 'contentious politics', to use the terminology associated with Charles Tilly and Sidney Tarrow.[54] Until very recently, however, social movements theory has shown little interest in the type of contentious politics emerging from the Muslim communities, and Islamism has often been brushed aside as 'ugly movements' coming from the Middle East.[55]

[52] Gudrun Kramer, 'Islamist notions of democracy', *Middle East Report* no. 183, 1993, pp. 2–8, at p. 5.

[53] Regarding the (re-)construction of a specifically Islamic economic system see Charles Tripp, *Islam in the Moral Economy* (Cambridge: Cambridge University Press, 2006).

[54] Charles Tilly and Sidney Tarrow, *Contentious Politics* (Boulder: Paradigm Publishers, 2006).

[55] Sidney Tarrow, *Power in Movement: Social Movements and Contentious Politics* (Cambridge: Cambridge University Press, 1998), p. 203. Tarrow's rather negative interpretation of social movements associated with Islamism is developed in his subsequent work on transnationalism, which is directly influenced by Gilles Kepel's interpretation of political Islam. See Sidney Tarrow, *The New Transnational Activism* (Cambridge: Cambridge University Press, 2005) For a more sanguine assessment of the potential of these movements see the contributors to Q. Wiktorowicz (ed.), *Islamic Activism: A Social Movement Theory Approach* (Bloomington: Indiana University Press, 2004).

As in the debate about democracy—see chapter five—common international studies descriptions of an Islamic state (or would-be Islamic state) are characterised mostly by what such a state lacks in relation to western institutions that constitute the teleological horizon. A 'Third-World' IR specialist like Mohamed Ayoob rightly criticises these assessments for being too heavily influenced by what is thought to be the norm in terms of state historical evolution and behaviour—i.e. a duplication of European state-making processes. In this respect, the demands and expectations of the dominant western state system are contributing to the difficulties of organisation faced by postcolonial states.[56] Some analysts, particularly from the developmentalist Left, have repeatedly suggested that one should stop blaming states in the developing world for their inability to meet western standards of institutionalization and ask instead how useful are current standards of state governance to address these predicaments.[57] Though this may be a worthy enterprise, to date, very few alternatives for state governance have been convincingly put forward. To a degree, the observation made earlier—that Islamism is not primarily concerned with standard models of political institutionalisation and theories of governance—contributes to this perceived absence of concrete alternatives. In relation to the Muslim world, much of the 'failed/weak state' literature focuses on the problems caused by political Islam rather than considers it as providing new resources for addressing the dilemmas faced by these polities.[58] The 'weak state' argument comes in many guises

---

[56] Mohammed Ayoob, *The Third World Security Predicament: Statemaking, Regional Conflict and the International System* (Boulder: Lynne Rienner, 1995); 'Subaltern realism: international relations theory meets the Third World', in S.G. Neuman (ed.) *International Relations Theory and the Third World* (New York: St. Martin's Press, 1998).

[57] See for example Arlene Tickner, 'Seeing IR differently: notes from the Third World', *Millennium*, 32 (2) 2003, pp. 295–324; Pinar Bilgin and Adam D. Morton, 'Historicising representations of "failed states": beyond the Cold War annexation of the social sciences?', *Third World Quarterly* 23 (1) 2002, pp. 55–80.

[58] The literature on the Saudi state and Saudi foreign policy is a good example of this trend, particularly from a security perspective in which the need to ensure that the Saudi states does not fail is paramount. See Sherifa D. Zuhur, *Saudi Arabia: Islamic Threat, Political Reform, and the Global War on Terror* (Carlisle: Strategic Studies Institute United States Army War College, 2005). There are

due to the different dependent and independent variables that are deemed to constitute the specificity of the Middle Eastern/Muslim-majority states' developmental and security dilemmas.[59] These schemes explicitly or implicitly support the view that political Islam compounds the usual problems of state-building and state cohesion, thereby weakening the role of the Muslim-majority countries in the international system.[60] Due to the peripheral role attributed to Islamism, much of the 'weak state' literature, regardless of its theoretical grounding, tends to provide rather reductionist accounts of political Islam. In particular, these approaches are by design squeezing the supra/trans-national aspects of Islamism into a more rigid framework based on sovereign interests (either in terms of domestic calculations of state survival or in terms of the balance of power at the regional level).

The theoretical haziness that exists regarding the nature of an 'Islamic state' is duplicated at the transnational level, where much miscomprehension is generated by the notion of 'Caliphate'. Here too, Islamic normative theory is only very loosely connected to notions of institutional practice. Very few serious Islamic thinkers and movements have spent time and energy specifying the institutional mechanisms of a modern caliphate. Many of the debates and conclusions that Muslim thinkers had reached in the aftermath of the abolition of the Ottoman caliphate commonly remain the current 'state of the art'.[61] The lack of solid modern references for the Caliphate in international politics ensures that IR scholars keep paying lip service to state-based international institutions like the Organization of the Islamic Conference (or even the Arab League despite the recognition that not all Arabs are Muslim, and not all Muslims Arabs).[62]

---

nonetheless alternative readings of the Saudi context that de-emphasise the role of Islamism. See Pascal Menoret, *The Saudi Enigma: A History*, Trans. P. Camiller (London: Zed Books, 2005).

[59] For a critique see, Bilgin and Morton, 'Historicising representations'..

[60] For a sweeping critique see, Mustapha K. Pasha, 'Islam, "soft" Orientalism and hegemony: a Gramscian rereading', *Critical Review of International Social and Political Philosophy* 8 (4) 2005, pp. 543–58.

[61] For an overview see, Hamid Enayat, *Modern Islamic Political Thought* (Austin: University of Texas Press 1982).

[62] See Naveed S. Sheikh, *The New Politics of Islam: Pan-Islamic Foreign Policy in a World of States* (London: RoutledgeCurzon, 2002).

Institutionalist bias toward the state-led structures is duplicated in the various United Nations' policy initiatives, notably on 'civilizations'. In marked contrast to the attention given to putative 'Islamic' regional organizations, few in the academic and policy-making communities pay much attention to organizations like the European Council for Fatwas and Research (ECFR), as institutions capable of addressing the changing normativity of international interactions. Only scholars of transnationalism note the relevance of such informal institutions in the global politics of Muslim communities.[63]

Constructivist approaches to the construction of the international community appear to be conceptually better equipped to address the transnational reconfiguration of Islamism. Yet, there is a thin line between 'thick' notions of international society that can explain and understand the relevant cultural underpinning of international society, and an endorsement of the culture of liberal modernity of a 'global elite'. This is a difficulty that Andrew Linklater faces frontally in the *Transformation of the Political Community*. Linklater is justifiably wary of the 'false universality' induced by a-historical approaches that are rooted in natural law, or by teleological interpretations of human progress and development.[64] Yet he himself offers few suggestions regarding how best to harness new processes of globalisation and stronger interpretations of human rights within a 'universal communication community'. Linklater may claim that 'intimations of the post-Westphalian world are apparent in Western Europe', but, despite an endorsement of dialogic cosmopolitanism, his own account leaves out supra-national religious schemes.[65] For

[63] See Peter Mandaville, *Transnational Muslim Politics: Reimagining the Umma* (London: Routledge, 2001); Jocelyne Cesari, *When Islam and Democracy Meet: Muslims in Europe and in the United States* (New York: Palgrave, 2006). I return to the relevance of these transnational aspects in chapter six in connection to multiculturalism.

[64] Andrew Linklater, *The Transformation of Political Community: Ethical Foundations of the Post-Westphalian Era* (Cambridge: Polity Press, 1998).

[65] Linklater, *The Transformation of Political Community*, p. 9. For alternative readings of such communities based on the Islamic practices see, Armando Salvatore, 'The exit from a Westphalian framing of political space and the emergence of a transnational Islamic public', *Theory, Culture & Society* 24 (4) 2007, pp. 45–52; Salman Sayyid, 'Beyond Westphalia: nations and diasporas: the case of the Muslim umma', in B. Hesse (ed.), *Un/settled Multicultural-*

critical IR studies to take contemporary global pluralism seriously, as Scott Thomas noted, they need at least to recognize the interests and concerns of transnational religious communities (especially in the non-western world). Like the categories of the 'political' and the 'religious', notions of what constitutes a relevant subject matter for international studies have shifting boundaries.[66] How should international notions of Islamic human rights be part of this picture? How do specific conceptions of (transnational) community welfare, or common good, form a specifically Islamic type of 'good governance'?[67] These issues remain on the fringes of constructivist debates despite some attempts at putting religious actors centre stage, as with Thomas' take on global interactions.[68] To date, the dominant tendency remains to invoke the manipulation of religion by states in order to achieve some pre-defined tactical or strategic gains.[69] In this context, religious norms are norms like any other, and as such, do not deserve to be given a particular explanatory status.

In foreign policy analysis in particular, this state-centric focus facilitates the assimilation of an Islamic foreign policy to the foreign policies of those Muslim-majority countries that present themselves as Islamic states. There is no easy framework for identifying what would be specifically Islamic in those countries, let alone in Muslim-minority countries where there is greater uncertainty regarding the political input of Muslims-as-Muslims (and not as migrants from particular countries of the Muslim world). How can foreign policy analysis treat for example, the issue of political Islam in the 'West', when traditionally these communities have been viewed primarily as ethno-national groups?[70] In recent

---

isms: Diasporas, Entanglements, Transruptions. (London: Zed Books, 2000), pp. 33–51.

[66] For an outline of these dilemmas see, Maia Carter Hallward, 'Situating the "secular": negotiating the boundary between religion and politics' *International Political Sociology* 2 (1) 2008, 1–16;.

[67] See Salvatore, 'The exit from a Westphalian framing of political space'.

[68] Thomas, *The Global Resurgence of Religion.*

[69] See Ann Elizabeth Mayer, *Islam and Human Rights: Tradition and Politics* (Westview Press, 2006); Dalacoura, *Islam, Liberalism and Human.* For a slightly more sanguine assessment see, Robert R. Bianchi, *Guests of God: Pilgrimage and Politics in the Islamic World* (New York Oxford University Press, 2004).

[70] From a US perspective see, Yossi Shain, *Marketing the Democratic Creed Abroad:*

years there has been a tendency to import insights from multiculturalism studies in order to account for the specifically religious component of the Muslim community. This reflects a changing emphasis within multiculturalism studies themselves, away from ethno-nationalist referents and toward religious ones—an issue that will be examined in chapter six. Analysts are beginning to explore this dimension of the foreign policy process in order to provide the building blocs of a behavioural or structural model for this religious input into foreign policy making.[71] One key difficulty remains to know how far it is possible to produce a systematic account of when a Muslim community acts as an 'Islamic' entity.[72] Foreign policy scholarship on the role of political Islam in foreign policy processes in western democracies is in its infancy and there is not (yet) any meaningful 'multiculturalist theory of foreign policy'. As discussed earlier, a principal stumbling block here remains the unwillingness to set aside common assumptions about religion and politics that are embedded Western secularist worldviews.[73]

Diasporas in the U.S. and their Homelands (Cambridge: Cambridge University Press, 1999); 'Multicultural foreign policy', *Foreign Policy*, No. 100, 1995, pp. 69–87. In this argument, Shain subsumes any putative 'Muslim' constituency into an 'Arab' one, with Asian and black communities being treated separately.

[71] See Elizabeth Shakman Hurd, *The Politics of Secularism in International Relations* (Princeton: Princeton University Press, 2007); Christopher Hill, 'Bringing war home: foreign policy-making in multicultural societies', *International Relations* 21 (3) 2007, pp. 259–83.

[72] See Lisbeth Aggestam and Christopher Hill, 'The challenge of multiculturalism in European foreign policy', *International Affairs* 84 (1) 2008, pp. 97–114; and compare the more critical assessments contained in Shane Brighton, 'British Muslims, multiculturalism and UK foreign policy: "integration" and "cohesion" in and beyond the state', *International Affairs*, 83 (1), 2007, pp. 1–17; Christoph Schumann, 'A Muslim "diaspora" in the United States?', *The Muslim World* 97 (1) 2007, pp. 11–32; and Frédéric Volpi, 'The European transnational Islamic nexus: The North-African "umma" between exit, voice, loyalty', *Government and Opposition*, 42 (3) 2007, pp. 451–70.

[73] For example, how far is it meaningful to represent French and American foreign policy choices in relation to Hamas' electoral victory in Palestine in 2005, as a direct outcome of domestic understandings of *laïcité* and multiculturalism, as Hurd suggests? Elizabeth S. Hurd, 'Political Islam and foreign policy in

Although religious considerations per se have not been replaced at the centre of IR theorising, since the closing years of the Cold War, the rise of various strands of constructivist thinking have introduced more complex socio-historical variables than before.[74] Typically, constructivist arguments highlight how interactions between individuals, social groups, or states involve not only material objects (resources, territory) but also subjective ones, like projecting or defending a certain ideal, such as a sense of who they are. These agents interact not only because of some underlying will to power, or because of the requirements of an anarchic international system, but also because they construct certain views of the kind of persons, societies, or institutions that they want to be. Usually these notions of identity-construction precede the formulation of interests, and therefore pre-shape the field of possible political actions. In these debates, religious elements can often be at odds with the tendency towards cosmopolitanism that is implicit or explicit in many of the efforts to make IR theory and practice less western-centric.[75] As indicated in the preceding chapter in relation to the move beyond orientalism, in IR the task of moving constructivism forward in such a way as to take proper consideration of religious narratives proves difficult for practical and conceptual reasons.

Moving forward with political Islam in IR

The practical difficulties of including a religious factor like Islamism in debates about international relations increased in the aftermath of 9/11, as many constructivist analyses failed to address the issued effectively. Approaches keen to retain a 'critical' dimension were reluctant to dip into narratives about Islamism that appeared to be tainted with essentialism.[76]

Europe and the United States', *Foreign Policy Analysis* 3 (4) 2007, pp. 345–67. For a more conventional interpretation that stresses instead the dynamics produced by a pro-Arab foreign policy in France since the 1960s, and conversely a pro-Israeli US foreign policy since that time see, Roy, *Globalized Islam*.

[74] See Mustapha Kamal Pasha, 'Liberalism, Islam and international relations', in B.G. Jones (ed.), *Decolonizing International Relations* (Lanham: Rowman & Littlefield, 2006), pp. 65–87.

[75] See Pinar Bilgin, 'Thinking past "Western" IR?', *Third World Quarterly*, 29 (1) 2008, pp. 5–23; Teti, 'Bridging the gap'.

[76] See Naeem Inayatullah and David L. Blaney, *International Relations and the Problem of Difference* (London: Routledge, 2004).

Some of the earlier reluctance of constructivism to be seen as developing a theory for 'culture' or 'identity' construction was exacerbated in this context. As scholars favouring more causal accounts of political interactions stressed, the rigour of constructivist accounts regarding the processes of the formation of the political does not apply to the choice of the more substantive matter of these processes.[77] In connection to political Islam, these choices directly impacted on the ability of constructivist authors to neutralize the appeal of 'civilizational' narratives. Constructivist accounts are better able to explain the processes of a cultural and normative 'clash' by detailing the power relations that articulate identity politics in situations of domination and subordination. In doing so, however, they commonly tend to reify the most visible manifestations of political Islam, thereby turning what Bernard Lewis presented as an 'irrational confrontation', into a logical interaction between two sets of structures, norms and practices. In so far as they are able to investigate the very process of formation of the notion of political Islam—both in the Muslim community and in the western academic/policy/media community—they have to downgrade accordingly the descriptive and predictive capabilities of their argument.

This tendency to naturalize a monolithic Islamism meant that the representations of an Islamist religious bogeyman grew exponentially after 9/11. Even those scholars who had previously introduced to the debate non-essentialist characterisations of identity formation fell prey to orientalist biases. In Jean Elshtain's later work—an apologia for US intervention in the Middle East—she depicted Islamists in sharp black and white terms as, 'those who believe in a literal understanding of the Qur'an and condemn all who disagree; Muslim and non-Muslim alike; who have hijacked Islam, in the view of many devout Muslims here and abroad; for their own intolerant purposes; who advocate militant theocracy; and who insist that there can be no distinction between civil law and the strict,

---

[77] For better *and* for worse, constructivist approaches do not usually seek to explain the precise nature of the main constitutive elements of political life—identities, norms, practices, structures—but indicate instead how these elements are positioned and constitutive of each other. See Jeffrey T. Checkel, 'The constructivist turn in international relations theory', *World Politics* 50 (2) 1998, pp. 324–48; Emanuel Adler, 'Seizing the middle ground: constructivism in world politics', *European Journal of International Relations* 3 (3) 1997, pp. 319–63.

fundamentalist Shari'a law, the ancient Islamic holy law.'[78] Turning on its head her earlier argument on the construction of war stereotypes for males and females, or on the role of ethics and norms in international interaction, Elshtain revived stereotypes of the bloodthirsty male Islamist radical, whose very being is the negation of everything which anyone decent could represent. Moving away from the specific inputs of identity into international practices, this signalled a return to modelling interactions on the basis of reified abstractions—something that constructivists were precisely trying to warn against.

Conceptually, political Islam is caught between two modes of thinking about the dynamics of change in contemporary international politics. On the one hand, one could point to a revival of public religions worldwide and locate political Islam within this scheme in order to explain new patterns of international relations. On the other hand, one could use an area-studies approach to identify localised adaptations of the international systems, with Islamism representing a Muslim regional variation. Commonly, the analysis of political Islam in international studies ends up being short-changed by both. From the revival of religion perspective, the difficulty is that it so happens that some revivals are politically more significant than others. After a while, the quest to produce a systematic mapping of 'fundamentalism' becomes so encompassing (and hazy) that it loses most of its practical relevance. Marty and Appleby's ambitious conclusions to the 'Fundamentalist Project' illustrate the benefits, and even more clearly the limitations, of the notion of 'fundamentalism' for political science and international studies.[79] For policy analysts in particular, not the overall parameters of the revival matter, but the specific factors affecting some public religions but not others. Neither the addi-

---

[78] Jean Bethke Elshtain, *Just War against Terror: The Burden of American Power in a Violent World* (New York: Basic Books, 2004) p. 3. Thus she concluded that 'when I claim that changes to our policies would not satisfy Islamists, the reason is quite basic: They loathe us because of who we are and what our society represents'.

[79] Compare, Gabriel A. Almond, Emmanuel Sivan, R. Scott Appleby, 'Explaining fundamentalisms', in M.E. Marty and R.S. Appleby (eds.), *Fundamentalisms Comprehended* (Chicago: Chicago University Press, 1995), pp. 425–44; with James P. Piscatori, 'Accounting for Islamic fundamentalisms', in M.E. Marty and R.S. Appleby (eds.), *Accounting for Fundamentalisms: The Dynamic Character of Movements* (Chicago: Chicago University Press, 1994), pp. 361–73.

tion of terms such as 'fundamentalism-like', nor the ingenious utilisation of hand-picked cases can convincingly sustain the grand structural explanation of fundamentalism that these comparative schemes propose.[80] Tellingly, at that level of generality, the social-movement perspective used by Rhys Williams to bring together various regional accounts in another section of the Fundamentalist Project conveys greater clarity to the debate than the very notion of fundamentalism itself.[81]

This situation is not particular to large-scale collaborative works like the 'Fundamentalism Project' but also applies to single-handed efforts at mapping out globalized religious revivals. In the early 1990s, Gilles Kepel and Bruce Lawrence also proposed some overarching themes to bring more structure to the study of similar-looking religious phenomena.[82] On close examination, however, these structural models faced an increasing amount of recalcitrant evidence over time that undermined their explanatory potential. Ultimately, Kepel had to stress the importance of differences rather than the similarities between 'revived' public religions in the *Revenge of God*. In particular, he contrasted the political relevance of Islamic activism taking place in non-secularized contexts to the subdued impact of Christian revivalism in secularized ones.[83]

The tension between emphasising differences or stressing diversity is palpable in Mark Jurgensmeyer's analysis. In *The New Cold War* he outlined the importance of understanding the specific pathways leading to the nationalistic transformation of religious movements in particular socio-historical contexts.[84] By contrast, in his subsequent *Terror in the Mind of God*, his analysis of Christianity and Islam stressed the similari-

[80] Gabriel A. Almond, Emmanuel Sivan, R. Scott Appleby, 'Fundamentalism: genus and species', pp. 339–424; 'Politics, ethnicity, and fundamentalism', pp. 483–504, in Marty and Appleby, *Fundamentalisms Comprehended*.

[81] Rhys H. Williams, 'Movement dynamics and social change: transforming fundamentalist ideology and institutions', in Marty and Appleby, *Accounting for Fundamentalisms*, pp. 785–834.

[82] Bruce B. Lawrence, *Defenders of God: The Fundamentalist Revolt Against the Modern Age* (London: I.B. Tauris, 1990).

[83] Gilles Kepel, *The Revenge of God: The Resurgence of Islam, Christianity and Judaism in the Modern World*, trans. A. Braley (University Park: Pennsylvania State University Press, 1994).

[84] Mark Jurgensmeyer, *The New Cold War?: Religious Nationalism Confronts the Secular State* (Berkeley: University of California Press, 1994).

ties between notions of Holy War in international confrontations. He noted how the theological dimension of each religion contributed to make the international behaviour of states belonging to one tradition unlike that of states from the other. Yet, the level of generality of this religious-based explanation is such that it is very difficult to point to the analytical gains that studying religious violence per se would provide in international politics. Jurgensmayer effectively concludes that although the relation between religion and violence:

has much to do with the nature of the religious imagination, which always has had the propensity to absolutize and to project images of cosmic war. It also has much to do with the social tensions of this moment of history that cry out for absolute solutions, and the sense of personal humiliation experienced by men who long to restore an integrity they perceive as lost in the wake of virtually global social and political shifts.[85]

In short, the attitude of Islamists toward international conflict appears to have as much to do with religious referents than it has with everything else.

While the attempt to outline the general parameters of religious revivals provides relatively limited insights for the study of international relations, the eagerness to devise an all-encompassing framework for religious factors may simply confuse the issue. A recent illustration of this difficulty is to be found in the pages of Timothy Byrnes and Peter Katzenstein's *Religion in an Expanding Europe*.[86] From a European comparative perspective, while the different religious factors and interactions with the state can be held together for the Catholic and Orthodox trends—primarily via an analysis of the role of the Church—the argument slackens considerably regarding the role played by political Islam, not least because the contributors point to opposing explanatory factors. From a more orientalist perspective, Tibi emphasizes the very different conception of politics in Islamism and in secular European states; while from a post-orientalist angle Yavuz emphasizes the fluidity of these representations and of their political relevance within and between states.[87] Ultimately,

[85] Mark Juergensmeyer, *Terror in the Mind of God: The Global Rise of Religious Violence (Berkeley: University of California Press, 2003), p. 248.*

[86] T.A. Byrnes and P.J. Katzenstein (eds.), *Religion in an Expanding Europe* (Cambridge: Cambridge University Press, 2006).

[87] Bassam Tibi, 'Europeanizing Islam or the Islamization of Europe: political

the overall framework proposed in this work can function as a general model only because it does not say much about the institutionalization of political Islam. As is commonly the case, the specificity of political Islam for IR is not meaningfully theorized, but rather reflects some salient observations proposed by Islamic specialists, who have outlined the political mechanisms corresponding to their preferred methodological perspective. This leaves the issue of the articulation of these mechanisms in the hands of IR specialists trying to make them fit into their own disciplinary paradigms.

Today, revitalized orientalist perspective still heavily influences common neo-realist and neo-liberal IR readings of political Islam via its depiction of the classical Islamic legal tradition of international relations. It is argued that because the classical Islamic tradition does not operate with the notion of nation-state, the more Islam intervenes in governance, the less a Muslim country will behave like a normal nation state. As detailed studies of the historical evolution of Islamic empires and societies have pointed out, this is a oversimplification in many important respects. Ira Lapidus points to the increasing differentiation between state and religion in the Umayyad and Abbasid period, and to the tendency for the integration of the state and religious community to be best applicable to Middle Eastern tribal settings.[88] Halliday stresses that over time differentiation of the religious from the political could be as easily promoted as the opposite trend. He suggests that 'a separation of religion and state, indeed a rejection of all worldly, political activity, is just as possible an interpretation of Islamic thinking as anything the Islamists now offer'.[89] The works of Ayubi and Zubaida mentioned earlier also develop at length this theme in relation to the Middle East and the modern Arab

---

[88] Ira M. Lapidus, *A History of Islamic Societies* (Cambridge: Cambridge University Press, 1988). Ayoob further stresses that 'the temporal authority's de facto primacy over the religious establishment continued through the reign of the three great Sunni dynasties—the Umayyad, the Abbasid, and the Ottoman'. Mohammed Ayoob, 'Political Islam: image and reality', *World Policy Journal* 21 (3) 2004, pp. 1–14.

[89] Fred Halliday, *Islam and the Myth of Confrontation*.

state specifically.[90] A more balanced reading of the historical role of Islam in international relations and state behaviour should be able to avoid the twin fallacies of either assuming that the fusion of 'politics' and 'religion' is a natural occurrence, or of portraying as 'normal', a trajectory of relative political quietism occasionally interrupted by 'abnormal' Islamic revivals.[91] From an area-studies perspective, the task is to highlight the different historical and intellectual traditions of Muslim societies in various parts of the world in order to show the commonalities and differences that are relevant to international affairs.[92]

James Piscatori has shown quite well that the historical process of inclusion, and more commonly of exclusion of religious matters from the political, is a complex convoluted affair that involves a fair dose of pragmatism and opportunism from Muslim rulers and religious leaders.[93] The decision to place Islam more or less centrally in state politics is not only a pragmatic choice in a specific international context, but also a response to a more substantive debate about how desirable it is for Islamic norms and practices to be closely associated with the potentially corrupting exercise of political power.[94] These debates and choices have implications for both the domestic-international aspects and the trans/supra-national dimensions of Islamism. From a political history perspective, Piscatori proposed some sophisticated analyses illustrating that these trends were not easily reducible to pro-system state actors versus system-challenging non-state actors (plus so-called 'rogue states').[95] This balance between state-centred and non-state centred frameworks is crucial to the appraisal of political Islam in International Relations. In the contemporary context,

---

[90] Ayubi, *Political Islam*; Sami Zubaida, *Islam, the People and the State: Political Ideas and Movements in the Middle East* (London: I.B. Tauris, 1993).

[91] For such a problematic model see L. Carl Brown, *Religion and State: The Muslim Approach to Politics* (New York: Columbia University Press, 2000).

[92] This is a large and important task that I do not propose to undertake in this short chapter. For some of the foundational work on this issue see, James P. Piscatori, *Islam in a World of Nation States* (Cambridge: Cambridge University Press 1986).

[93] Piscatori, *Islam in a World of Nation States*.

[94] Regarding the latter see for example, Abdolkarim Soroush, *Reason, Freedom and Democracy in Islam: The Essential Writings of Abdolkarim Soroush* (New York: Oxford University Press, 2000).

[95] Piscatori, *Islam in a World of Nation States*.

Piscatori links his argument to post-orientalist explanations of the 'modern' nature of Islamism described earlier. He points out that behind the fiery rhetoric deployed by many movements there is also a de facto acceptance of the current conditions of modernity, which include the international system and institutions based on state sovereignty.[96] At the same time there is clearly what could be identified as a 'solidarist' agenda and practice in an Islamist worldview. This aspect of the phenomenon cannot be put back in its box simply by suppressing unruly transnational movements and other would-be 'rogue states', as might have been thought using Cold War examples. Yet, such insights do not amount to an overall analytical scheme that would readily insert political Islam into standard international relations accounts of contemporary world politics. Once more, in such debates, it is less Islamism per se that appears to matter most, but rather the various consequential aspects of it as perceived by IR specialists.

[96] James Piscatori, 'Order, justice and global Islam', in R. Foot, J.L. Gaddis and A. Hurrell (eds.), *Order and Justice in International Relations* (Oxford: Oxford University Press, 2003), pp. 262–86.

4

THE SOCIOLOGY OF RELIGION
IN THE MUSLIM WORLD

FROM SECULAR MODERNIZATION
TO ISLAMIZATION

Moving past orientalist sociology

For most of the nineteenth century, as sociology established itself as a distinct discipline, the sociological approach to the study of religion was meant to cover as broad a spectrum of religious phenomena as possible. The works of Max Weber at the turn of the century are indicative of these attempts at providing exhaustive explanations of the religious. They addressed everything from the rise of Protestantism and the 'spirit of capitalism' in Renaissance Europe to the predicaments of the main world religions at the beginning of the twentieth century. Although it quickly became clear that Weber's framework contained serious flaws, sociological inquiries have been heavily influenced by this broad agenda throughout much of the twentieth century. Peter Berger, once a leading proponent of modernization theory recently commented that 'it is fair to say that, for close to a century now, the ghost of Max Weber has been hovering over the enterprise that we have come to call the sociology of religion'.[1] Over the years, many have pointed out that this grand approach to religion was over-ambitious from the start; leading Weber and his followers to make

[1] Peter L. Berger, 'Reflections on the sociology of religion today', *Sociology of Religion* 62 (4) 2001, pp. 443–54, on p. 447.

crude simplifications regarding the historical development and homoge-
nization of cultural norms. The limitations of Weber's own analysis of
Islam are well known and there is little need to rehearse the problems
associated with his views here. What is worth stressing however, are the
continuing failures in the comparative analysis of secularization in the
Muslim world. The criticisms directed at Weber on the grounds of his
orientalist assumptions are probably less relevant in the case of Weber
himself—his views being a reflection of the knowledge available at the
time—than they are for subsequent Weberian analyses of Islamism.[2]

Weber had suggested that modern societies were going through a process of disenchantment as scientific advances turned into mundane affairs
an increasing number of issues previously cloaked in mystery and tied to
religious/supernatural explanations. This transformation of social consciousness was for Weber directly linked to the increased autonomy of
the state apparatus and market institutions from the religious establishment. In this perspective, what happened to the Christian societies of
Europe was bound to happen to other societies around the world as modern rational-scientific approaches were slowly but surely replacing beliefs
in supernatural mechanisms. From social theory to social anthropology,
from Berger to Wallace, by the middle of the twentieth century there was
a strong suspicion that religion was bound to become a quaint cultural
artefact.[3] At that time, sociological narratives presented Islamism primarily as an anachronistic 'anti-modern' movement illustrating a rearguard
action by traditionalist religious actors. The processes of such a religious
collapse in the face of what could be called 'deep secularization, were outlined in the early works of Berger. Marginally at first, then more deci-
sively, new arguments began to challenge such linear accounts by
proposing that Islamism was a modern phenomenon illustrative of one
particular articulation of religion and modernity. These accounts of what
might be termed 'secularization lite' concentrated on explaining how the

---

[2] For insightful critiques see, Bryan S Turner, *Weber and Islam: A Critical Study*
(London: Routledge and Keegan Paul, 1973); Mohammad Nafissi, 'Reframing
Orientalism: Weber and Islam', *Economy and Society* 27 (1) 1998, pp. 97–118.

[3] A.F.C. Wallace, *Religion: An anthropological view* (New York: Random House,
1966); Peter L. Berger, *The Sacred Canopy: Elements of a Sociological Theory of
Religion* (Garden City: Doubleday, 1967); D.E. Smith, *Religion, Politics, and
Social Change in the Third World* (New York: Free Press, 1971).

institutionalization of religion could be weakened without necessarily undermining the informal religious networks and individual commitments that developed alongside scientific-secular worldviews.[4]

In the last couple of decades it has become increasingly clear that the question of how widespread and deep the processes of secularization are in non-western countries is immensely difficult to answer due to the scope of the inquiry and paucity of reliable data. Although the Muslim world caught the attention of scholars from very early on, mainstream sociological analyses of the region up to the 1980s still relied heavily on Weberian frameworks to assess the developments taking place there. Few accounts moved past the standard models of secularization and modernization theory that presented Islamism as a rearguard reaction doomed to failure. One influential, empirically informed rephrasing of this model was provided by Ernest Gellner in *Muslim Society*, where he suggested that key aspects of Islamism were highly compatible with modernity. He emphasised that contemporary Islamist movements attempted to embody a scriptural and orthodox 'High Islam' in opposition to various forms of mystical 'Folk Islam'. As such, this type of urban, egalitarian and puritanical Islamism was not too distant from Weber's Protestant ethic and quite compatible with modernization. Indeed, it was precisely through the growth of mass literacy and mass communication that this modern Islamic orthodoxy could fully overcome 'Folk Islam'.[5] This distinction between high and low Islam, fed into another distinction between Islamism from above and Islamism from below that was increasingly favoured by political scientists and area studies specialists at the time. In the 1980s, most analyses focused on the rise of political Islam through an examination of parties and movements aiming for state power. These movements were

---

[4] See particularly José Casanova, *Public Religions in the Modern World* (Chicago: University of Chicago Press, 1994). From a theoretical perspective, however, it is important to note that most leading scholars in the sociology of religion are still concentrating on Christian, Euro-American issues to develop their analytical frameworks.

[5] Ernest Gellner, *Muslim Society* (Cambridge: Cambridge University Press, 1981). See also Bryan S. Turner, 'Towards an economic model of virtuoso religion', in E. Gellner (ed.), *Islamic Dilemmas: Reformers, Nationalists and Industrialization: The Southern Shore of the Mediterranean* (Berlin: Mouton De Gruyter, 1985), pp. 49–72.

seen as the political embodiments of the formalist 'High Islam' that Gellner said was compatible with modernity. By contrast, grassroots Islamization was relatively under-studied, except by social anthropologists; as it was not perceived to be significant as a primary framework of analysis (as well as being too heterogeneous to frame in relation to modernity).[6] Even Gilles Kepel, who had emphasized the relevance of grassroots movements Islamization for the success of revolutionary Islamist parties shaped his account of the rise of Islamism primarily in relation to this revolutionist political dimension.[7] More uncompromisingly, Olivier Roy suggested that one of the reasons why one could talk about the failure of political Islam was that 'during the 1980s there was an observable drift of political Islam toward a "neofundamentalism". Militants who were previously striving for the Islamic revolution are becoming involved in a process of re-Islamization from below'.[8] In this perspective, Islamization from below debases the activities of politicized movements, which then re-focus their energy on individual activities and morality in the social sphere.

A growing appreciation of the complex transformation of religiosity in social theorizing came more from empirical studies conducted in western settings than from analyses of Muslim-majority countries where a revitalization of religious practices was most visibly taking place.[9] Subtler accounts of secularization theory began to gain ground in the 1990s that stressed the plural nature of modern societies rather than the uniformity of the scientific worldview.[10] Niklas Luhman suggested in particular that

[6] For clear signs that these views were being modified in the 1980s see Dale F. Eickelman, 'Changing interpretations of Islamic movements', in W.R. Roff (ed.) *Islam and the Political Economy of Meaning* (London: Routledge, 1987), pp. 13–30.

[7] Gilles Kepel, *The Revenge of God: The Resurgence of Islam, Christianity and Judaism in the Modern World*, trans. A. Braley (University Park: Pennsylvania State University Press, 1994); *Prophet and Pharaoh: Muslim Extremism in Egypt*, trans. J. Rothschild (Berkeley: University of California Press, 1986).

[8] Olivier Roy, *The Failure of Political Islam*, trans. C. Volk (Cambridge: Harvard University Press, 1996).

[9] For an early critique see Ibrahim Abu-Lughod, 'Retreat from the secular path? Islamic dilemmas of Arab politics', *The Review of Politics* 28 (4) 1966, pp. 447–76.

[10] See for example Karel Dobbelaere, 'Secularization: a multi-dimensional concept', *Current Sociology*. 29 (2) 1981, pp. 1–213; 'Secularization theories and so-

the key characteristic of modernity was less the rationalism inherited from the Enlightenment than a particular combination of structural differentiation, technical specialization, and pluralization of life-worlds.[11] Analysts began to be wary of the bias being introduced in the debates about secularization, and about the relationship between religious and secular institutions, by the over-emphasis placed on Christian contexts.[12] Turning common views of the relation between European modernity and religiosity on its head, Grace Davies would later suggest that Europe's religious life 'is not a prototype of global religiosity; it is rather one strand among many which make up what it means to be European'.[13] In the 1990s, the strengthening of postmodern views that undermined grand narratives about social evolution challenged linear notions of secularization, and emphasized the plurality of norms and ethics in postmodern public spheres.[14]

In the following, I do not primarily address the literature of transnationalism that frames a distinct set of mechanisms contributing to the evolution of political Islam in a global *ummah*—these aspects will be considered in more detail in the chapter on globalization. Instead, I focus on those national-based comparative analyses that constitute the basis of most theoretical generalizations in the sociology of Islamism. The rise of political Islam in Muslim-majority countries alongside its growth in western settings stresses the pertinence of trying to rephrase more carefully the secularization-modernization argument in a global context.

---

ciological paradigms: a reformulation of the private-public dichotomy and the problem of societal integration', *Sociological Analysis* 46 (4) 1985, pp. 377–86.

[11] Niklas Luhmann, *Religious Dogmatics and the Evolution of Societies* (New York: Mellen Press, 1984).

[12] See however the useful comparative perspectives provided by the contributors to S.A. Arjomand (ed.), *The Political Dimensions of Religion* (Albany: State University of New York Press, 1993).

[13] Grace Davies, *Religion in Modern Europe: A Memory Mutates* (Oxford: Oxford University Press, 2000).

[14] See, Jean François Lyotard, *The Postmodern Condition: A Report on Knowledge*, (Minneapolis: University of Minnesota Press, 1984); Zygmund Bauman, *Legislators and Interpreters: On Modernity, Post-Modernity, Intellectuals* (Ithaca: Cornell University Press, 1987). In Muslim contexts see, Akbar S. Ahmed, *Postmodernism and Islam: Predicament and Promise*, revised edition (London: Routledge, 2004); Bryan S. Turner, *Orientalism, Postmodernism and Globalism* (London: Routledge, 1994).

Nonetheless, the processes taking place in Muslim-majority countries and among Muslims worldwide are still usually analyzed separately in the bulk of the literature on Islamism.[15] In the first instance, I will therefore also keep these analyses separated in order to map out the state of the research as it is currently structured. It must be stressed in addition in relation to the issue of Islamization, that to take seriously the idea of a 'true' Islam struggling against other ideologies and the relativism of postmodern culture, is not to fall back on Gellner's notion of 'High Islam'. Analysts of the 'postmodern condition' note the elusive character of any putative orthodoxy, but stress that the quest for a truer Islam is nonetheless sociologically significant and a key element for understanding the reflexive constructions of political Islam today. In this perspective, as Sayyid suggests, 'Islam' becomes a kind of empty malleable 'master signifier' about which every Muslim can agree upon with having to or being able to attribute to it a specific meaning.[16]

From deep secularization to Islamic activism

In its most ambitious mode, secularization is tightly connected to notions of modernization of society and the disenchantment of the world.[17] In this perspective, socio-economic developments (industrialization, urbanization), administrative rationalization and educational transformation (rise in literacy, in scientific methods) combine to ensure that the place of religious explanations as well as religiosity decrease. In Berger's early secularization thesis, the material power of religious institutions and the subjective religiosity of individuals are interdependent, and if the Church loses its influence, piety will weaken, and so on. Berger concluded that 'as there is a secularization of society and culture, so there is a secularization

---

[15] See *passim* John R Bowen, 'Shari'a, state and social norms in France and Indonesia', ISIM Papers no. 3, Leiden, 2001; Naim, Abd Allah Ahmad, 'Human Rights and Islamic Identity in France and Uzbekistan: Mediation of the Local and Global', *Human Rights Quarterly* 22 (4) 2000, pp. 906–41.

[16] Salman Sayyid, *A Fundamental Fear: Eurocentrism and the Emergence of Islamism*, revised edition (London: Zed Books, 2003).

[17] See Roy Wallis and Steve Bruce, 'Secularization: the orthodox model', in S. Bruce (ed.), *Religion and Modernization: Sociologists and Historians Debate the Secularization Thesis* (Oxford: Clarendon Press, 1992), pp. 8–30.

of consciousness'.[18] The other key argument of these early accounts of modernization and secularization is that societal changes observed mainly in Christian Europe were not only bound to happen in other societies and religions, but also constituted an irreversible process—once the world is disenchanted, there is no going back. Certainly, when such far reaching accounts of secularization and modernization were proposed some doubts were voiced regarding their accuracy. At the time, the specific difficulties encountered by these narratives were generally not directly addressed; or it was estimated that the risks were worth taking. As Robert Bellah's conclusion in the mid-1960s regarding such religious transformations, 'construction of a wide-ranging evolutionary scheme [...] is an extremely risky enterprise. Nevertheless such efforts are justifiable if, by throwing light on perplexing developmental problems they contribute to modern men's effort at self interpretation'.[19]

In the footsteps of Weber, many analysts viewed modernity and tradition as polar opposites. It was a small step from this view to arguing that the kind of modernization process that Muslim societies were going through necessarily had to take the form it had taken in the Christian 'West'. By the 1960s, traditional Muslim societies were judged to be as good as gone in the modern world. Daniel Lerner's views of Muslims having a choice between 'mechanization or Mecca' was in fact no choice at all; simply a case of survival of the fittest, which left little doubt as to the outcome. By and large, religious and traditional forms of social affiliations were viewed as impediments to the proper functioning of a modern state, as they were hindrances to national integration and undermined loyalty to the nation-state.[20] Islamic movements were thus seen as anachronistic forces in society, largely drawing into their ranks the poor and disenfranchised who did not manage to adapt to modern conditions. Such individuals were seen as the victims of modernization and Islamism was merely an expression of their discontent; and a fleeting or relatively inconsequential one at that. The solution to this predicament was simply that the local political elites would provide more social mobility and more

---

[18] Berger, *The Sacred Canopy*, p. 107.
[19] Robert N. Bellah, 'Religious evolution', *American Sociological Review* 29 (3) 1964, pp. 358–74, at p. 374.
[20] Daniel Lerner, *The Passing of Traditional Society: Modernizing the Middle East* (Glencoe: Free Press, 1958), p. 405.

opportunity for economic and political integration of the masses in order to make Islamism go away.[21]

It is noticeable that these arguments were repeatedly put forward by many intellectuals not only outside but also inside the Muslim world. In Turkey, they were particularly fashionable and were the basis of many policy decisions from the 1920s onwards.[22] As Albert Hourani's study of the Middle Eastern intellectual scene in the nineteenth century indicates, advocates of western secularization were present in that century too, but outside a few urban elites they went relatively unheeded.[23] These notions came back with greater strength in the twentieth century, as they were endorsed by many post-colonial elites. And what is noticeable to this day, is the enduring appeal of these notions for the ruling elites in the region, even in the face of the repeated failures of modernizing and secularizing programmes in many polities (Egypt under Nasser, Iran under the Pahlavis, etc.). At the turn of the twenty-first century, there still are lingering echoes of this developmentalist drive, particularly in connection to the idea of Islamic Reformation. As Saad Eddin Ibrahim noted in the contemporary Egyptian context, liberal analysts are no longer suggesting that 'Islam without a Martin Luther-like reformation would be antithetical to any socio-economic and political development'.[24] Nonetheless, with the benefit of hindsight, one can easily see that the religious and political ecology of modernizing Muslim societies was always more complex than what Lerner had anticipated. The idiosyncratic pattern of socio-economic development driven by oil exports and the globalization of markets that structured changes in the Gulf States and Saudi Arabia from the 1970s onward, showed for example, that a straightforward 'westernization' of the socio-cultural dynamics of Muslim societies was wishful thinking.[25]

---

[21] For a useful critique see Hasan Kosebalaban, 'The rise of Anatolian cities and the failure of the modernization paradigm', *Critique: Critical Middle Eastern Studies* 16 (3) 2007 pp. 229–40.

[22] See Niyazi Berkes, *The Development of Secularism in Turkey* (Montreal: McGill University Press, 1964).

[23] Albert Hourani, *Arabic Thought in the Liberal Age 1798–1939* (Cambridge: Cambridge University Press, 1983).

[24] Saad Eddin Ibrahim, *Egypt, Islam and Democracy: Critical Essays* (American University in Cairo Press, 2002), p. 1.

[25] See the contributors to J.W. Fox, N. Mourtada-Sabbah and M. Al-Mutawa (eds.), *Globalization and the Gulf* (London: Routledge, 2006).

Quite distinctly, the notion of a linear connection between the socio-economic aspects of modernization and the process of secularization had come under so much strain in the closing decades of the twentieth century that it could no longer be taken at face value.[26]

In those circumstances, an alternative set of explanations favoured by the advocates of a grand narrative about secularization is often framed in terms of the institutional retreat of religious structures, which is taken to be the sign that secularization is progressing. Modernization theory argued that over time the institutions of the modern state would eventually become accepted and recognised as legitimate by the masses, first out of necessity then out of habit, then eventually out of conviction. For orientalist-minded political scientists it is precisely the secular dimension of the state institutions and ideology that ensured the relevance of the western model of nation-state for the Muslim world, as with Turkey.[27] In spite of growing criticisms, it is not until the Iranian revolution that political scientists seriously questioned the modernization-secularization model of institutional development. In the 1960s and 1970s, with most attention being given to the State, its ideology, its developmental strategy and so on, analyses presented primarily in neo-Weberian and neo-Marxist terms emphasized the evolution of the new political elite, as well as the reasons for their legitimacy deficit (clientelism, (neo)patriarchy, (neo)patrimonialism, etc.).[28] Islamism, whenever mentioned, was relegated to the category of symptoms characterizing a much deeper socio-economic and political problem. In the main, such accounts of state-led modernization suffered from the generic problems of offering at once over-specific and over-generalized accounts of social change.[29] The general claim that the processes of modernization and secularization observed in Europe were a template for the rest of the world, remained more often than not just that, a claim not particularly well-substantiated by

[26] For a sophisticated overview of the interactions between economic developments and Islamist doctrines see Charles Tripp, *Islam and the Moral Economy: The Challenge of Capitalism* (Cambridge: Cambridge University Press, 2006).

[27] See Serif Mardin, *The Genesis of Young Ottoman Thought* (Princeton: Princeton University Press, 1962); Niyazi Berkes, *Secularism*.

[28] See Michael C. Hudson, *Arab Politics: The Search for Legitimacy* (New Haven: Yale University Press, 1979).

[29] For a blunt critique see Rodney Stark, 'Secularization, R.I.P. (rest in peace)', *Sociology of Religion* 60 (3) 1999, pp. 249–73.

detailed studies.[30] The specific claims regarding the unidirectionality of these processes was undermined by the clear revival of religious institutions and practices in many places, and quite visibly after 1991 in the former communist bloc after many decades of official state-promoted atheism.

In countries of the former Communist bloc, the relevant observation is not about the re-enchantment of the social sphere but about the kind of disenchantment that was engineered by the secular/atheist state institutions.[31] In many parts of the former USSR, whether predominantly Christian or Muslim, personal and communal forms of piety remained present below the institutional level, and they were given public recognition and re-institutionalized after the collapse of the Soviet regime. Some of the early post-1991 grand narratives about a return of Islam in Central Asia after the collapse of the Soviet Union had been operating on the premises that a thorough process of secularization did in fact occur as a result of Soviet policies.[32] More critical assessments have questioned how wide and how deep was the Soviet impact on Islamic practices; particularly non-institutionalized ones and those operating in informal institutions (e.g. Sufi brotherhoods).[33] Yet, in the aftermath of the collapse of the USSR, as much as in the aftermath of the Islamic revolution in Iran, it was clear that a working knowledge of those Muslim societies was often lacking. Commenting on the state of this 'expert knowledge' after

---

[30] See for example, Robert N. Bellah, 'Religious aspects of modernization in Turkey and Japan' *The American Journal of Sociology*, LXIV (1) 1958, pp. 1–5; Robert E. Ward and Dankwart A. Rustow, *Political Modernization In Japan and Turkey* (Princeton: Princeton University Press, 1964).

[31] See John Anderson, *Religion, State and Politics in the Soviet Union and Successor States* (Cambridge: Cambridge University Press, 1994).

[32] See for example Ahmed Rashid, *The Resurgence of Central Asia: Islam or Nationalism?* (London: Zed Books 1995).

[33] See Alexandre A. Bennigsen and S. Enders Wimbush, *Mystics and Commissars: Sufism in the Soviet Union* (London: Hurst & Co, 1985); Sergei P. Poliakov, *Everyday Islam: Religion and Tradition in Rural Central Asia*, trans. A. Olcott (Armonk: M.E. Sharpe, 1992); Alexei V. Malashenko, 'Islam versus Communism', pp. 63–78, in D.F. Eickelman (ed.), *Russia's Muslim Frontiers: New Directions in Cross-cultural Analysis* (Indianapolis: Indiana University Press, 1993). What became clear, nonetheless, is that the post-1991 versions of Islamic orthodoxy and orthopraxy that are promoted and popular in the region are quite different from the ones that prevailed before the Soviet experience.

1991, Muhammad Khalid Masud emphasizes that the too great concern with formal politics and institutions had led to understudying the informal social and political dynamics of Muslim communities in the region.[34]

If the perception of a linkage between institutional or economic modernization and secularization decreased over time, that of the connection between political/religious modernization and secularization remains central in the debates about the Muslim world in the post-Cold War context. Whilst the spread of formally secular state institutions progressively ceased to be seen as a reliable indicator of general secularizing trends, the growth of particular discourses regarding the respective roles of religion and politics has been proposed instead as a more reliable indicator of such trends. Ronald Inglehart and Pippa Norris' *Sacred and Secular* provide a recent illustration of this approach, and of its shortcomings.[35] Though the interest in the Muslim world and in political religion is fairly recent in this type of quantitative approach, the methodology has been well tested in western polities for quite some time. As with the democratization debates that will be addressed in the next chapter, it has become fashionable in recent decades to use survey techniques to attempt to develop some general framework for the region, despite the paucity of reliable data concerning the mechanisms of formation of political and religious opinion.[36] These problems with data are quite apparent in the model that Inglehart and Norris use to frame and test traditional secularist propositions like 'growing up in societies in which survival is uncertain is conducive to a strong emphasis on religion'; or 'as a society moves past the early stages of industrialization and life becomes less nasty, less brutish, and longer, people tend to become more secular in their orientations'.[37] Operating from such premises, they can claim to 'demonstrate

---

[34] Sombrely, Masud reiterates the comments made by Piscatori after the Iranian revolution that 'to date there have been only a few empirical studies that try to go beyond the impressionistic and the general, and take the measure of Islam's current political activity'. Quoted in Muhammad Khalid Masud, 'Conclusion: the limits of expert knowledge', pp. 190–200, in Eickelman, *Russia's Muslim Frontiers*, at p. 190.

[35] Ronald Inglehart and Pippa Norris, *Sacred and Secular: Religion and Politics Worldwide*, (Cambridge: Cambridge University Press, 2004).

[36] See Moataz A. Fattah, *Democratic Values in the Muslim World* (Boulder: Lynne Rienner, 2006).

[37] Inglehart and Norris, *Sacred and Secular*, pp. 219–20.

that the process of secularization—a systematic erosion of religious practices, values and beliefs—has occurred most clearly among the most prosperous social sectors living in affluent and secure post industrial nations'. They can therefore conclude that 'secularization is not a deterministic process, but it is still one that is largely predictable, based on knowing just a few facts about levels of human development and socioeconomic equality in each country.'[38] Using a developmentalist structural framework, Inglehart and Norris argue that since a key factor driving religiosity are feelings of vulnerability to social and personal risks, as these decrease, secularization increases. This explanation is grounded on a straightforward interpretation of the Enlightenment heritage that suggests that the structural transformation of the public sphere requires the privatization of religious choices. Conceptually, the most serious inconvenience of this type of approach is the tendency to infer structural change from (more or less well-documented) changes in belief when the overall argument outlines causation mainly in the opposite direction. As in many survey-based analyses, there also remains a tendency to revert to orientalist clichés about the flaws of these societies—e.g. the fate of women, the condition of the poor—due to the absence of empirical analysis of micro-social and micro-political processes of identity formation.[39]

The quest for an elusive Islamic Reformation

The processes of secularization in Turkey or in the Central Asian republics of the former USSR hardly provided analysts with a clear model for understanding changes in other Muslim-majority polities. Considering the evolution of Turkish Islamic movements Hakan Yavuz outlines how simplistic it is to view the progressive return of more public forms of Islam as a mere reaction to changing political and economic circum-

[38] Inglehart and Norris, *Sacred and Secular*, pp. 5, 109. In their scenario, however, the argument about an 'existential security' form of development is undermined by the slippery character of their preferred notion of security.

[39] Infusing a dose of Eurocentric feminism, they suggest that 'if this theory is applied to cultural contrasts between modern and traditional societies, it suggests that we would expect one of the key differences between the Western and Islamic worlds to focus around the issues of gender equality and sexual liberalization'. Inglehart and Norris, *Sacred and Secular*, p. 138.

stances. Instead, he suggests that 'moral questions and values in Turkish politics have been articulated in Islamic terms because the Kemalist cultural revolution did not produce an alternative shared moral language, and Islamic references and idioms remain the depository for the moral debate'.[40] This line of argument feeds into a larger debate concerned with understanding the trajectory of Islamic movements as reflecting primarily an evolving indigenous political tradition that can generate order, meaning and legitimacy based on the Islamic revelation.[41] For a scholar of these alternative Islamic versions of modernity like John Esposito it is clear that 'modernization as Westernization and secularization remained primarily the preserve of a small minority elite of society. More important, the secularization of processes and institutions did not easily translate into the secularization of minds and culture'.[42] This assessment is probably too rigid, as many post-orientalist scholars have pointed out that secularization has changed the ways in which Muslim communities and Islamic activists perceive themselves to be connected to their religious commitments. They stress that there is a self-reflective process of objectification of what it means to be a Muslim community, which is posited in contradistinction to what secularization represents.[43] If secularization did not unfold as it was meant to according to earlier sociological views, it did nonetheless impact Muslim communities—primarily via the actions of the state—and it did shape the formation of alternatives to western secularism. In this context, the issue of an Islamic Reformation—as distinct from ordinary reforms in Islamic jurisprudence—has been repeatedly evoked in various intellectual and policy-making circles.[44] To date, it is not yet clear how far these issues and debates are superseding or con-

---

[40] M. Hakan Yavuz, *Islamic Political Identity in Turkey* (New York: Oxford University Press, 2003), p. 220.

[41] See Roxanne L Euben, *Enemy in the Mirror: Islamic Fundamentalism and the Limits of Modern Rationalism* (Princeton: Princeton University Press, 1999); Armando Salvatore, *Islam and the Political Discourse of Modernity* (Reading: Ithaca Press, 1999).

[42] John L. Esposito, *The Islamic Threat* (New York: Oxford University Press, 1992), p. 9.

[43] See for example, Eickelman and Piscatori, *Muslim Politics*.

[44] See Robin B. Wright, 'Two visions of reformation', pp. 64–75; and Abdou Filali-Ansary, 'The challenge of secularization', pp. 76–80, both in *Journal of Democracy* 7 (2) 1996.

tributing to those directly concerned with secularization as Westerniza-tion. Indeed, Abdullahi An-Naim, one of the most articulate current commentators on this theme, initially argued that secularism was receding as reformation progressed, but subsequently developed the argument that Islamic politics could be best served by a formally secular institu-tional system.[45]

Undoubtedly, interesting parallels can be drawn between the flurry of modern reformist activities among Islamic scholars and the Christian brand of reformation. There is in addition a set of arguments and debates about the specific heritage of the so-called 'Reform Movement' spear-headed by Mohammed Abduh and Jamal al-Afghani in the late nine-teenth.[46] Their opposition to an unquestioned acceptance of tradition and their push for a more scientific process of hermeneutic interpretation of the sacred texts points to a thematic convergence in reformist thinking. However, this rapprochement also highlights a key difference between the two reforming contexts, namely the lack of an established Church that one can oppose and try to restructure in the Muslim tradition— except to a degree in specific communities like the Twelver Shi'a. In this context, it has been repeatedly asked whether the presence of many reformist thinkers amount to a Reformation. The arguments developed by An-Naim suggest that the quest for a unity of reforms is not high on the Islamic agenda. Even when there are similarities between thinkers, it hardly produces the linear conception of religious 'enlightenment' that western observers commonly have in mind when debating reformation— especially when it comes to the topic of the public-private distinction that is central to liberal thinking.[47] For Dale Eickelman, the changing forms of communication and the role of the media in Muslim society unmistak-ably facilitate a reformation of the scripturalism that used to structure religious authority in earlier Muslim communities.[48] He suggests that in

---

[45] Compare Abdullahi Ahmed An-Naim, *Toward an Islamic Reformation: Civil Liberties, Human Rights, and International Law* (Syracuse: Syracuse University Press, 1990) with Abdullahi Ahmed An-Naim, *Islam and the Secular State* (Cambridge: Harvard University Press, 2008).

[46] See Salvatore, *Islam and the Political Discourse of Modernity*.

[47] See Saba Mahmood, 'Ethical formation and politics of individual autonomy in contemporary Egypt', pp. 837–68; and Nilufer Gole, 'The voluntary adoption of Islamic stigma symbols', pp. 809–30, both in *Social Research* 70 (3) 2003.

[48] Dale F. Eickelman, 'Who speak for Islam? Inside the Islamic Reformation',

the long term, 'rising literacy and education, together with the proliferation of new media, may well foster the growth of pluralism, tolerance,
and civility'.[49] Eickelman's work uncovered some important factors driving the process of reformation by focusing on changing forms of mass-
communication and the associated growth of the public sphere. His
collaborations with Jon Anderson on the new media in the Muslim world
and with Armando Salvatore on the Islamic public were useful in outlin-
ing sociologically grounded accounts of such transformative practices in
many polities of the Muslim world.[50] Nonetheless, as Eickelman himself
recognises, even in the most promising situations, the analogy with the
Protestant Reformation remains imperfect.[51] The main value of these
analyses therefore is to highlight the concrete mechanisms involved in
the restructuration of the public sphere and public debate. Whether this
amounts to a reformation may not be that relevant after all; as the most
that can be hoped for by drawing analogies with the Protestant Reformation are pointers for new research, not a set of analogous conclusions.

For Olivier Roy, the observation that there are Muslim theologians
who advocate some form of reformation from a doctrinal perspective is
neither necessarily connected to, nor a prerequisite for, a western-type
modernization process. Rather, he sees the mechanisms of social transformation along western lines already at work in the increased de-linking
of Islamic religious and cultural identity, as well as in the shift away from
dogma and toward everyday practice among 'neo-fundamentalist' movements.[52] In the political domain it may well be, as Abdelwahab al-Effendi
suggests, that 'an "Islamic Reformation" is neither necessary nor sufficient
for enabling Muslims to build stable and consensual political institutions.

---

in M. Browers and C. Kurzman (eds.), *An Islamic Reformation?* (Lanham:
Lexington Books, 2004).

[49] Dale F. Eickelman, 'Inside the Islamic Reformation', *Wilson Quarterly* 22 (1)
1998, pp. 80–89, at p. 88.

[50] D.F. Eickelman and J.W. Anderson (eds.), *New Media in the Muslim World: The
Emerging Public Sphere* (Bloomington: Indiana University Press, 1999); A. Sal-
vatore and D.F. Eickelman (eds.), *Public Islam and the Common Good* (Leiden:
Brill, 2004).

[51] Eickelman, 'Inside the Islamic Reformation', p. 89.

[52] Olivier Roy, *Globalized Islam: The Search for a New Ummah* (London: Hurst &
Co., 2004).

A reformation may be a desirable thing; that is a matter for Muslim believers to decide. But its prospect is unlikely to improve the outlook for political stability in the short term'.[53] Undoubtedly, the relationship between the 'desirable' aspect of reformist endeavours and political 'stability' has received much interest from policy-makers in recent years. Unfortunately, this interest has itself introduced new difficulties into these debates. A recent policy report for the Rand Corporation encouraging the US government to visualize the contemporary religious transformation in Islam through the lenses of the Protestant Reformation, and proposing policies designed to support fully the 'modernists', selectively the 'secularists', and tactically the 'traditionalists' in order to counter the 'fundamentalists', provides a good example of this trend.[54] As Saba Mahmood remarks, the attempt to tie together the political interests of liberal democratic states with an 'accurate' and 'modern' interpretation of the religious texts by specific intellectuals is quite specious. Not only are there no necessary connections between these two elements, but also the very notion of a 'proper' understanding of the Islamic corpus is heavily and problematically tainted by the secular and liberal preferences of these state actors.[55]

Secularization light or Islamic modernity?

Just as many 'truths' of orientalism proved to be not as solid as they were meant to be, so too a large section of the scholarship on secularization had to be downgraded in recent years to the level of unsubstantiated generalizations. A repentant Berger suggested that 'a whole body of literature by historians and social scientists loosely labelled "secularization theory" is essentially mistaken'.[56] Sociologists of religion like Rodney Stark and Roger Finke even argued that it was 'time to carry the secularization

---

[53] Abdelwahab El-Affendi, 'The elusive reformation', *Journal of Democracy* 14 (2) 2003, pp. 34–44, at p. 38.

[54] Cheryl Benard, *Civil Democratic Islam: Partners, Resources, and Strategies* (Santa Monica: RAND, 2004).

[55] Saba Mahmood, 'Secularism, hermeneutics, and empire: the politics of Islamic reformation', *Public Culture* 18 (2) 2006, pp. 323–47.

[56] P.L. Berger (ed.), *The Desecularization of the World* (Washington, DC: Ethics and Public Policy Center, 1999), p. 2.

doctrine to the graveyard of failed theories'.[57] In its stead they proposed their own version of the political economy of faith that indicated how, as pluralism increases in society, faith and religious movements also grow in strength. It may well be, however, that these damning assessments of the contemporary situation are too harsh regarding secularization theory. In partial defence of notions of secularization, Jose Casanova argues that there is still some life in this body of scholarship. In particular, he suggests that an analytical distinction ought to be made between three different connotations of the theory. First there is an account of the decline in religious belief and practices, second there is a descriptive and normative narrative about the privatization of religion, and third there is a description of the increased differentiation of the secular and religious sphere at the institutional level. Casanova's suggestion is that maximalist narratives about secularization are fundamentally flawed because they attempt to borrow evidence from one set of processes to support their claim regarding another one, for which direct evidence is harder to come by. For him, the best strategy is to abandon wholesale debates about secularization and to re-focus the discussion on more specific secularization issues in a comparative social and historical perspective.[58]

Regarding Muslim polities, two types of scholarship heeded the call for more modest accounts of secularization: studies focusing on institutionalization of Islam, and the research on the new practices of religiosity. In the first category, scholars chose to concern themselves not primarily with belief but with the institutionalized structures of religious life. In particular they consider the separation between 'Church' and 'State'— though both notions remain problematic in developing countries—and the authority of religious leaders in a secularized social and political field. This perspective enables them to avoid many of the teleological biases of

---

[57] Rodney Stark and Roger Finke, *Acts of Faith: Explaining the Human Side of Religion* (Berkeley: University of California Press, 2000), p. 79.

[58] See Casanova, *Public Religions in the Modern World*. The 'maximalist' flaw is well illustrated in the works of Inglehart and Norris previously mentionned. In Casanova's own comparative framework, the more modest account of secularization proposed focuses primarily on institutional differentiation as a meaningful way of identifying common trends in Christianity and Islam. José Casanova, 'The long, difficult, and tortuous journey of Turkey into Europe and the dilemmas of European civilization', *Constellations* 13 (2) 2006, pp. 234–47.

earlier studies and to propose more pragmatic accounts of religious dynamics—a pragmatic reading that undermines various claims of exceptionalism regarding the Muslim world. Such studies indicate that the battle-lines between religious and secular institutions are shifting over-time not only because of changing views of what is acceptable and appropriate, but also because of particular power struggles for short or long term benefits.[59] From this non-exceptionalist perspective, as John Ruedy summarizes in the North African context, 'the struggle over the frontier between the secular and the religious is one characterized by continuous tension [and] up to now, the exact line of the frontier between the two has never been agreed upon'. Ruedy adds that in western settings too, 'there has seldom been agreement among secularists as a group, nor among the religious as a group, as to where exactly that frontier should be'.[60] Even in the case of Turkey, which is usually invoked as a case of deep social transformation introduced by secular policies, the retreat of institutionalized Islam from the public sphere did not make Islam an entirely 'private' affair. As Andrew Davison indicated, 'Islam was not disestablished, it was differently established'.[61] Although the public role of an institutionalized Islamic tradition was redefined by the secularized institutions of the Turkish Republic, the tradition still operated as a forum for associational networks and community building. Ultimately, Yavuz noted that following a broadening of 'opportunity spaces' for social net-working during the process of democratization in the 1980s, political Islam visibly came back in the Turkish public and political sphere.[62] In Turkey as much as in the former Soviet Republics of Central Asia, or even in Iraq under Baathism, the forceful interventions of the state to define the proper place of the religious and the secular in public life do

---

[59] See José Casanova, 'Civil society and religion: retrospective reflections on Catholicism and prospective reflections on Islam', *Social Research* 68 (4) 2001, pp. 1041–82; 'Catholic and Muslim politics in comparative perspective', *Taiwan Journal of Democracy* 1 (2) 2005, pp. 89–108.

[60] John Ruedy, 'Introduction', in J. Ruedy (ed.), *Islamism and Secularism in North Africa* (New York: Palgrave 1994), p.xiv.

[61] Andrew Davison, 'Turkey, a "secular state"? The challenge of description', *South Atlantic Quarterly* 102 (2/3) 2003, pp. 333–50, at p. 341; Andrew Davison and Taha Parla, *Corporatist Ideology in Kemalist Turkey: Progress or Order?* (Syracuse: Syracuse University Press, 2004).

[62] Yavuz, *Islamic Political Identity in Turkey*, p. 24.

not provide very reliable information regarding the process of long-term institutional secularization. Clearly too, the harsh enforcement of a nationalist secular creed can also be matched by an equally brutal intervention of a religiously-construed state, as in the case of Afghanistan in the late 1990s when the Taliban strove to 'deprivatize' religion and decree its public practice a national obligation.

In the post-colonial context as much as before, the authoritarian nature of the state, which usually promoted such swift and wide-ranging changes, also ensured that the social acceptance of these new interactions was not well entrenched. It promoted a grudging quiescence by threatening would-be dissenters with violence. In the 1960s already some analysts had begun to question certain common assumptions about the institutional modernization of religion in the Middle East. Ibrahim Abu-Lughod noted 'the resurgence of Islam in Arab politics as a force having significant impact on internal, and to a lesser extent, on external politics [that was] reflected in the institutional and juridical structure of the Arab States, as well as in social patterns of behaviour'. He argued that after decolonization there was increased secularization because 'there has been a much greater fusion between politics and religion, in which certain religious tasks are being performed by the state in its "secular" aspect, while other political and quasi-political tasks are being performed by the sacred arm of the state'.[63] For Abu-Lughod, in the 1960s there was a readjustment in the relationship between religion and politics that produced relative gains for both. In subsequent decades, area specialists produced new explanations for this 'legitimisation crisis' and for the relative gains of institutionalized religion. Regardless of other socioeconomic, political and cultural factors—rent, authoritarianism, patronage, etc.—what these 'non-standard' institutional practices were deemed to highlight was the role of the social sphere in 'distorting' political processes. In particular, it was thought to be a clear case of colonization of modern-secular practices by traditional religious ones.[64] For most scholars, regardless of their preferred analytical approach this situation made political Islam unavoidably part of the problem, and not part of a solution. From Gellner to Kepel some of the most astute observers of Islamism still fell back on a standard

---

[63] Abu-Lughod, 'Retreat from the secular path?', pp. 449, 468.
[64] See Joel S. Migdal, *Strong Societies and Weak States* (Princeton: Princeton University Press, 1988).

view of secularization and modernization of social and political life informed by the European model as the natural way forward for the Muslim world. Such arguments reinforced policy perceptions that under favourable circumstances the importation of liberal democratic institutions and principles, the emergence of a secular civil society and the separation of Church and State were the means to ensure that Islam became compatible with political modernity, at least in institutional terms. Evidently, these accounts were not meant to be merely descriptive, they were quite prescriptive.[65]

At this juncture, institutionalist accounts of religion and the state connect with anthropological narratives about the transformation of religiosity. Initially, such readings had been framed by the dominant Weberian views regarding the role of the modern nation-state as the enforcer of claims to constitute legitimate social entities and arenas. Yet, despite expectations that value-judgements would be kept at distance, the tendency to see Europe's religious life as a prototype of global religiosity meant that the progress of secularism in Muslim polities was assessed in relation to norms that had no necessary relevance in that particular context.[66] Asad's work on the interaction between the religious and the secular outlines the problematic nature of the public-private distinction that has been forcefully promoted by these 'western' narratives. Asad notes that the secular 'should not be thought of as the space in which real human life gradually emancipates itself from the controlling power of "religion" and thus achieves the latter's relocation'.[67] He stresses that initially, the 'secular' was a category created by theological discourse, and that in modern times there has been a role reversal that made the 'religious' constituted by political secularism and by the positive sciences; and as such a

[65] Even today Kepel still argues that the 'separation of the secular and religious domains is the prerequisite for liberating the forces of reform in the Muslim world'. Gilles Kepel, *The War for Muslim Minds: Islam and the West* (Cambridge: Belknap Press, 2004), p. 295.

[66] See for some varying appraisals of the interaction between secularism and modernity in Muslim communities, J.L. Esposito and F. Burgat (eds.), *Modernising Islam: Religion in the Public Sphere in Europe and the Middle East* (London: Hurst, 2002); A. Tamimi and J.L. Esposito (eds.), *Islam and secularism in the Middle East* (London: Hurst, 2000).

[67] Talal Asad, *Formations of the Secular: Christianity, Islam, Modernity* (Stanford: Stanford University Press, 2003), pp. 191–2.

subjective construct of Western modernity. Politically, Asad suggests that 'secularism is invoked to prevent two very different kinds of transgression: the perversion of politics by religious forces, on the one hand, and the state's restriction of religious freedom, on the other.'[68] For much of the post-colonial period in the Arab Middle East in particular, he stresses that the secularized ideology of Arabism primarily tried to define Islamism and to put it in its proper place. Increasingly in the last few years, many analysts of Muslim politics, as well as comparative sociologists have placed a greater emphasis on the constitutive role of secularism in the contemporary representation of the religious in general and of Islamism in particular. They recognize that earlier analyses all too readily assumed that the expansion of the apparatus of the colonial and neo-colonial state was a natural part of the modernization process and that the secularization of public (and in some cases private) life would naturally follow. Hence, they sought to contextualize better the unexpected strength of an Islamic political 'revival' and the 'colonization' by Islamists of social spheres that were deemed to be beyond the remit of religious discourse.

Saba Mahmood stresses that with secularizing discourses it 'is not simply a question of ideological bias, but rather the way these critiques function within a vast number of institutional sites and practices aimed at transforming economic, political, and moral life in the Middle East— from international financial institutions to human rights associations to national and local administrative bureaucracies'.[69] In this context, she notes that Islamism is viewed 'as an eruption of religion outside the supposedly 'normal' domain of private worship, and thus as a historical anomaly requiring explanation if not rectification'. To avoid the normative bias contained in institutionalist approaches, post-orientalist social anthropologists and area specialists have increasingly turned their attention to the behavioural and ethical embodiments of the power dynamics

---

[68] Talal Asad, 'Trying to understand French secularism', in H. de Vries and L. Sullivan (eds.), *Political Theologies: Public Religions in a Post-Secular World* (New York: Fordham University Press, 2006), pp. 494–526, at p. 524.

[69] Saba Mahmood, *Politics of Piety: The Islamic Revival and the Feminist Subject* (Princeton: Princeton University Press, 2004), p. 191. These observations dovetail with those of Mitchell regarding the workings of the modern Egyptian state system, as an anarchic instigator of new forms of social governance. See Timothy Mitchell, *Rule of Experts: Egypt, Techno-Politics, Modernity* (Berkeley: University of California Press, 2002).

enacted between religious and secular actors. In her study of the 'vernacular politics' of Islamist mobilization in Turkey, Jenny White urges the
reader to question 'the usefulness of analytically separating "modern" civil
society and party politics from "traditional" communalistic institutional
practices, from individual relations, or political ideology from cultural
beliefs', and to 'think outside the categories we have inherited for understanding political life'.[70] Clearly, although one cannot question everything
at once, White's suggestion is valuable in the sense that considering the
repeated failures at explaining the evolution of political Islam, there may
be more to be gained by working outside conventional social and political
frameworks than by insisting on using them. This is not an argument in
favour of Islamic exceptionalism, but rather a critique of the secular-based
sociological explanations, and an incentive to devise better ones. From a
social anthropology perspective, the argument has already moved beyond
what religious and areas specialists called for a decade earlier—namely
revising our views of how religious movements articulated themselves in
national politics via Islamo-nationalist parties.[71] Now the issue becomes
that of revising what basic principles of socio-political organisation can
be meaningfully invoked in those polities to make sense of religiosity.
Clearly, this is not without problems, since what Islamism (and now 'post-
Islamism') means is rapidly evolving, and clarity is needed in order not
to talk past one another.[72]

In attributing much of the current social predicaments in the Muslim
world to the evolution of modern politics, one should not go so far as to
turn political Islam once again into a mere congregation of losers in the
process of nation building. White's comparative work on secularized and

[70] Jenny White, *Islamist Mobilization in Turkey: A Study in Vernacular Politics* (Seattle: University of Washington Press, 2002), p. 6.

[71] See Mark Juergensmeyer, *The New Cold War?: Religious Nationalism Confronts
the Secular State* (Berkeley: University of California Press, 1994); 'The new religious state', *Comparative Politics* 27 (4) 1995, pp. 379–91.

[72] See M. Hakan Yavuz, 'Introduction: the role of the new bourgeoisie in the
transformation of the Turkish Islamic movement', in M.H. Yavuz (ed.), *The
Emergence of a New Turkey: Democracy and AK Parti* (Salt Lake City: Univer-
sity of Utah Press, 2006), pp. 1–22; Umit Cizre, 'Introduction: the Justice and
Development Party—making choices, revisions and reversals interactively', in
U. Cizre (ed.), *Secular and Islamic Politics in Turkey: The Making of Justice and
Development Party* (London: Routledge, 2008).

Islamized social mobilization in contemporary Turkey illustrates the variations and the similitude between these two types of activism; thereby avoiding caricaturing the Islamic-inspired practices. By focusing on these micro-practices one may better understand how a subtle reor-ganisation of power can occur over time, and how it can influence the legal and legislative system. Studies looking at the framing of Islamic practices in the everyday politics of the believers highlight the deep and potentially significant work of identity reconstruction that takes place 'below the radar' of national politics. As with Mahmood's study, a new light on these processes has been shed recently by works that either approached Islamism from a feminist angle, or looked at the issue of the Islamist 'female subject' and the modalities of her insertion in the social sphere.[73] In recent years, there is also a growing body of literature that investigates the 'Islamic human right' dimension of Islamism and details how such rights are embedded in everyday practices.[74] Although I will return to this issue in more details in the chapter on globalization, it is worth noting here that at the local level too, there is a significant entrenchment of a self-reflective discourse on personal freedoms, and religious and public liberties. How far an effective and durable reworking of the public-private interaction can be put in place through these pro-cesses will depend on the success of the social and political movements mediating them. At the same time, the extent to which these movements can be seen by both individuals and institutions to have legitimate grounds for revising the public-private boundaries is a key component of their success. In such a context, the debate over new forms of religios-ity and 'authentic' Muslim selves that is particularly prevalent among the more conservative advocates of the Islamist project is also positioned to provide answers to the abovementioned secularization debates. Many Islamist movements struggling for political recognition in Muslim-majority countries nowadays still firmly emphasize a unitary model of Islamism that could replace what nationalism and socialism previously offered—and their public discourse often reflects primarily this aspect

[73] Mahmood, *Politics of Piety*.

[74] See *passim* Ann Elizabeth Mayer, *Islam and Human Rights: Tradition and Pol-itics* (Boulder: Westview Press, 2007). See also the chapters by Fred Halliday; Ali Mohammadi, Charles Kurzman and Mahmood Monshipouri in Ali Mo-hammadi (ed.), *Islam Encountering Globalisation* (London: Routledge, 2002).

of their programme.[75] Yet, closer investigations of the internal dynamics of these movements reveal that there a recognition of heterogeneity, especially among a new generation of activists. In the case of well-established organizations, like the Egyptian Muslim Brotherhood, these internal debates may lead to a kind 'auto reform', as outlined by Carrie Rosefsky Wickham, or it may result in the formation of new (liberalized) offshoots, as Raymond Baker suggested.[76]

One dimension of this debate on internal political reorientations that is well scrutinized today in the context of the interaction between Turkey and the European Union, is how the Justice and Development Party redefines the terms of Islamic activism in secular democratic settings.[77] In this particular context, scholars in the secularization tradition tend to argue that the current evolution of Islamist-minded political parties in Turkey is not to be trusted, and that their strategy of democratization and Europeanization is only a subterfuge. By contrast, post-orientalist analysts suggest that the tactical and strategic choices of the AKP could be better understood through a sociological and historical comparison with the European Christian Democratic parties of the 1950s.[78] Beyond the issue of party politics, however, these debates point to the need to analyze better the social construction of Islamism outside the formal political sphere. The move toward what some analysts call post-Islamism, is presented by some scholars like Bayat or Roy as a sizing down of the political aspirations of an earlier generation of Islamist revolutionaries.[79] This assessment

---

[75] See Nicola Pratt, *Democracy and Authoritarianism in the Arab World* (Boulder: Lynne Rienner, 2007).

[76] Carrie Rosefsky Wickham, *Mobilizing Islam: Religion, Activism, and Political Change in Egypt* (New York: Columbia University Press, 2002); Raymond William Baker, *Islam without Fear: Egypt and the New Islamists* (Cambridge, MA: Harvard University Press, 2003).

[77] See Yavuz, *The Emergence of a New Turkey*; Cizre, *Secular and Islamic Politics in Turkey*; Cihan Tugal, *Passive Revolution: Absorbing the Islamic Challenge to Capitalism* (Stanford: Stanford University Press, 2009).

[78] Compare, for the former, Bassam Tibi, 'Europeanizing Islam or the Islamization of Europe: political democracy vs. cultural difference', with, for the latter, M. Hakan Yavuz, 'Islam and Europeanization in Turkish-Muslim socio-political movements', in P. Katzenstein and T. Byrnes (eds.), *Religion in an Expanded Europe* (Cambridge: Cambridge University Press, 2006).

[79] Asef Bayat, *Making Islam Democratic: Social Movements and the Post-Islamist Turn* (Stanford: Stanford University Press, 2007); Roy, *Globalized Islam*.

may well be accurate but only in so far as the focus remains firmly on formal political institutions and mechanisms. Using a micro-social perspective instead of an institutionalist one, scholars like Ismail, Mahmood, Whickam or White have documented how a revived emphasis on ethics, piety and welfare contribute to a re-composition of priorities in a dynamic Islamic tradition. This focus on the self may involve a different set of background assumptions regarding individualism and its political and social expression, but it does not necessarily constitute a lesser form of socio-political involvement simply because it does not meet western standards for institutionalized politics.

5

LOCATING POLITICAL ISLAM
IN DEMOCRATIZATION STUDIES

The historicity of the study of democratization in 'Muslimstan'

Over the last few decades, the issue of the absence of common models of democracy in Muslim-majority countries has been at the centre of much debate in political science. This situation is remarkable since before that, the 'Muslim world' and political Islam were not deemed to be very worthy research topics. If it was not dealt with using the traditional tools of modernization theory, it was a matter left to areas study specialists and, regarding the specifically 'Islamic' aspects, to orientalist scholars with training in philology. It is significant that the most emblematic Islamic political movement of the twentieth century, the Muslim Brotherhood, hardly featured on the political sciences' horizon until Richard Mitchell's pioneering study published in 1969.[1] In practice, political science research on Islamic movements, when it existed, received little attention beyond specialist debates before the Iranian Revolution of 1979. Then in the space of two decades political Islam moved from being a quaint anachronism to being one of the leading features of political life and institutional change in Muslim polities. From the 1980s onward, two relatively new bodies of literature attempting to explain political change in the developing world have grown exponentially, namely democratization studies and studies on Islamism.[2] These two specialities met in the closing

[1] Richard P. Mitchell, *The Society of the Muslim Brothers* (Oxford: Oxford University Press, 1969).
[2] See Leonard Binder, *Islamic Liberalism: A Critique of Developmental Ideologies*

stages of the Cold War, when many believed that authoritarian regimes worldwide would soon disappear to be replaced by Western-style liberal democracies. Since that time, however, due to the largely disappointing results of democratization in most of the Muslim-majority countries and in the Middle East in particular, scholars and policy-makers have concentrated their attention on the putative causes that ensured the continuing absence of substantial democratic reforms in those regions. Repeatedly, one of the most conspicuous answers to this noted lack of 'progress' in Muslim polities has been construed in terms of the intrinsically regressive and authoritarian nature of Islam as beliefs system and of Islamism as a socio-political organization.[3]

Progressively in the 1990s, the research on political democratization in Muslim polities began nonetheless to shift the grounds of the inquiry away from narratives informed by orientalism and toward more empirical methods of assessment. Scholars started to refocus their explanations to answer practical dilemmas about the processes of Islamization and democratization, and not meta-questions about the nature of Islam and Democracy. Analyzes became concerned more with the issue of the practical role played by Islamist movements as institutional actors for political mobilization, and less with the diffuse cultural and religious underpinnings of social identity.[4] Undoubtedly, at the turn of the century, the events of 9/11 facilitated a return to meta-theoretical considerations about Islamism, particularly in the field of foreign policy analysis and democracy promotion. More than ever, the 'radical' edge of political Islam was presented as a major security challenge to the very idea of Democracy, as well as to individual democracies or would-be democracies. In the subsequent decade of the 'War on Terror', democracy and democracy promotion were reaffirmed as the mirror image of the institutions and practices of the European and North American liberal democracies. At the same time, in-depth considerations of what might constitute viable demotic-based institutional alternatives to these domi-

---

(Chicago: University of Chicago Press, 1988); W.R. Roff (ed.), *Islam and the Political Economy of Meaning* (London: Routledge, 1987).

[3] See Samuel P. Huntington, *The Clash of Civilizations: And the Remaking of World Order* (New York: Free Press, 2002).

[4] For a clear statement see Daniel Brumberg, 'Islamists and the politics of consensus', *Journal of Democracy* 13 (3) 2002, pp. 109–15.

nant models receded into the background. This discursive buttressing of what were perceived to be standard frameworks of both Democracy and Islamism structured the debates regarding the future prospects of these phenomena.

Contemporary debates about the interaction between political Islam and democracy display clearly the historicity of the answers that have accumulated over time in this field of research. In particular, one can recognize the continuing impact of orientalist attempts to build a comprehensive and systematic picture of an Islamic civilization, with its own logic and system of value.[5] This influence is strongest in the description of specifically Islamic dynamics through the lenses of western concepts and methodology which are presented as rational universals. As such, orientalist narratives have no difficulty in finding their place in related paradigms and explanations in other social sciences disciplines. As indicated earlier, from this perspective, there is an object 'out there' called Islam or the Muslim world that can be systematically studied; and the task of the analyst is precisely to contribute little by little to building a grand picture of the political mechanisms of this society. As both critiques and proponents of this scholarship have argued, traditional orientalists have (had) a sophisticated knowledge of many aspects of the Islam that they studied. Indeed, in the early days of political science research in the Middle East, it seemed difficult and unwise directly to challenge the findings of orientalist scholarship. Manfred Halpern's pioneering work on the Middle East and North Africa in the early 1960s provides a clear illustration of this attitude.[6] Rather than directly questioning the narratives put forward by orientalists, Halpern attempted to supplement them with a more empirical analysis of political and institutional behaviour in the postcolonial states of the region. Reviewing the state of the field at that time, Halpern concluded that 'it would be quite impossible for students of political modernization to do any sensible work without, for example, drawing upon the works of H. A. R. Gibb, Gustave von Grunebaum, or Wilfred Cantwell Smith'.[7] Hence, he was concerned with devel-

---

[5] For a critical analysis see Salman Sayyid, *A Fundamental Fear: Eurocentrism and the Emergence of Islamism*, revised edition (London: Zed Books, 2003).

[6] Manfred Halpern, *The Politics of Social Change in the Middle East and North Africa* (Princeton: Princeton University Press, 1963).

[7] Manfred Halpern, 'Middle Eastern studies: a review of the state of the field with a few examples', *World Politics* 15 (1) 1962, pp. 108–22, at p. 111.

oping what he called a 'new orientology' more attuned to the paradigms of modern political science and more grounded on quantitative methods. At the time, most social scientists did not see a contradiction between the two types of scholarship; rather they expected to find a complementary relationship. This tendency is illustrated in the works of many leading social and political science experts in the 1960s and 1970s, from Leonard Binder to Dankwart Rustow, who provided empirically grounded elaborations of traditional orientalist arguments about the dynamics of the political culture of the Muslim world and the Middle East.[8]

For political scientists, the legacy of orientalism has a dual set of philosophical and political implications. From a philosophical perspective, approaches informed by orientalism seek to construct a paradigmatic reading of Islam that would structure the freedom of action of Muslim social and political actors—what they can or cannot do and say, what they should or should not do and say. This framing was particularly important up to the 1960s, as orientalist scholarship was deemed to be more reliable on all things Islamic than any explanations indigenous actors and scholars could come up with.[9] Typically, this framework for Islam was contrasted to a similarly rigid account of liberal democratic principles that could not accommodate, or be accommodated by, the Islamic tradition in some fundamental ways. While traditional orientalism focused on religious dogma and theological exegesis, subsequent neo-orientalist analyses concentrated instead on the politicized pronouncements of various Islamic ideologues. From a political perspective, orientalist readings of Islamism are directly connecting theological interpretations to political action. Put crudely such views indicate that there are some key Islamic issues which the leadership of the Islamist movements 'ought to' consider, and that politics therefore will be organized around those issues by an Islamist regime. This particular take on Islamism accommodates itself well, and is also partly constitutive of, a traditional 'realist' account of power construction and projection in

[8] See Leonard Binder, *The Ideological Revolution in the Middle East* (Chicago: University of Chicago Press, 1964); Dankwart A. Rustow, 'Turkey: the modernity of tradition', in L.W. Pye and S. Verba (eds.), *Political Culture and Political Development* (Princeton: Princeton University Press, 1965).

[9] As Halpern indicated at the time, orientalists are 'largely responsible for having given Middle Easterners themselves an accurate appreciation of their past'. Halpern, 'Middle Eastern Studies', p. 117.

international relations.[10] Unsurprisingly, in the Muslim world, for most of the Cold War, political Islam was presented as a dependent variable in an international context where realist/neorealist views of international relations seemed adequate to map out patterns of conflicts and alliances. At the domestic level, the choices for Islamism were framed in a dualistic mode: either it was the source of a radical exceptionalism to modernization theory—as in the Islamic Republic of Iran—or it was an object that could be accommodated within what this theory predicted in terms of societal change, as in Turkey.

Because narratives on the modernization and secularization of institutions and of social life constituted the dominant developmental paradigm, comparisons with democratic developments in the 'West' were not only useful to understand 'Muslimstan' but they were in fact necessary. As developmentalists had argued, since the religious glue of Muslim society was bound to be dissolved by modernization, any revival of religious activism was ultimately doomed to failure. Hence, political sociology was better advised to focus on modern political forces that duplicated those existing in western societies.[11] Some early critiques noted that since these processes of institutional modernization were often forcefully put in place by authoritarian regimes, a return of the repressed social and political forces, particularly Islamic ones, was likely to happen should the resolve and capabilities of the regimes weaken.[12] By and large, however, this eventuality was not deemed to be significant enough to actually warrant much research on Islamism itself. Resistance to the process of social and political secularization and modernization was deemed largely futile before 1979 and at best marginally significant after the Iranian revolution. Conceptually, it is not until well after the emergence of the Islamic Republic of Iran, that scholars began seriously to consider the over-stretch of the modernization-secularization theory, especially when applied to largely under-studied social forces in Muslim majority countries.[13] Still, for

[10] See L. Carl Brown, *International Politics and the Middle East: Old Rules, Dangerous Game* (London: I B Tauris, 1984).

[11] As Lerner suggested, in this context, the apparent choice between Mecca or Mecchanisation is in fact no choice at all. Daniel Lerner, *The Passing of Traditional Society in the Middle East* (New York: Free Press, 1958).

[12] See Ibrahim Abu-Lughod, 'Retreat from the secular path? Islamic dilemmas of Arab politics', *The Review of Politics* 28 (4) 1966, pp. 447–76.

[13] See Binder, *Islamic Liberalism*.

decidedly orientalist scholars like Elie Kedourie or Bernard Lewis the democratization debate remained a non-starter for Islamist movements because of both the weight of the Islamic tradition and the fact that Islamist ideologues repeatedly spoke against the notion of Democracy.[14] Their analyses emphasized the role of key theological resources in Islam that undermined basic concepts of democratic organization, such as popular sovereignty. These authors presented the domestic and international politics of Muslim-majority societies against the backdrop of a fairly unitary notion of national interest stigmatised by an anti-liberal and anti-western Islamist ideology. In this context, for many scholars of comparative politics, the merging of orientalist scholarship and empirical political sociology remained largely a matter of commonsense. In a standard Middle East textbook from the 1980s, James Bill and Carl Leiden could therefore argue that because of the continuing relevance of Islam and the example set by the Prophet, 'twentieth-century Muslim political leaders often have styles and use strategies that are very similar to those instituted by the Prophet Muhammad in Arabia some 1,400 years ago'.[15] Contemporary democratization dilemmas were not uncommonly assumed to be more dependent upon the 'Muslimness' of the agents and the socio-historical and cultural weight of Islam, than shaped by the modern nationalist ideologies and military-administrative reorganizations that most rulers in the region produced in the postcolonial period.

The end of the Cold War and the rise of democratization as a particular Muslim problem

In international politics there have been repeated attempts to subsume the case of Muslim-majority countries under a regionalist approach to Middle East politics. Commonly, these approaches emphasized an 'Iranian model' of Islamist take over, with variations on this theme such as the Algerian scenario.[16] While these perspectives also took note of arguments developed

---

[14] Elie Kedourie, *Democracy and Arab Political Culture* (Washington DC: Washington Institute for Near East Policy, 1992); Bernard Lewis, *The Political Language of Islam* (Chicago: Chicago University Press, 1988).

[15] James Bill and Carl Leiden, *Politics in the Middle East*, 2nd ed. (Boston: Little, Brown and Co., 1984), p. 133.

[16] For a critique see Frédéric Volpi, *Islam and Democracy: The Failure of Dialogue in Algeria* (London: Pluto Press, 2003).

by post-orientalist scholars, area study specialists were more directly influenced by the dominant realist and neo-realist paradigms of the day.[17] Hence, interpretations involving political Islam remained mainly a second-order tool of analysis for most of the 1980s as the dynamics of the Cold War constituted a first-order *explanandum* for regional geopolitics and domestic developments. The realist influence on the study of the Middle East and the Muslim world shaped the evolution of the democratization debates from the 1980s onwards. In particular, it facilitated the continuation of grand narratives about Muslim politics underpinned by culturalist views that gave an air of causality to many weak correlations in the region—such as the alleged resistance of 'Islamic political culture' to democratic ideas. Illustrative of this situation are the positions of Samuel Huntington regarding the 'third wave' of democratization in the Middle Eastern and 'Islamic' context. From his 1984 article, 'will more countries become democratic' to his 1991 book, *The Third Wave*, Huntington views the spread of liberal democracy to the Middle East and the Muslim world as difficult yet probably unavoidable in the long term, considering the direction of world politics. He warns against a particularly difficult set of structural factors stacking up against rapid democratization in many of the key Muslim-majority societies due to 'Islamic culture'. Yet, this situation does not constitute for him a qualitatively different democratization dilemma altogether.[18] In this context, the Middle East/Muslim world may be 'exceptional' as suggested by orientalists, but not exceptional enough to evade the dominant political paradigms of the day.

The reliance on vague notions of 'Islamic political culture' as a generic explanation provides a common thread between the modernization accounts of the 1950s and 1960s, the realist analyses of the Cold War and the post-Cold War narratives about Muslim democratic exceptionalism.[19]

---

[17] This is one strand of argument proposed by both Roy and Kepel—though both authors subsequently added correctives to their early narratives on the development of Islamism. See Olivier Roy, *The Failure of Political Islam*, trans. C. Volk (Cambridge: Harvard University Press, 1996); Gilles Kepel, *The Revenge of God: Resurgence of Islam, Christianity and Judaism in the Modern World*, tr. A. Braley (Cambridge: Polity Press, 1993).

[18] Samuel P. Huntington, 'Will more countries become democratic', *Political Science Quarterly* 99 (2) 1984, pp. 193–218; *The Third Wave: Democratization in the Late Twentieth Century* (Norman: University of Oklahoma Press, 1991).

[19] This is not to say that notions of 'political culture' cannot be deployed usefully

In practice, many democratization specialists would little revise their positions regarding the Muslim world after the collapse of the communist bloc. Adrian Karatnycky's 2001 Freedom House democracy survey still emphasizes that 'Islamic countries' are lagging behind all the others in terms of advances in democracy and civil liberties. Quoting approvingly Bernard Lewis on the paucity of the democratic lexicon in Arabic and on the merging of religion and politics, Karatnycky refers back to the idea that it simply takes time for democratic principles to take root in an 'Islamic political culture'.[20] In such accounts, the 'political Islam problem' in the post-Cold War situation is mainly a reification of the Middle East problem. Bernard Lewis' *What Went Wrong* provides a good illustration of this trend. In this work, Lewis proposes general insights into political Islam, despite having an empirical focus limited to Middle East politics.[21] Partial amendments were proposed by democratization specialists who argued that it was more an 'Arab culture' problem than an 'Islamic' one; but this revision did not really address some of the main over-generalizations regarding the specifically 'Arab' character of these dynamics.[22] Instead, after the collapse of the USSR and the rise of Islamic militancy in Central Asia, neo-orientalist and neo-realist analysts joined forces to propose the notion of a 'Greater Middle East' which presented these developments within known frames of references and security practices (i.e. military alliances with nationalist autocrats to secure oil resources and hold Islamism in check).[23] In the post Cold War period there is an

---

in the region, particularly to provide accounts of political change that avoid various forms of socio-economic determinism. See Michael C. Hudson, 'The political culture approach to Arab democratization: the case for bringing it back, carefully', in B. Korany, R. Brynen and P. Noble (eds.), *Political Liberalization and Democratization in the Arab World: Theoretical Perspectives*, (Boulder: Lynne Rienner, 1995), pp. 61–76.

[20] Adrian Karatnycky, 'The 2001 Freedom House survey: Muslim countries and the democracy gap', *Journal of Democracy* 13 (1) 2002, pp. 99–112.

[21] Bernard Lewis, *What Went Wrong Western impact and Middle Eastern response* (Oxford: Oxford University Press, 2002).

[22] See Alfred Stepan with Graeme B. Robertson, 'An "Arab" more than a "Muslim" democracy gap', *Journal of Democracy* 14 (3) 2003, pp. 30–44.

[23] See R.D. Blackwill and M. Stürmer (eds.), *Allies Divided: Transatlantic Policies for the Greater Middle East* (Cambridge: MIT Press, 1997); Völker Perthes, 'America's "Greater Middle East" and Europe: key issues for dialogue', *Middle*

increased polarization between on the one hand, neo-orientalist and neo-realist approaches to democratization in the Muslim world, and on the other, post-orientalist and constructivist interpretations. In part, this polarization is informed by the debate in the sociology of religion that addresses the issue of the de-privatization of religion.[24] As indicated earlier, this sociological re-assessment undermined the premises of the modernization theories that many analysts had used to explain social and political change in the developing world. From the mid-1990s onward, there is an emergence of a new set of more un-compromising neo-realist interpretations of democratization in the Muslim world, that consider the project in jeopardy in the light of the strengthening of political Islam. For these authors, as Islamism becomes the first level of analysis, the narrative that they propose tries very hard to link (liberal) democracy to political Islam (or Islam *tout court*) in order to show the incompatibility of these two organizing principles of political life.[25] In this context, their constructivist opponents are led to formulate their response using similar terms.

In the 1990s the debates concerning political Islam tends to become polarized between those whom Fred Halliday calls 'essentialists' and 'contingencists'.[26] Essentialists develop an argument with a strong orientalist favour that attributes to the 'fundamentals' of Islam the cause of systemic clashes with western notions of liberal democracy. Contigencists on the other hand, argue that like any other religious doctrine, Islam is malleable enough to be interpreted in such a way as to minimize the frictions with liberal notions of democracy. This tension also indicates that each 'camp' has embarked upon rather different intellectual endeavours that cannot be unified by mere reference to the data. For some, the task is to construct a usable framework for representing 'national interests' from the discourse of political Islam, and therefore to find unity in diversity. For others, the

---

East Policy XI (3) 2004, pp. 85–97. And compare Pinar Bilgin, 'Whose "Middle East"? Geopolitical inventions and practices of security', *International Relations* 18 (1) 2004, pp. 25–41.

[24] See José Casanova, *Public Religions in the Modern World* (Chicago: University of Chicago Press, 1994).

[25] See Huntington, *The Clash of Civilizations*.

[26] Fred Halliday, 'The politics of Islam: a second look', *British Journal of Political Science* 25 (3) 1995, pp. 399–417.

task is to unmask the alternative articulations of the Islamist discourse and show where and when the resources of the Islamic tradition can be combined with other resources (including from the liberal democratic tradition). In democratization studies these debates are also structured by two earlier perspectives on political change. On the one hand there are those agency-based studies that became fashionable in the 1980s and that emphasized the role of political players during the transition period. On the other hand there are those slightly older accounts of democratization based on structural pre-conditions for change that have their roots in modernization theory.[27] For 'essentialists' the core virtues of the Islamic and liberal-democratic tradition are too different to allow agents to build a system that would satisfy both sets of skills and expectations—no matter how much good fortune one may have. The case of the Islamic republic of Iran under Khomeini, as well as the evolution of Afghanistan under the Taliban or the rise of Turabi in the Sudan, provided a good backdrop against which to deploy such narratives. For 'contingencists', by contrast, given the right circumstances and despite having different traditions, individuals can find interpretations of their own values and practices that generate political synergies rather than conflicts. In this perspective, episodes like the rise of Khatami in Iran showed that the attribution of 'Islamic' national interests was not as straightforward as once thought. Evidently, the mere possibility of a convergence does not imply that it will necessarily happen in practice, as some well-crafted post-orientalist narratives stressed.[28]

In all those narratives, simply referring to the 'facts' in the region does not provide an easy way of resolving the abovementioned dilemmas. Due to the limited number of examples and counter-examples invoked in each scenario, what counts as a meaningful generalization and what represents an exception to the rule is strongly determined by the type of explanation that the analyst wants to propose. The debate regarding democratization in Turkey provides a good illustration of how either narrative can be supported by the evolution of a polity. For analysts attributing a benign role

---

[27] See Guillermo O'Donnell and Philippe C. Schmitter, *Transitions from Authoritarian Rule: Tentative Conclusions about Uncertain Democracies* (Baltimore: Johns Hopkins University Press, 1986).

[28] Compare Kepel, *The Revenge of God*, and Roy, *The Failure of Political Islam*, with John L. Esposito and John O. Voll, *Islam and Democracy* (Oxford: Oxford University Press, 1996).

to political Islam, the fact that the country has been governed by a political party with Islamist inclinations in 1996–97 and since 2002 is a clear indication that democratization can proceed smoothly even in the presence of an Islamic-minded political party and public discourse. Yet Turkey also proclaims its republican credentials forcefully, as well as promoting its own brand of republicanism (Kemalism) as the state ideology. On the basis of those evidences, neo-realist and neo-orientalist authors are able to articulate developmentalist and primordialist arguments regarding the relationship between Islamism and modern liberal democracies. Lewis argues in particular that there is a prior requirement for a radical ideational change in order to enable the organization of democratic politics, since even words like citizen and citizenship had until recently no direct equivalent in the Arabic, Persian or Turkic languages.[29] From this perspective, the current situation in Turkey is not an example of Islamic moderation but one of the success of political secularisation. Evidently, faced with such assertions, 'contingencists' would reply that the presence of a specific vocabulary is less important than the meaning that words actually acquire in particular socio-historical contexts. Although the western political lexicon long possessed those terms, their political meaning has been re-constructed from the Enlightenment onwards to resonate with new practices corresponding to modern political sensibilities.[30]

To avoid these conceptual dilemmas, some comparative studies have tried to quantify political and social preferences of citizens in these polities. From the mid 1990s onward, there has been an increasingly fashionable strand of survey-based research that investigated the attitudes of 'Muslims' toward 'democracy' in order to assess the degree of compatibility between the two.[31] A wide array of more or less well-designed surveys and analyses indicated that the religious beliefs held by citizens throughout the Muslim world did not in themselves preclude people from taking

[29] Bernard Lewis, *The Emergence of Modern Turkey* (Oxford: Oxford University Press, 1968); 'Islam and liberal democracy: a historical overview', *Journal of Democracy* 7 (2) 1996, pp. 52–63.

[30] For a general outline of those crucial semantic and conceptual changes, see, T. Ball, J. Farr and R.L. Hanson (eds.), *Political Innovation and Conceptual Change* (Cambridge: Cambridge University Press, 1989).

[31] See for example the outputs of the Pew Global Attitudes Project, http://pewglobal.org and the World Values Survey, http://www.worldvaluessurvey.org.

an interest in 'democracy'.[32] Although these studies have the advantage of avoiding the (pseudo)philosophical problems that flourish in the abovementioned debates by focusing on what local people actually say, they face a different kind of methodological problems. The notion of democracy is simply not as rigid and/or self-evident as many of these analyses take it to be. These analyses do not thoroughly investigate what respondents actually mean when they use the words that are suggested to them by these surveys. These survey-based studies point to a notion of liberal democracy that is reconstructed by the analysts from the basic social and political preferences voiced by the respondents. Yet, because of the methods used and the nature of the data obtained, the analysts do not and cannot describe the deliberative processes that produce a socially embedded account of what a word like 'democracy' actually means for the citizens locally. Instead, what these studies show is how compatible local preferences are with existing liberal democratic practices, based on the rational choice models that would work in already established liberal democracies. All that seems to be certain from these analyses is that terms like democracy and democratization are far more fashionable political expressions than they were twenty years ago. Yet, the lack of characterization of how these ideas are socially constructed and turned into practices undermines the explanatory powers of the survey-based approaches, especially for forecasting purposes.

Beyond the 'democratization paradigm' for political Islam

Trying to measure 'really existing democracy' in Muslim-majority polities indirectly contributed to reinforce pre-existing dilemmas in explanations of political change (or the lack of it) in the region. Two related sets of arguments have shaped these debates in the post-Cold War context. One side of the debate has a long tradition in developmental studies and

[32] See Mark Tessler, 'Islam and democracy in the Middle East: the impact of religious orientations on attitudes toward democracy in four Arab countries', *Comparative Politics*, 34 (3) 2002, pp. 337–54; 'Do Islamic orientations influence attitudes toward democracy in the Arab world: evidence from the World Values Survey in Egypt, Jordan, Morocco, and Algeria', *International Journal of Comparative Sociology* 44 (2) 2003, pp. 229–49; Moataz A. Fattah, *Democratic Values in the Muslim World* (Boulder: Lynne Rienner, 2006).

focuses on the structural impediments to democratization, primarily from socio-economic and institutional perspectives. In recent years, it is the issue of the (re)institutionalisation of authoritarian regimes in democratic guise which has become the object of particular discussion. The other side of the debate is more attuned to studies of civic activism and the role of civil society in political transformations. Building on the insights about democratization obtained in Latin America and Eastern Europe, these analyses focus on the similarities and differences with Islamic social activism.

In the civil society/civic activism debate, the principal difference that is commonly highlighted is the lack of the strong liberal trend that existed in the other regions where democratization processes occurred in recent years. However, Guillermo O'Donnell noted that even in the Latin American context, analysts had a tendency to let their normative preferences and teleological inclinations gloss over as irrelevant some inconsistencies in the processes of transition and consolidation.[33] In analyses of Latin American and Eastern European transitions, such lapses appeared not to have been too consequential because the voluntarist drive of the analyses commonly reflected the views of the civil society groups and political counter-elites that were on the ascendancy at the time—though these difficulties proved to be quite relevant in the consolidation period. In most Muslim polities today, similar assumptions about the liberal nature of civil and political activism are not prevalent, though the opposite expectation does have an impact on many analyses in the same fashion. Typically, from rather orientalist premises, Ernest Gellner presses the point that whatever associative life there may exist in Muslim polities, it is not of the right kind and therefore unpropitious to the emergence of a genuine democratic order.[34] There are evidently different types of 'civil society' or 'civil sphere' in different parts of the Muslim world. Yet, even the rather sanguine studies of Augustus Norton and his collaborators highlighted that in the 1990s the presence of a recognisably liberal civil society project in the Middle East often amounted to a mere twinkle in the eyes of an active minority.[35] Nonetheless, it has been noted over the

---

[33] Guillermo O'Donnell, *Counterpoints: Selected Essays on Authoritarianism and Democratization* (Notre Dame: University of Notre Dame Press, 1999).

[34] Ernest Gellner, *Conditions of Liberty: Civil Society and its Rivals* (London: Hamish Hamilton, 1994).

[35] A. R. Norton (ed.), *Civil Society in the Middle East* (Leiden: Brill, 1995).

years that the positions of Islamist movements have moved away from a general condemnation of liberalism as incompatible with Islam—though this view also remains common. Increasingly, it is noticeable that these movements either suggest that liberalism and democracy are essentially Islamic—though this remains often a very rhetorical point—or, more convincingly, that if there are conflicts between liberalism and Islamism they can be resolved through a process of mutual reinterpretation.[36]

The debates to date on the practical and conceptual developments in civil society in the Muslim world remain tentatively optimistic, but proponents of a new 'civil society' paradigm advance their argument with extreme prudence.[37] At the turn of this century, the dominant view appears to be that civil society cannot play the role of the dominant democratization paradigm in the Muslim context in the same way that it could be invoked in the 1980s and 1990s in Latin America and Eastern Europe. Only in a few specific cases, is this argument being invoked as one of the main explanatory tools for democratic transition, as in Robert Hefner's analysis of the Indonesian case. Working from observations on grassroots organization, Hefner is able to argue quite convincingly that Indonesian 'civil society', partly led by Islamic associations, was conducive to a recognisably liberal democracy slowly being created in a Muslim polity.[38] Yet, apart from a few 'exceptional' polities, the dominant perception remains that there are fewer opportunities for the authoritarian elite to hand over power 'gracefully' on the model of the Latin American pacted transitions, because of the uncompromising ideological discourse held by the most powerful Islamist opposition movements in most Muslim-majority countries. The situation in Southeast Asia might have been the most propitious for such a process, but elsewhere in the Muslim world, only the better-run parliamentary monarchies, like Morocco or Jordan, appear to provide the kind of exit strategy for the ruling elite that

[36] See Charles Kurzman, 'Liberal Islam: prospects and challenges', *Middle East Review of International Affairs* 3 (3) 1999, pp. 11–19.

[37] See Amy Hawthorne, 'Is civil society the answer?', in T. Carothers and M.S. Ottaway (eds.), *Uncharted Journey: Promoting Democracy in the Middle East* (Washington: Carnegie Endowment for International Peace, 2005), pp. 81–114.

[38] Robert W. Hefner, *Civil Islam: Muslims and Democratization in Indonesia* (Princeton: Princeton University Press, 2000).

might avoid a brutal democratic transition. In other cases, what is estimated to embolden the determination of the ruling elite to stay in power is the assessment that dramatic consequences would follow were they to relinquish power to the Islamist opposition, as in the Algerian scenario.[39]

The second set of arguments about contemporary processes of democratization in Muslim polities is structured mainly on the mechanisms of institutionalisation of authoritarian regimes. In many countries of the Muslim world it is being argued that there is an enduring situation of stalled transitions. Some democratization specialists from Larry Diamond to Thomas Carothers have argued that this situation is becoming such a common political condition in the developing world that it is now a state of normality rather than of exception.[40] From this perspective, hybrid authoritarian regimes are not a deviation from a liberal democratic framework but a distinct analytical category and political phenomenon. They are the main feature of the democratization conundrums of the Muslim world where, in addition to the nature of the political opposition, processes of securitization, as well as political and financial institutionalization, create specific democratization dilemmas. Because of the apparent weakness of civil society, analysts have be keen to stress the particular structural organization of state power in the Middle East—and these arguments have been transposed to several other parts of the Muslim world. Regarding security institutionalization, Marsha Posusney and Eva Bellin have emphasized the role of the authoritarian elite. In the main, they have argued that the strength of the coercive apparatus in the Arab world has been the principal inhibitor of democracy change.[41] Commonly, this secu-

---

[39] See William Case, 'Revisiting elites, transitions and founding elections: an unexpected caller from Indonesia', *Democratization* 7 (4) 2000, pp. 51–80; Abdeslam Maghraoui, 'Monarchy and political reform in Morocco', *Journal of Democracy*, 12 (1) 2001, pp 73–86; Mansoor Moaddel, 'Religion and the state: the singularity of the Jordanian religious experience', *International Journal of Politics, Culture and Society* 15 (4) 2002, pp 527–68.

[40] Larry Diamond, 'Thinking about hybrid regimes', *Journal of Democracy* 13 (2) 2002, pp. 21–35; Thomas Carothers, 'The end of the transition paradigm', *Journal of Democracy* 13 (1) 2002, pp. 5–21; David Collier and Steven Levitsky, 'Democracy with adjectives: conceptual innovation in comparative research', *World Politics*, 49 (3) 1997, pp. 430–451.

[41] Marsha Pripstein Posusney, 'Enduring authoritarianism: Middle East lessons for comparative theory', *Comparative Politics* 36 (2) 2004, pp. 127–38; Eva

rity argument is supported by references to the notion of *asabiyya* as a crucial structuring factor in Middle East politics.[42] Akbar Ahmed has suggested that a notion of 'hyper-asabiyya' could also be used in order to understand the new regional security dynamics post-9/11.[43] Regarding political institutionalization, Volker Perthes and Ellen Lust-Okar stress how elites have managed to restructure and co-opt their opponents, as well as exploiting and manipulating the cleavages between opposition groups (especially the secular/Islamist divide), so as to neutralize demands for democracy from the masses.[44] This trend is reinforced by the fact that historically, these polities are generally latecomers to the democratization process. As autocrats learn from past mistakes, we witness the rise of more competitive forms of authoritarianism in relation to liberal democracy.[45] Finally, explanations focusing on structural state power find additional support for their case by incorporating in their argument a political economy perspective that shows how oil wealth in the contemporary international and geopolitical context reduces the necessity to liberalise politically.[46]

Bellin, 'The robustness of authoritarianism in the Middle East: exceptionalism in comparative perspective', *Comparative Politics* 36 (2) 2004, pp. 139–57.

[42] See Olivier Roy, 'Patronage and solidarity groups: survival or reformation', in G. Salamé (ed.), *Democracy without Democrats* (London: IB Tauris, 1994); Kathleen Collins, 'The political role of clans in Central Asia', *Comparative Politics* 35 (2) 2003, pp. 171–90.

[43] Akbar S. Ahmed, *Islam under Siege: Living Dangerously in a Post-Honor World* (Cambridge: Polity Press, 2003).

[44] V. Perthes (ed.), *Arab Elites: Negotiating the Politics of Change* (Boulder: Lynne Rienner, 2004); Ellen Lust-Okar, *Structuring Conflict in the Arab World: Incumbents, Opponents, and Institutions* (Cambridge: Cambridge University Press, 2007).

[45] Repeatedly too, it has been noted how the efforts to liberalize and democratize the political system of Muslim countries have induced a refinement of the authoritarian skills of the ruling elite. See Daniel Brumberg, 'The trap of liberalized autocracy', *Journal of Democracy* 13 (4) 2002, pp. 46–68; Frédéric Volpi, 'Algeria's pseudo-democratic politics: lessons for democratization in the Middle East', *Democratization* 13 (3) 2006, pp. 442–55.

[46] See Raymond Hinnebusch, 'Authoritarian persistence, democratization theory and the Middle East: An overview and critique', in F. Volpi and F. Cavatorta (eds.), *Democratization in the Muslim World: Changing Patterns of Power and Authority* (London: Routledge, 2007), pp. 11–34; Michael L Ross, 'Does

From pseudo-democracy to rethinking democratic transformation

The problem that Islamic movements create for common explanations of democratization is that their democratizing potential challenges some basic assumptions about the relationship between contemporary forms of liberalism and democracy. For quite some time, analysts on the 'clash' side of the debate have maintained that all the discrete cases of opposition between Islamist views and 'western' liberal democratic views are only the surface manifestations of a deeper and all-inclusive illiberal and undemocratic Islamist worldview. However, such arguments show such a degree of over-generalization regarding what constitutes liberalism and democracy and what makes an illiberal and undemocratic Islamic worldview, that their explanatory powers are significantly reduced. Their parsimony and easiness of use ensure nonetheless that they have been relatively well conveyed to policy-makers and the mass media. In this context, post-orientalist critiques of arguments about clashing political cultures can only point out that there are benign alternatives by emphasizing the more 'democratic' and 'liberal' forms of political Islam.[47]

What is still missing from many analyses of democratization processes in Muslim polities is a detailed consideration of what conceptual compromises are needed for a meaningful dialogue between opposition and government (both in and outside the polity). This situation helps to explain to some degree the current lack of options for (liberal) democracy promotion at the policy level. Due to the limited scope of these conceptual inquiries, it is commonly perceived in policy circles that any deviation from the liberal democratic model in the Muslim context unavoidably leads to the emergence of what Fareed Zakaria calls 'illiberal democracies'.[48] The alternative to the notion of illiberal democracy is to talk about 'grey areas' of democracy, thereby suggesting the partial convergence of

---

oil hinder democracy?', *World Politics* 53 (3) 2001, pp. 325–61. This point is evidently most powerfully made in relation to some of the wealthier Gulf States. See Michael Herb, *All in the Family: Absolutism, Revolution, and Democratic Prospects in the Middle Eastern Monarchies* (Albany: State University of New York Press, 1999).

[47] See A. Salvatore and D.F. Eickelman (eds.), *Public Islam and the Common Good* (Leiden: Brill, 2006); Esposito and Voll, *Islam and Democracy*.

[48] Fareed Zakaria, *The Future of Freedom: Illiberal Democracy at Home and Abroad* (New York: W.W. Norton, 2003).

Islamist and liberal-democratic political agendas. Nathan Brown, Marina Ottaway and Amr Hamzawy provide detailed illustrations of these processes, in which the principal difficulty is deemed to be the ethos of political and civil society that needs to be reformed (liberalized and democratized) alongside the institutional structure.[49] The main difficulty of democratization in the Muslim world is thus seen as this disjunction between a rapid top-down reform of the political mechanisms that allow people to express their choices (via free and fair elections), and the protracted bottom-up process of civic education that gives them the opportunity to acquire the aforementioned liberal democratic skills and habits. Problematically, however, the very notion of convergence that is suggested between Islamic and liberal perspectives is, more often than not, viewed as a prelude to the full acceptance of liberal democratic models of governance. These analyses do not habitually delve into the alternative political realities that Islamist movements are constructing—both ideologically and socially—nor do they consider how far these models constitute viable and locally acceptable versions of 'democracy'. What remains understated in explanations of 'grey zone' democracy, is that the 'clarity' that has been achieved in established liberal-democracies is not merely a deliberative process of enlightenment, where legally backed discursive constructs ensure that an acceptable consensus on individual rights and collective duties is reached. While Islamist players may welcome political liberalization as leading one step closer to their preferred model of democracy, once they reach the tipping point beyond which their democracy is no longer synergetic with the liberal democratic standard currently promoted by the international community, new and unpredictable forms of oppositions and alliances emerge, which undermine previous assumptions about democratic political development.[50] This is not however a straightforward process as, in itself, challenging the dominant liberal democratic consensus in the name of a more religiously framed notion of demotic power may constitute a valid and useful form of criticism.[51]

---

[49] See Nathan Brown, Amr Hamzawy and Marina S. Ottaway, 'Islamist Movements and the Democratic Process in the Arab World: Exploring Gray Zones', Carnegie Paper no. 67, March 2006.

[50] See Frédéric Volpi, 'Pseudo-Democracy in the Muslim world', *Third World Quarterly* 25 (6) 2004, pp. 1061–78.

[51] According to Stepan, the 'lesson' from Western Europe 'lies not in the need for a "wall of separation" between church and state but in the constant political

Charles Hirschkind's study of dialogues between Islamists and non-Islamists in Egypt, illustrates that there are nonetheless coercive undertones in all these dialogical political interactions.[52] Yet, whether these social forces appear to be genuinely 'civil' or quite 'uncivil' from a western perspective, they are to be reckoned with, as they are able to durably shape local at, at times, national politics.[53] In this context, the issue of knowing how far Islamist parties should then become 'normal' players in state politics remains far more a problem of presentation for local autocrats and their international backers who have demonized these parties in the past than it is for everyday politics in the region. Beyond the Turkish case—where the Justice and Development party has chosen to stop presenting itself as a primarily Islamic party—there have now been more systematic analyses of the (possibility of) involvement of Islamist parties in genuine governing coalitions.[54] In rethinking the acceptable parameters of a democratic system there is also unavoidably a struggle on issues where consensus cannot possibly be reached.[55] This tension is also exacerbated by the type of liberal democratic order that had become the norm in the second half of the twentieth century, and whose function was to place restraints on majority rule with the view to protect very specific individual

---

construction and reconstruction of the "twin tolerations"'. Stepan nonetheless recognized that historically the reconfiguration of State–Church interaction did not happen without periods of serious crisis and confrontations. Alfred Stepan, 'Religion, democracy and the "twin tolerations"', *Journal of Democracy* 11 (4) 2000, pp. 37–57, at p. 42.

[52] Charles Hirschkind, 'Civic virtue and religious reason: an Islamic counterpublic', *Cultural Anthropology* 16 (1) 2001, pp. 3–34. See also in the Turkish context, Cihan Tuğal, 'The appeal of Islamic politics: ritual and dialogue in a poor district of Turkey', *Sociological Quarterly* 47 (2) 2006, pp. 245–73.

[53] See Maha Abdel Rahman, 'The politics of "uncivil" society in Egypt', *Review of African Political Economy* 29 (91) 2002, pp. 21–35; Francesco Cavatorta, 'Civil society, Islamism and democratisation: the case of Morocco', *The Journal of Modern African Studies* 44 (2) 2006, pp. 203–22.

[54] See for example in connection to Yemen and Egypt, Michaelle L. Browers, *Political Ideology in the Arab World: Accommodation and Transformation* (Cambridge: Cambridge University Press, 2009).

[55] This debate is particularly relevant in connection to constitutionalism. See Abdullahi Ahmed An-Naim, *Islam and the Secular State: Negotiating the Future of Shari'a* (Cambridge: Harvard University Press, 2008).

rights and civil liberties.[56] The imposition of constraints on rights and liberties—both individual and collective—is a substantive feature of governance that promotes a distinct political ethos; and it should come as no surprise that Islamists propose to do the same with an ethos that need not be defined primarily in terms of its liberal character.

As the postcolonial literature emphasizes, it is conceptually hazardous to equate democratization with modernization and secularization—i.e. westernization.[57] Talal Asad notes that modernity is a set of interlinked projects for the institutionalization of principles such as constitutionalism, moral autonomy, democracy, human rights, civil equality, industry, consumerism, freedom of market, and secularism.[58] This idea of modernity encapsulates what western policy-makers and public opinion—and even some scholars—understand to be a 'democracy'. In this context, democratization may (and is likely to) entail curtailing some of the prerogatives of the demos for the benefit of a liberal constitutional ideal. Although from a western perspective there are no particular difficulties in conceiving that a 'universalistic' notion like individual human rights may 'trump' majoritarian forms of democracy, serious difficulties emerge when more communitarian notions of public virtue or religious orthodoxy are invoked to 'trump' civil liberty issues.[59] In most parts of the Muslim world, the process of democratic reinvention and institutionalization of 'a-liberal' Islamic practices is specifically harnessed to the diffusion of an ethos that portrays them as virtuous components of a social and political project. As Saba Mahmood notes, these two components can be expressed very differently within a polity, and more social-minded pietist movements may effectively oppose more political-minded Islamist parties.[60] Either way, from a western perspective, Islamist approaches are perceived to be blurring the distinction between the public and the private that is central to the functioning of contemporary liberal democratic institu-

---

[56] See James Tully, *Strange Multiplicity: Constitutionalism in an Age of Diversity* (Cambridge: Cambridge University Press, 1995).

[57] See Sayyid, *A Fundamental Fear.*

[58] Talal Asad, *Formations of the Secular: Christianity, Islam, Modernity* (Stanford: Stanford University Press, 2003), p. 13.

[59] See Hirschkind, 'Civic virtue and religious reason'.

[60] Saba Mahmood, *Politics of Piety: The Islamic Revival and the Feminist Subject* (Princeton: Princeton University Press, 2004).

tions—as well as potentially introducing a 'dangerous' positive definition of liberty grounded on religious normativity.

To understand these new trends in the region, democratization studies have begun to move past the functionalist explanations that previously dominated the field. The collapse of much of modernization-secularization theory in sociology, which underpinned linear accounts of democratic transitions over the last two decades, has left nonetheless a vacuum in contemporary explanatory frameworks of democratization in Muslim polities. In the Middle East in particular, the weakness of 'civil society' based explanations reopened the way for analyses based on structural factors—usually the role of security apparatuses and the oil rent—which form the backbone of many recent accounts of the slow pace of political change in the region. Internationally, particularly in the aftermath of 9/11, democratization processes have been portrayed once more as a dependent variable in a neo-realist geostrategic balance of power, with hard security (terrorism) and energy security (oil) being the key structuring factors. In this context, domestically, the processes of moderation of Islamist movements have been viewed as a functional adaptation to state repression and the spread of 'western' democratic discursive tools. These narratives are predicated upon a fairly static political order and only marginally consider the process of democratization as an engine of change in domestic and international systems—thus contributing to a shrinkage of the interested in democracy promotion. To date, only a limited number of democratization analysts take the risk to emphasize a more substantive transformation of Islamic ideas of governance and political practice, due mainly to the paucity of empirically solid data on these issues.[61] Those analyses that move past traditional liberal interpretation of democratization have nonetheless a greater potential to comprehend how these new political articulations can transform the relationships between state and society in the flawed democratizing settings of contemporary Muslim communities.

[61] But see in the Turkish context, M. Hakan Yavuz, *Islamic Political Identity in Turkey* (New York: Oxford University Press, 2003). The case of Shi'a governance in Iraq might also prove to be an interesting case in point. See Robert Gleave, 'Conceptions of authority in Iraqi Shi'ism: Baqir al-Hakim, Ha'iri and Sistani on ijtihad, taqlid and marja'iyya' *Theory Culture and Society* 24 (2) 2007, pp. 59–78; Juan Cole, 'The Ayatollahs and democracy in Iraq', ISIM Paper no. 7, Leiden, 2006.

6

MULTICULTURALISM INSIDE/OUTSIDE
POLITICAL ISLAM

Just as in Muslim-majority countries, in recent decades there have been increasingly vocal political demands for better inclusion of Islamic views in the national cultural sphere of polities where Muslims are a minority. This process has been particularly noticeable in western democracies, due to the ability of social and political actors to voice their claims and be heard by political institutions with a reasonable level of success.[1] Though similar trends are witnessed in both Muslim-majority and Muslim-minority countries, it has not commonly been the case, that this phenomenon has been addressed either by the same scholars or within the same comparative frameworks. This is problematic, as Olivier Roy points out, since any general view about the evolution of political Islam today should not assume that the analytical distinction between Muslim-majority and Muslim-minority countries has an intrinsic sociological value—still less that there are methodologically well-founded reasons for analyzing the two separately.[2] Yet,

---

[1] See for example, Jorgen S. Nielsen, *Muslims in Western Europe* (Edinburgh: Edinburgh University Press 1992); B. Metcalf (ed.), *Making Muslim Space in North America and Europe*, Berkeley (Berkeley: University of Berkeley Press, 1996); G. Nonneman, T. Niblock, B. Szajkowski (eds.), *Muslim Communities in the New Europe* (London: Ithaca Press, 1996); Y. Haddad (ed.), *Muslims in the West: From Sojourners to Citizens* (Oxford, Oxford University Press, 2002); S. Allievi and J.S. Nielsen (eds.), *Muslim networks and transnational communities in and across Europe* (Leiden: Brill. 2003).

[2] Olivier Roy, *Globalized Islam: The Search for a New Ummah* (London: Hurst & Co., 2004).

there is a palpable disconnection between the literature on political Islam in the core regions of the Muslim world, and the literature focusing of political Islam in fringe regions like Europe or the United States. In terms of political analysis, while the focus is on the processes of political democratization in Muslim-majority polities, it is firmly on the sociology of multiculturalism in western polities. In this respect, anthropologists and sociologists of religion are commonly hindered by methodological and area specialism boundaries. As Robert Hefner stresses, scholars who 'rightly challenge the application of secular-modernization narratives to the non-Western world are sometimes less critical of these theories' portrayal of religion in the modern West'.[3]

Today, there are still few systematic attempts to bridge the gap between political and anthropological studies in Muslim-majority countries and sociological multiculturalist approaches to Muslim minorities in western settings. John Bowen's work on socio-legal reforms in the Muslim communities of Indonesia and France is a notable exception to this trend.[4] However, it is noticeable that in framing his research, Bowen starts with a detailed analysis of the socio-cultural and politico-legal dynamics of norms formulation and rules implementation in each national context before venturing to analyze global and transnational trends. To obtain a sufficiently detailed knowledge of different national communities is a challenge for analysts, be they social anthropologists or political scientists.[5] Hence for the sociology of religion, the paucity of such global analyses of Islamism constitutes a hindrance to the construction, not only of comparative narratives, but also of a general theoretical argument that includes insights from all relevant contexts. Bowen himself stresses that

---

[3] Robert W. Hefner, 'Multiple modernities: Christianity, Islam, and Hinduism in a globalizing age', *Annual Review of Anthropology* vol. 27, 1998, pp. 83–104.

[4] John R. Bowen, *Islam, law, and Equality in Indonesia an Anthropology of Public Reasoning* (Cambridge: Cambridge University Press, 2003); *Why the French Don't Like Headscarves: Islam, the State, and Public Space* (Princeton: Princeton University Press, 2007); 'Does French Islam have borders? Dilemmas of domestication in a global religious field', *American Anthropologist* 106 (1) 2004, pp. 43–55; 'Beyond migration: Islam as a transnational public space', *Journal of Ethnic and Migration Studies* 30 (5) 2004, pp. 879–94

[5] Another notable exception from an international study perspective are the works of Mandaville on transnational Islamism. See Peter Mandaville, *Transnational Muslim Politics: Reimagining the Umma* (London: Routledge, 2001).

he views these developments 'not only as a case for comparative Islamic studies, but as part of something broader—an interlocking set of conversations across nations and world-areas about the place of diverse social norms in a political community'.[6] In his study, the institutional and ideational structures that shape public deliberations do not have the same political and religious boundaries but still interact meaningfully with each other. For example, regarding the articulation of arguments about the shari'a onto particular national legal frameworks, Bowen insists that 'the continuing challenge to social science and to normative political theory is to grasp the similarity of these thrusts across the dissimilarities of their languages'.[7]

Scholars such as Roy or Kepel have also developed a similar research agenda by extending their area studies expertise. In this way they proposed grand explanations that cut across the usual divisions between studying the dynamics of Muslim communities in the 'West' and those of Muslim-majority countries. Nonetheless, their approaches do not seek to provide the kind of framework for the sociological and ideational transformation of political Islam that Bowen evoked.[8] Instead their research trajectories illustrate a sophisticated adaptation of the theses developed in their earlier works on Islamist politics in the core regions of the Muslim world to the situation of Muslim minorities in the 'West'. This evolution is well illustrated by the shift in emphasis in Roy's analysis of the direction taken by political Islam from the nationalist Islamists aiming at gaining state power through revolution (à la Khomeini) to the activism of ummah-centric militants enforcing a 'deculturalized' Islamization through their globalized networks.[9] For the latter, Roy and Kepel concur with mainstream sociologists of religion regarding the new dilemmas of the political institutionalization of religiosity in a context of

---

[6] John R Bowen, 'Shari'a, state and social norms in France and Indonesia, ISIM Papers no. 3, Leiden, 2001, p. 1.

[7] Bowen, 'Shari'a, state and social norms', p. 25.

[8] Compare Gilles Kepel, *The War for Muslim Minds: Islam and the West*, trans. P. Ghazaleh (Cambridge: Belknap Press, 2004) with Gilles Kepel, *Le Prophète et le Pharaon: Aux sources des mouvements islamistes* (Paris: Le Seuil, 1984) and Gilles Kepel, *Les banlieus de l'islam: Naissance d'une religion en France* (Paris: Le Seuil, 1987).

[9] Compare Roy, *Globalized Islam* with Olivier Roy, *The Failure of Political Islam*, trans. C. Volk (Cambridge: Harvard University Press, 1996)

de-institutionalization of the churches and the emancipation of the believers from the tutelage of their traditional religious authorities. From José Casanova to Daniele Hervieu-Léger, religious specialists identify two interconnected trends in explanations of Islamism in western multiculturalist contexts. The first one articulates concerns regarding religious institutionalization; the other deals primarily with the evolution of religiosity in (post)modern societies.[10] In this respect, the perspective of comparative sociology of religions usefully shows how the articulation of the relationship between Muslim communities and the secular democratic state is informed by the formal set of interactions that have already been set in place for pre-existing (Christian and Jewish) religious communities.[11]

Multiculturalism and the institutionalization of political Islam

Homi Bhabha suggested over a decade ago that:

multiculturalism—a portmanteau term for anything from minority discourse to postcolonial critique, from gay and lesbian studies to chicano/a fiction—has become the most charged sign for describing the scattered social contingencies that characterise contemporary *kulturkritik*. The multicultural has itself become a 'floating signifier' whose enigma lies less in itself than in the discursive uses of it to mark social processes where differentiation and condensation seem to happen almost synchronically.[12]

In the last decade or so, it has become commonplace for western institutional actors to frame and engage with the issue of political Islam and with the 'Muslim community' under the general heading of multiculturalism. It has become increasingly noticed that the impact of these multicultural policies on western secular identities, is an important factor in the response of those Islamic communities which are the designated targets of the policies. In this respect, the policy and media communities'

---

[10] José Casanova, *Public Religions in the Modern World* (Chicago: University of Chicago Press, 1994); Danièle Hervieu-Léger, *Religion as a Chain of Memory* (Cambridge: Polity Press, 2000).

[11] See J. Malik (ed.), *Muslims in Europe: From the Margin to the Centre* (Münster: LIT-Verlag, 2006).

[12] Homi K. Bhabha, 'Culture's in between', in S. Hall and P. du Gay (eds.), *Questions of Cultural Identity* (Sage Publications, 1996), pp. 53–60, at p. 55.

initial interest in the notion of multiculturalism and their subsequent doubts (particularly pronounced after 9/11), can be in themselves a relevant matter for sociological inquiry. As analysts of migration have noted, what has been particularly remarkable since the 1980s is the emergence of the category of 'Muslim community' whereas previously scholars, policy-makers and the media were using ethno-national referents to identify such minorities.[13] It is also significant that some of the trend-setting scholarly works on Muslims in the 'West' were initiated in a French context of *laïcité*, with its strong integrationist drive, and not in a 'standard' form of multiculturalism.[14] This situation contributed to generating a debate about the issue of how many models of secularism (and multiculturalism) actually shaped the contemporary social and political situation.[15] Despite many developments in multiculturalism in recent years, when it comes to dealing with political Islam, the commonalities between various liberal approaches to the issue of secular-religious interactions override national differences.[16] A common thread among most contemporary perspectives is the focus on possible revisions of the liberal-democratic insti-

---

[13] See the early contributions contained in Tomas Gerholm and Yngve Georg Lithman, *The New Islamic Presence in Western Europe* (London: Mansell, 1988), and compare the more recent stocktaking exercise undertaken by Ralph Grillo, 'Islam and transnationalism', *Journal of Ethnic and Migration Studies* 30 (5) 2004, pp. 861–78.

[14] See Kepel, *Les Banlieus de l'Islam; A l'Ouest d'Allah.*

[15] Not only are different European polities proposing slightly different views and policies but they are also not dealing with quite the same set of concerns than in North America; let alone those of more authoritarian systems like Russia or China. For a contrast between Europe and North America see, Y. Haddad (ed.), *Muslims in the West.* For Russia and China see, H. Pilkington and G.M. Yemelianova (eds.), *Islam in Post-Soviet Russia* (London: RoutledgeCurzon, 2002); Dru C. Gladney, *Dislocating China: Muslims, Minorities and Other Subaltern Subjects* (London: Hurst & Co, 2004)

[16] See C. Joppke and E. Morawska (eds.), *Toward Assimilation and Citizenship: Immigrants in Liberal Nation-States* (Basingstoke: PalgraveMacmillan, 2004); Christian Joppke, 'Transformation of immigrant integration in western Europe: civic integration and antidiscrimination policies in the Netherlands, France, and Germany', *World Politics* 59 (2) 2007, pp. 243–73; Jytte Klausen, *The Islamic Challenge: Politics and Religion in Western Europe* (Oxford: Oxford University Press, 2005).

tutions and practices to accommodate the needs of minority communities in the public space. Yet, in those debates, the positioning of religious communities—as distinct from ethnic, racial or gendered communities—is deemed particularly problematic; and that of the 'Muslim community' even more so.[17]

As many analysts in Europe and North America have noted, there is a widespread perception that Muslims are voicing politically unreasonable claims, and making religiously backward and unacceptable demands on western governments and societies.[18] This is commonly translated into various fears and uneasiness ranging from the perception that Muslims are particularly reluctant to integrate in their host society, to the fear that they may constitute a 'fifth column' ready to strike against the host community.[19] The object of suspicion, as we will see below—and in the chapter on security and terrorism subsequently—is not confined to an original migrant Muslim community. There is also unease at the possibility of contamination of people, particularly 'young' and 'vulnerable' individuals—hence the intense focus on issues of education, internet communication and the role of women. These fears are heightened by suggestions from the more alarmist security analysts that some of the more radical Islamist organisations (e.g. al-Qaeda) have a relatively high number of converts in their midst.[20] More broadly, beyond specific security concerns,

---

[17] See the differing perspectives offered by the contributors to S.M. Okin (ed.), *Is Multiculturalism Bad for Women?* (Princeton: Princeton University Press, 1999). See also Lucas A. Swaine, 'How ought liberal democracies to treat theocratic communities?' *Ethics* 111 (1) 2001, pp. 302–43.

[18] See the contributors to T. Modood, A. Triandafyllidou and R. Zapata-Barrero (eds.), *Multiculturalism, Muslims and Citizenship: A European Approach* (London: Routledge, 2006). For non-western contexts, see W. Kymlicka and B. He (eds.), *Multiculturalism in Asia: Theoretical Perspectives* (Oxford: Oxford University Press, 2005).

[19] These concerns were especially high in the United Kingdom after the 2005 London bombings, as the focus was placed on 'home-grown terrorists'. See, House of Commons, *Report into the official account of the bombings in London on 7th July 2005* (London: Stationery Office, 2006); Milan Rai, *7/7: the London bombings and the Iraq War* (London: Pluto, 2006).

[20] Unsurprisingly, analysts approaching this issue from the perspective of terrorism studies stress what the potential risks are on a worst-case scenario basis. See Rohan Gunaratna, 'The post-Madrid face of Al Qaeda', *The Washington Quarterly* 27 (3) 2004, pp. 91–100; Jessica Stern, 'The protean enemy', *Foreign*

this uneasiness towards the 'Muslim community' translates into an argument that multiculturalism may have over-stretched itself and needs to be re-defined more restrictively in order to be workable.[21] In this context, there is a direct relationship between political Islam and multiculturalism in the sense that, as Will Kymlicka notes, 'public support for multiculturalism has declined as Muslims have come to be seen as the main proponents or beneficiaries of the policy'.[22] Beyond media headlines, the increased prominence of the Islamic tradition in the debate on multiculturalism is perceived by many scholars to create a problem for equality (and especially gender equality) in liberal settings.[23] At stake is not merely the practical question of how to deal with various forms of 'Islamophobia'—be they explicit or implicit, individualized or institutionalizsed, real or imagined—but also the philosophical conundrums regarding the limits of the liberal democratic tradition.[24] Pnina Werbner indicates how looking at Islamophobia's connections with other social myths, reveals serious and enduring political tensions within liberalism.[25] Undoubtedly,

---

Affairs 82 (4) 2003, pp. 27–40; Javier Jordan and Luisa Boix, 'Al-Qaeda and Western Islam', *Terrorism and Political Violence* 16 (1) 2004, pp. 1–17.

[21] Compare Christian Joppke, 'The retreat of multiculturalism in the liberal state: theory and policy', *British Journal of Sociology* 55 (2) 2004, with the more nuanced assessment contained in Ralph Grillo, 'An excess of alterity? Debating difference in a multicultural society', *Ethnic and Racial Studies* 30 (6) 2007, pp. 979–98.

[22] Will Kymlicka, *Multicultural Odysseys: Navigating the New International Politics of Diversity* (Oxford: Oxford University Press, 2007), p. 126.

[23] For a black and white argument on the flaws of an Islamic input in multiculturalism see, Susan Moller Okin, 'Is multiculturalism bad for women?', in Okin, *Is Multiculturalism Bad For Women?*, pp. 9–31,. For a more nuanced account of what issues are at stakes and what are some common misperceptions, see Azizah Y. Al-Hibri, 'Is Western patriarchal feminism good for Third World/ minority women?', in Ibid, pp. 41–6.

[24] See Christian Joppke, *Veil: Mirror of Identity* (Cambridge: Polity Press, 2009); Tahar Abbas (ed.), *Islamic political radicalism: a European comparative perspective* (Edinburgh: Edinburgh University Press, 2007); C. Allen and J. Nielsen, *Summary report on Islamophobia in the EU after 11 September 2001* (Vienna: European Union Monitoring Centre on Racism and Xenophobia, 2002).

[25] Pnina Werbner, 'The predicament of diaspora and millennial Islam: reflections on September 11, 2001', *Ethnicities* 4 (4) 2004, pp. 451–76.

the reflections regarding multiculturalism in western settings tend to be more sophisticated than those regarding the nature of 'Democracy' in Muslim-majority countries mentioned earlier. Yet, as Tariq Modood notes, it remains often unclear what these theoretical debates actually imply for improving the situation of really existing communities and really existing states.[26]

It has been a common argument of many critics of the culturalist slant in multiculturalist approaches to say that political philosophers and theorists—and in their wake politicians and policy makers—make too much of culturally framed political claims at the expense of universalistic democratic norms.[27] A sophisticated version of this argument is proposed by Sheila Benhabib, who indicates that those who argue that liberal democracies ought to accord greater political rights to communities defined by their 'culture', misconceive the notion of culture itself, especially in its social and political representations. She argues that those endorsing 'the claims of culture' end up creating abstract sociological entities with clear lines of demarcation that serve to identify communities for the purpose of governance—a process particularly relevant for alleged 'group rights'.[28] Benhabib concludes that 'it is the epistemic interest in power [...] that leads to the silencing of dissenting opinions and contradictory perspectives, and yields dominant master narratives of what the cultural tradition is, who is in, and who is out'.[29] As an alternative informed by discourse ethics, Benhabib presents culture as a process of perpetual negotiation and constant change of imaginary boundaries. Because her suggestion is underpinned by a liberal version of democratic theory that enshrines the primacy of the individuals determining their cultural identity/belonging—therefore prioritising democratic universalism over cultural auton-

---

[26] Tariq Modood, *Multicultural Politics: Racism, Ethnicity and Muslims in Britain,* (Edinburgh: Edinburgh University Press, 2005).

[27] See for example Brian Barry, *Culture and Equality: An Egalitarian Critique of Multiculturalism* (Cambridge: Polity, 2001).

[28] Here one could point to Rawls' attempt to define a good non-liberal society—the fictional Muslim polity of Kazanistan—based on the principle of a decent, consultative hierarchy, which ensures that the interests of all groups are represented, albeit through institutionalized inequality. John Rawls, *The Law of Peoples* (Cambridge: Harvard University Press, 1999).

[29] Seyla Benhabib, *The Claims of Culture: Equality and Diversity in the Global Era* (Princeton: Princeton University Press, 2002), p. 102.

omy—Benhabib could be criticized for forcing the hand of the individuals concerned. Whether or not we endorse Benhabib's preferred social construct, her critique highlights nonetheless the difficulty of linking up normative ideals and practical policies without over-determining societal options *excathedra*—a potentially unwelcome reversion to orientalist declarations about 'proper' Islam.[30]

As Benhabib has hinted, the institutionalization of multicultural views risks producing a reimagination, reclassification and re-empowerment of religious structures to which citizens are meant to belong merely for administrative purposes. In this process, not all the individual believers may have their say on the matter. This observation is certainly not very new in relation to earlier integration processes and multicultural policies. Bikhu Parekh's detailed examination of the idea of multiculturalism illustrated that earlier patterns of national integration were placing very high demands on migrants—demands that currently clash with liberal views concerned with a dialogical construction of societal unity.[31] In these earlier contexts, host states and societies were simply demanding that migrants should endorse dominant social practices, and only retain theirs in so far as they were compatible with the dominant mores, without having much opportunity to change the parameters of the debate. To expect Muslims and other minorities to follow this path is probably not ethically desirable, even when it is practically feasible. This leaves common liberal approaches to integration with serious dilemmas since in the main they still expect national political unity to be based on a common public culture. Yet, such public culture cannot be neatly separated from varied and diverse sub-national cultures. To address this dilemma, multiculturalist specialists have proposed notions of 'thin' integration that would enable minorities to step back from full integration whenever public culture

---

[30] In another notable critique of 'identity politics', Brubaker and Cooper questioned the sociological foundations of 'group-centered representation of the social world' which are now fashionable in multicultural political thinking. They suggested that 'the identitarian language and groupist social ontology that informs much contemporary political theory occludes the problematic nature of "groupness" itself and forecloses other ways of conceptualizing particular affiliations and affinities'. Rogers Brubaker and Frederick Cooper 'Beyond "identity"', *Theory and Society* 29 (1) 2000, pp. 1–47, at p. 31.

[31] Bhikhu *Parekh, Rethinking Multiculturalism: Cultural Diversity and Political Theory* (Cambridge: Harvard University Press, 2000).

might be harmful to their communal views.[32] Similar proposals have also been developed in relation to religious communities that outline some of the discursive and institutional practices that could enable this cohabitation.[33] In the post-9/11 context, however, the bulk of these analyses clearly favour a retreat from, rather than a development of multiculturalist frameworks.[34]

The recent much-publicized debates in France about the issue of the Islamic veil illustrate well the tensions between an official public culture and communal preferences—a tension assertively resolved in favour of the former in this case. This assertion of the epistemic and material power of the state, leads Asad to conclude that:

what seems to emerge from this discourse is not that secularism ensures equality and freedom but that particular versions of 'equality' and 'freedom' ensure laïcité. Laïcité is the mode in which the Republic teaches the subjects in its care about what counts as real, and what they themselves really are, in order better to govern them by letting them govern themselves.[35]

For Asad, the difficulties of institutionalized multiculturalism have to be considered in relation to the perception that secularization is no longer a 'natural' form of social evolution. The politics of the secular, of which multiculturalism is part, are re-presented as a dynamic set of power relations. Asad notes that secularism is specifically invoked to 'prevent two very different kinds of transgression: the perversion of politics by religious forces, on the one hand, and the state's restriction of religious freedom, on the other'. He concludes that:

---

[32] See Will Kymlicka, *Politics in the Vernacular: Nationalism, Multiculturalism, and Citizenship* (Oxford: Oxford University Press, 2001); Kymlicka 'Immigration, citizenship, multiculturalism: exploring the links', *The Political Quarterly* 74 (s1) 2003, pp. 195–208.

[33] See Lucas A. Swaine, *The Liberal Conscience: Politics and Principle in a World of Religious Pluralism* (New York: Columbia University Press, 2006).

[34] See for example Olivier Roy, *Secularism Confronts Islam* (New York: Columbia University Press, 2007).

[35] Talal Asad, 'Trying to understand French secularism', in H. de Vries and L. Sullivan (eds.), *Political Theologies: Public Religions in a Post-Secular World* (New York: Fordham University Press, 2006), pp. 494–526, at p. 521. See also Commission présidée par Bernard Stasi, *Laicite et Republique* (Paris: La Documentation Française, 2004).

in order to protect politics from religion (and especially certain kinds of religiously motivated behavior), in order to determine its acceptable forms within the polity, the state must identify "religion". To the extent that this work of identification becomes a matter for the law, the Republic acquires the theological function of defining religious signs and the power of imposing that definition on its subjects, of "assimilating" them.[36]

The practice of multiculturalism in the face of political Islam

The evolution of modern forms of Muslim religiosity in secularized settings is complicated by the state-led efforts at institutionalizing the Muslim constituency. As many analysts have shown, the multiplicity of meanings associated with public religious practice (e.g. veiling) creates political and policy dilemmas.[37] Vincent Geisser suggests that the heavy-handed intervention of the French state in the name of secularism is meant to address two types of fears, and redress two types of wrong.[38] Initially, in line with the earlier headscarf affairs of the late 1980s, the official (and media) concern was about the social pressures forcing women to display religiosity publicly by wearing the veil, against their wishes. Subsequently, however, there was a new and heightened fear generated by the perception that such public expression of religiosity was a conscious social and political choice made by these women. Geisser argues that it is precisely the autonomous nature of the women's decision to wear the Islamic veil that made them more 'dangerous'; as they were no longer unwitting accomplices but instead fanatical supporters of the Islamization of society. In the United Kingdom, despite having far more flexible multicultural policy options, there was a similar realization—especially after

---

[36] Asad, 'Trying to understand French secularism', p. 524. See also *passim* Talal Asad, *Genealogies of Religion: Discipline and Reasons of Power in Christianity and Islam* (Baltimore: John Hopkins University Press, 1993); Roy, *Secularism Confronts Islam*.

[37] See Françoise Gaspard and Farhad Khosrokhavar, *Le foulard et la République* (Paris, La Découverte, 1995); Valérie Amiraux, 'Discours voilés sur les musulmanes en Europe: comment les musulmans sont-ils devenus des musulmanes?', *Social Compass* 50 (1) 2003, pp. 85–96; Pnina Werbner, 'Veiled interventions in pure space: honour, shame and embodied struggles among Muslims in Britain and France', *Theory, Culture & Society* 24 (2) 2007, pp. 161–86.

[38] Vincent Geisser, *La nouvelle islamophobie* (Paris: La Découverte, 2003).

the 2004 London bombings—that since Muslim women self-reflectively endorsed uncompromising Islamist discourses, their religiosity made them potential security threats that needed to be securitized.[39] Here too, the simple 'good Muslim/bad Muslim' dichotomy that was commonly invoked to differentiate between peaceful women's values versus aggressive males' behaviour appeared to be under threat—and with it the security of the entire community.[40] In various guises, these dilemmas were replicated in other polities throughout the 'West', from the more accomodationist policy settings of the UK, Holland or the USA, to the more rigid frameworks in place in France, Belgium or Germany.[41]

Scholars as different as Parekh, Asad or Euben have stressed repeatedly that the acceptable face of religious accommodation that emerged during the rise of secularism in western settings was heavily influenced by the Judeo-Christian heritage.[42] This impact goes beyond the traditional problem of keeping religion private, as even when public demands might be 'acceptable' they are not so easily understood when coming from the Islamic tradition. Kymlicka notes that in relation to the balance between the values of tolerance and the fears of diversity in contemporary western democracies, 'many citizens are willing to accept multiculturalism policies when they are perceived as low risk, but oppose them when they are perceived as high risks'.[43] Institutionally, socially and intellectually acceptable differences in western liberal democracy that have been tailored to the

[39] See Katherine Brown, 'The promise and perils of women's participation in UK mosques: the impact of securitisation agendas on identity, gender and community', *British Journal of Politics & International Relations* 10 (3) 2008, pp. 472–91.

[40] Unsurprisingly, these debates parallel the ones evoked in the previous chapter regarding securitization in Muslim-majority countries.

[41] See Ian Buruma, *Murder in Amsterdam: The Death of Theo Van Gogh and the Limits of Tolerance* (New York: The Penguin Press, 2006); P. M. Sniderman and L. Hagendoorn (eds.), *When Ways of Life Collide: Multiculturalism and its Discontents in the Netherlands* (Princeton: Princeton University Press, 2007); Valerie Amiraux, 'Considering Islam for the West', *Contemporary European History* 15 (1) 2006, pp. 85–101.

[42] See Roxanne L. Euben, *Enemy in the Mirror: Islamic Fundamentalism and the Limits of Modern Rationalism* (Princeton, NJ: Princeton University Press, 1999); Parekh, *Rethinking Multiculturalism*; Asad, *Genealogies of Religion*.

[43] Kymlicka, *Multicultural Odysseys*, p. 127.

experiences of Christianity or Judaism are not necessarily well suited to Islam. This observation applies particularly to the articulation of Islamism in relation to the secular nature of the state.[44] Hervieu-Léger notes that in the case of France, 'the problem of the assimilability of Islam, artificially represented as an immutable, monolithic whole, in the very abstract environment of *laïcité* (secularism), hides the fact that the legal and administrative framework within which these values are supposedly inscribed is itself the result of a historical compromise'.[45] Very modest reforms have indeed been initiated by Nicolas Sarkozy during his time as Interior Minister, notably in relation to the creation of a supervising body for Muslims in France that could receive state funding for the administration of prayer rooms and other religious duties, like the certifying of *halal* meat, in the same way as Christian and Jewish institutions benefited from state recognition.[46] In this context, the key issue is not that of the possibility of integration within the existing institutional framework, but rather that of the transformation of *laïcité* in the face of new religious processes. Such arguments about the need to understand better the historical rationale behind the concept of *laïcité* dovetail with calls for developing a genealogy of the 'secular'.

In earlier stages of the debate on multiculturalism, institutional actors found it convenient to assume that a light multiculturalist option—coinciding with a social behaviour that Grace Davie termed 'believing without belonging'—was well served by the weak degree of control provided by existing religious institutions.[47] Such an attitude was supported by assumptions regarding the process of modernization of society that would supposedly induce changes among Muslim minorities. Yet, as re-composed grassroots religious communities vocally re-entered the public

[44] There are nonetheless interesting exceptions to this trend. See for example Abdullahi Ahmed An-Naim, *Islam and the Secular State* (Cambridge: Harvard University Press, 2008).

[45] Danièle Hervieu-Léger, 'Islam and the Republic: the French case', in T. Banchoff (ed.), *Democracy and the New Religious Pluralism* (New York: Oxford University Press, 2007), pp. 203–21, at p. 205.

[46] For the general tone of the reforms proposed see, Nicolas Sarkozy, Thibaud Collin and Philippe Verdin, *La République, les religions, l'espérance* (Paris: Cerf, 2004).

[47] Grace Davie, *Religion in Britain Since 1945: Believing Without Belonging* (Oxford: Wiley-Blackwell, 1994).

sphere, state institutions were suddenly found wanting for more appropriate means of addressing these new social trends. Suddenly, the supposed role of modernization in smoothing over cultural and religious differences into a form of 'multiculturalism light' became a factor responsible for radicalizing and dis-embedding religious traditions. Once an over-optimistic narrator of the spread of liberal-democratic values, Francis Fukuyama assessed that in the circumstances, 'radical Islamism itself does not come out of traditional Muslim societies, but rather is a manifestation of modern identity politics, a by-product of the modernization process itself'.[48] Kymlicka makes a more precise observation by noting the presence of a feedback loop that operates between two of the pillars of multiculturalism, namely the 'liberal expectancy' and the 'desecuritization of ethnic relations'.[49] These dynamics were already at work before but, as Mahmood Mamdani observes, they were presented in the context of a distinction between the public activities of 'troublesome Islamists' in foreign policy versus the private role of Islam in the domestic context. Post-9/11, the distinction is re-drawn between good and bad Muslims, depending on whether they enthusiastically subscribe to the set liberal values that are meant to constitute a 'civilized' society or whether they appear to be reluctant to do so.[50] In this perspective, Islamophobia reformulates some old orientalist clichés and becomes a marker of the 'other' in a post-colonial situation where geographical/spatial divisions are less pronounced.

The apparent 'coming out' of the politics of identity in minority communities worldwide facilitated a greater democratization of the religious sphere, as individuals began to take into their own hands what the 'authorities' were apparently unable to do.[51] In the United States, because the fears raised by multiculturalism have less to do with the Muslim 'Other' than with the growth of the ethno-linguistic divides, there remains

[48] Francis Fukuyama, 'Identity, immigration, and liberal democracy', *Journal of Democracy* 17 (2) 2006, pp. 5–17, at p. 6.

[49] See Kymlicka, *Multicultural Odysseys*, particularly chapter four.

[50] Mahmood Mamdani, *Good Muslim, Bad Muslim: America, the Cold War, and the Roots of Terror* (New York: Three Leaves Publishing, 2004); 'Good Muslim, bad Muslim: a political perspective on culture and terrorism', *American Anthropologist* 104 (3) 2002, pp. 766–75. See also Werbner, 'The predicament of diaspora'

[51] Nilufer Gole, 'Islam in public: new visibilities and new imaginaries', *Public Culture* 14 (1) 2002, pp. 173–90.

a reasonable optimism about these multiculturalist trends.[52] In many European countries by contrast, there is a convergence of ideological and institutional tensions with strong migratory pressures from Muslim-majority countries that contribute to make the political challenge of the 'Muslim community' more substantial. In parallel, analyses of Muslim communities in the 'West' have recorded in detail the patterns of decline of 'traditional' Islamic institutions in Europe and the United States, mainly as a result of generational change.[53] Parekh has stressed the importance of this generational transformation, as Islam moved from being a taken-for-granted way of life for an older generation to become a conscious public statement of Islamic identity for the new one.[54] Pre-existing 'official' and/or 'traditional' religious organizations continue nonetheless to be privileged partners for the state institutions despite falling attendance numbers and increasingly weak grassroots legitimacy. Jocelyne Césari's analyses provide a useful survey of the trends towards a greater institutionalization of Islam in Europe and the United States, and of their shortcomings.[55] In particular, she notes how institutional inertia ensures the perceived continuing relevance of the older Islamic institutions even when they may be empty shells, as well as a tangible state interest in creating what are perceived to be 'responsible' (i.e. government friendly) institutions.

As indicated earlier, because of the legal distinction between the public and the private sphere made by the state, the recognition of Islamic institutions and groups in the public space is ultimately the prerogative of the secular state. In recent years, western policy makers provided important

[52] See Samuel P. Huntington, *Who Are We? The Challenges to America's National Identity* (New York: Simon and Schuster, 2004); Fukuyama, 'Identity, immigration, and liberal democracy'.

[53] See Metcalf, *Making Muslim Space*; Haddad, *Muslims in the West*; T. Modood and P. Werbner (eds.), *The Politics of Multiculturalism in the New Europe* (London: Zed Books, 1997); S.T. Hunter (ed.), *Islam, Europe's Second Religion: The New Social, Cultural, and Political Landscape* (Westport: Praeger, 2002).

[54] Parekh, *Identity, Culture and Dialogue*; Parekh 'Europe, liberalism and the Muslim question', in Modood, *Multiculturalism, Muslims and Citizenship*, pp. 179–203.

[55] Jocelyne Cesari, *When Islam and Democracy Meet: Muslims in Europe and in the United States* (New York: Palgrave, 2004); J. Cesari and S. McLoughlin (eds.), *European Muslims and the Secular State* (Aldershot: Ashgate, 2005).

incentives for creating various forms of 'national Islams'.[56] This institutionalization of Islam in its turn structured in part the avenues for Islamic discourses within the community.[57] In this debate, one main policy issue is where the impulse for more representative institutions should come from and under which framework such institutions should operate in order to engage meaningfully with a secular democratic state. Most conspicuously in European polities this has been translated into a thrust by governments to create national instances for the representation of their 'Muslim community'.[58] From the tentative construction of consultative Islamic bodies by the Spanish or Italian states to the more institutionalized systems like those supported by the French and Belgian governments, these new structures have received a fair amount of attention (and criticism). In the main, the lack of well-established and widely accepted institutionalized Islamic authority outside the core regions of the Muslim world ensures that state recognition of specific religious actors intensify the struggle for leadership within the Muslim communities. In this context, the fear of instrumentalization by state authorities is underpinned by the explicit objectives of western governments to create national Islams through the active endorsement and support of specific organizations, often with scant regards for the size of their following.[59]

[56] This is, for example, the debate about creating French Islam or being a British Muslim. From a policy perspective, see the essay written by Nicolas Sarkozy the current French President, when he still was Interior Minister. Sarkozy, Collin and Verdin, *La République, les religions, l'espérance*. For more scholarly treatments see, Franck Frégosi, *Penser l'islam dans la laïcité: Les musulmans de France et la République* (Paris: Fayard, 2008); Roy, *Secularism Confronts Islam*.

[57] See Frank Peter, 'Leading the community of the middle way: a study of the Muslim field in France', *The Muslim World* 96 (4) 2006, pp. 707–36.

[58] This process also operates at the micro level, for example in the identification of 'good' versus 'bad' imams. See Jonathan Birt, 'Good imam, bad imam: civic religion and national integration in Britain post-9/11', *The Muslim World* 96 (4) 2006, pp. 687–705; 'Wahhabism in the United Kingdom: manifestations and reactions', in M. Al-Rasheed (ed.), *Transnational Connections and the Arab Gulf* (London: Routledge, 2005), pp. 168–84.

[59] See Alexandre Caeiro, 'Religious authorities or political actors? The Muslim leaders of the French representative body of Islam', in Cesari and McLoughlin, *European Muslims*, pp. 71–84; Sara Silvestri, 'The institutionalization of Islam in Europe: a case study of Italy', Council For European Studies News-

There are at least two main dimensions to this internal struggle for leadership. First, there is a competition between members of these communities about which Islamic practices (and exponents thereof) should be endorsed. Second, there is competition between foreign-based and transnational Islamic organizations; especially between those that are state-controlled and opposition movements. Historically, the second dimension of this struggle over authority was the most relevant in the context of a limited potential for religious leadership coming from Muslims who spent all or most of their lives, outside the core regions of the Muslim world. From the 1980s onward, however, due to both the evolving socio-demographics of the Muslim diasporas and the shifts in identity politics from ethno-nationalist concerns toward religious normativity, the domestic versus transinternational aspect of the competition for religious leadership became increasingly important.[60] These 'new voices' of the diasporas have been struggling over the last quarter of century to find formal and informal institutional settings in which to express their Islamic practices, whilst selectively involving both external Islamic players and domestic secular authorities. Increasingly, many western-based Islamic intellectuals contribute to the declining influence of the traditional voices of authority of Islam in the 'West' (e.g. state-approved imams, classically-trained scholars, etc.). Tariq Ramadan's scholarly and policy efforts in this field are probably some of the most visible at the turn of the century in Europe. For Ramadan and other western-based Muslim thinkers like Taha Jabir al Alwani, the former Chairman of the North American Fiqh Council, new forms of political and religious authority have to be devised and implemented, not least through making good use of the opportunities for political participation provided by liberal democratic systems. In this perspective, it is argued that social and political participation is not so much a possibility as it is a duty for Muslims, as Muslims.[61] Islamic

---

letter, September 2004; Elena Arigita, 'Representing Islam in Spain: Muslim identities and the contestation of leadership', *The Muslim World* 96 (4) 2006, pp. 563–84.

[60] See for example in the French case, F. Frégosi (ed.), *La formation des cadres religieux musulmans en France: approches socio-juridiques* (Paris: L'Harmattan, 1998); Vincent Geisser and Aziz Zemouri, *Marianne et Allah: Les politiques français face à la "question musulmane"* (Paris: La Découverte, 2006).

[61] Tariq Ramadan, *Western Muslims and the Future of Islam* (New York: Oxford

intellectuals also operating within the framework of western academia are contributing to the debate on multiculturalism, even though their policy influence remains limited.[62]

The emerging theological and legal influence of Islamic religious councils in the 'West', such as the European Council for Fatwas and Research (ECFR), represent an alternative development to the national Islamic institutions. At heart, the legal scholars who form this 'European' body are providing new answers to old questions, but tailoring them to the need of Muslim communities living in the 'West'. Under the leadership of Yusuf al-Qaradawi, they developed a body of Islamic legal guidance for minorities by actualizing old juridical opinions and by formulating new ones in response to new issues.[63] Even though this Council, created in 1997, claims that its ambitions regarding legal authority are limited to the jurisprudence regarding minority populations, analysts indicate that there are implications for the rest of the Muslim world, especially because most of Islamic jurisprudence there is tightly controlled by regimes with weak legitimacy. Alexandre Caeiro notes that because they are 'struggling to integrate the European context into Islamic normativity, scholars engaged in this reflection are forced to search for the elusive distinction between tradition and religion, and risk in turn further destabilizing the edifice of Islamic fiqh, already under pressure in the Muslim world'.[64] To assuage the fears of the leading Islamic institutions in Muslim-majority

---

University Press, 2003); M.S. Seddan, D. Hussain and N. Mallik (eds.), *British Muslims between Assimilation and Segregation* (Leicester, The Islamic Foundation 2004.); Taha Jabir Al-Alwani, *Issues in Contemporary Islamic Thought* (Herndon: International Institute of Islamic Thought, 2005).

[62] See Abdulaziz Sachedina, *The Islamic Roots of Democratic Pluralism* (Oxford University Press, 2001); Abdolkarim Soroush, *Reason, Freedom, and Democracy in Islam*, trans. M. Sadri and A. Sadri (Oxford University Press, 2002); O. Safi (ed.), *Progressive Muslims: On Justice, Gender, and Pluralism* (Oxford: Oneworld Publications, 2003); Khaled Abou El Fadl, with J. Cohen and D. Chasman, *Islam and the Challenge of Democracy* (Princeton: Princeton University Press, 2004).

[63] On Qaradawi see, J. Skovgaard-Petersen and B. Graf (eds.), *The Global Mufti: The Phenomenon of Yusuf Al-Qaradawi* (London: Hurst & Co., 2009)

[64] Alexandre Caeiro, 'Adjusting Islamic law to migration', ISIM Newsletter no. 12, June 2003, p. 26.

countries concerned that the Council would undermine their authority at home, the ECFR had to encourage more members from these institutions to join in, thereby creating an organization with a greater Middle Eastern outlook than it initially planned. As Caeiro highlights:

the ECFR is playing a greater role in Islamic jurisprudential debates. In a globalized world, the members are deeply aware of the media impact of a fatwa, and very explicitly take it into consideration. The relations with the other, older councils of fiqh in Egypt and Saudi Arabia, mindfully established by the Council from the start, are already under strain. According to one member, the Council is now receiving questions from the Muslim world and, along with that, warnings against issuing fatwas towards the East.[65]

Unsurprisingly, the ECFR is also viewed with suspicion by European governments that would much rather prefer dealing with their own state-approved national Islamic councils.

For many analysts, there is an expectation that such an evolution in Islamic thinking is indicative of a more liberal articulation of the Islamic tradition in western settings. Some scholars emphasize the connection between these contemporary liberal and critical trends and the reformist agenda that have emerged in the Muslim world since the end of the nineteenth century.[66] Others, using different sociological premises stress instead the transformative impact of migration and the emergence of independent local voices.[67] Whether the emphasis is placed on intellectual continuities with previous reform movements or on the impulse given by practical interactions taking place in secularized western polities, these developments are viewed by analysts in a rather positive light. Yet, such

---

[65] Caeiro, 'Adjusting Islamic Law to migration', p. 26. The relations between various national and regional councils tentatively developed under the leadership of al-Qaradawi into a more formal organization, the International Association of Muslim Scholars (IAMS).

[66] See passim J.L. Esposito and F. Burgat (eds,), *Modernizing Islam: Religion and the Public Sphere in the Middle East and Europe* (London: Hurst & Co., 2003); John L. Esposito, 'America's Muslims: issues of identity, religious diversity, and pluralism', in Banchoff, *Democracy and the New Religious Pluralism*, pp. 133–50; Armando Salvatore, *Islam and the Political Discourse of Modernity* (Reading: Ithaca, 1997).

[67] Mandaville, *Transnational Muslim Politics*; Cesari, *When Islam and Democracy Meet*.

a causal link between a decline in traditional institutional authorities and the rise of a more liberal Islamic practice has not been recognised by all specialists. Many have pointed instead to the potentially large gap that can develop between the two phenomena. Having considered briefly the possibility that western-based Muslim communities could lead the way in the production of more democratic forms of Islamism which may be exported to the Muslim world, Kepel dismisses this option as currently unrealisable. In a similar way, Roy argues that although these develop-ments may generate more reflection on what Islam ought to be, more often than not they lead to the reaffirmation of conservative and neo-scripturalist versions of Islam—not least because they appear to be the ones with the greatest defensive potential for the Faith. In the end, Roy comes close to turning on its head the argument about the de-institu-tionalization of traditional religious authorities and the deregulation of Islamic practices. In his view, yes there is a weakening of pre-existing structures of authority, but no, this does not lead to a liberalized Islamic tradition, since nothing really original is being proposed in its place—it is merely a reflective endorsement of dogma.[68]

Do new forms of religiosity imply the end of multiculturalism as we know it?

The debate over whether there is a more liberal or critical form of Islamic tradition emerging in the 'West' under the conditions of modernity, is putting a particular twist on the study of the transformation of religious practices in Muslim communities.[69] Clearly, the more critical forms of Islamic tradition facilitate the formulation of more open-ended analyses of the patterns of religious change than the early debates generated by multiculturalism allowed. Mohammed Arkoun is a well-known propo-nent of such a wide-ranging critique of contemporary Islamic thinking; thinking which in his view does not yet overcome the conceptual hin-drances that have plagued the Islamic tradition over the centuries.[70] Yet,

[68] Roy, *Globalized Islam*, p. 92–3; See also Kepel, *The War for Muslim Minds*

[69] See Frank Peter, 'Individualization and religious authority in Western Euro-pean Islam', *Islam and Christian-Muslim Relations* 17 (1) 2006, pp. 105–18.

[70] See Mohammed Arkoun, *Islam: To Reform or to Subvert* (London: Saqi Books, 2006).

many current inquiries into the liberal nature of Islam are pursuing a relatively narrow political and conceptual agenda that has more to do with the insecurities of liberalism in the contemporary democratic and secular settings, than with the Islamic tradition per se. In the debate informed by multiculturalism, one issue remains central to the arguments developed in most narratives—the re-configuration of religiosity in post-industrial western settings. Some of the arguments in these debates constitute a reworking of Durkheim's notion of anomie and highlight that the breakdown of traditional social relationships produces deprivation and loss of membership in institutions validated by tradition. The individualization of religiosity is therefore seen to be a process tightly connected to the modernization and 'postmodernization' of society.[71]

The process of de-institutionalisation of the churches and the emancipation of the believers from the tutelage of their traditional shepherds does not eradicate the need for the faithful to testify of their experiences and to communicate in order to share their certainties. Hence there is a difficult process of construction required from new communities of faith in order to answer this demand. As Hervieu-Léger documented, there is a distinct reconfiguration of traditional modes of religious experience in the European context. Traditional religious worldviews can no longer be passed on as a matter of fact, but have to be reconstructed in the face of a secular alternative. For Hervieu-Léger, the crucial question that the sociology of religious modernity must answer is: 'what are the modalities capable of structuring both the quasi-unlimited itineraries of belief identification and the continuity of a tradition that is no longer—or less and less—expressed in the discourse of a religious authority or acknowledged as the sole guardian of this continuity?'[72] This reorganisation is itself shaped by an inter-generational breakdown in the transmission of the symbolic heritage. This reconfiguration of faith is therefore characterised by a high degree of bricolage, not only in the way religiosity is implemented but also in the way it is transmitted over time and between communities.[73] Here, religiosity is primarily malleable, individualistic, little regulated by norms, and external to the everyday life routines of the faith-

---

[71] See Berger, 'Reflections on the sociology of religion today', p. 450.

[72] Daniele Hervieu-Léger, 'In search of certainties: the paradoxes of religiosity in societies of high modernity', *The Hedgehog Review* 8 (1–2) 2006, pp. 59–69, at p. 62.

[73] Hervieu-Léger, *Religion as a Chain of Memory*.

ful. Alongside the bricolage that individuals have to do for themselves, there is a less individualistic process of sedimentation and transmission of a recomposed tradition. Cohesiveness remains because specific individuals are better positioned to produce and transmit recomposed forms of religiosity than others—due to factors like class, race, gender, education, etc. In this context, the central theme of religiosity is the convergence of, and dialectics between, individualized spiritual quests and the standardization of spiritual goods. Hervieu-Léger concludes that the paradox of the situation is that 'the more beliefs circulate, the less they determine tangible affiliations and the more they further a desire for community liable to evolve into intensive forms of religious socialization'. In this context, she notes that 'the bond that one chooses to preserve with some kind of spiritual family is now supported by no more than, one could almost say, minimal references, shared on a worldwide scale'.[74]

The issue of transmission of 'heterodox' Islamic discourses and practices is at the heart of contemporary debates over the Islamic revival in the 'West'.[75] Not secularization in the earlier sense of the term, but a secularizing effect is at work, as the unquestioned transmission of traditional Islamic views and practices is no longer an option. In the face of the apparent retreat of traditional Islamic institutions worldwide, individual Muslims are forced to come out to explicitly 'defend Islam' against a wide array of secularized institutions and practices.[76] Theological positions evolve in relation to the spread of unorthodox beliefs in order to restore religious credibility in a secular environment. This point is made particularly salient by the role played by the new media (internet, satellite TV), which stretch the possibility of conceiving extended forms of belonging, and yet undermine the consolidation of belief communities due to an ever-increasing background noise about all things Islamic. There is a ready availability, and free access to multifarious symbolic repositories (publications, television, films, websites) that leads to a weakening of the prescrip-

---

[74] Hervieu-Léger, 'In search of certainties', p. 66–7.

[75] This issue is evidently also crucial in other parts of the Muslim world, as earlier mechanisms of transmission of religious heritage are also being challenged and transformed. An indicative case is that of the evolution of religious teaching institutions. See R.W. Hefner and M.Q. Zaman (eds.), *Schooling Islam: The Culture and Politics of Modern Muslim Education* (Princeton: Princeton University Press, 2006).

[76] See Roy, *Globalized Islam*.

tive power of familial and other traditional religious references. In this context, many political analyses of the phenomenon have noted that if Islamist movements and their interpretations appeal to large modern constituencies it is because they place a greater emphasis on direct access to the rational 'Truth' of the Holy Scriptures at the expense of institutionalized or formal theological expertise.[77]

Hervieu-Leger notes that the plurality of answers that emerge in today's minority communities illustrate two main trends. 'On by one hand, it is a flexible, tolerant and fluid system of mutual faith validation, in which individuals authenticate for one another their common belonging to a faith lineage. On the other hand, it is a crystallization of small community systems of faith validation that offer to the religiously regenerated an absolute certainty: a body of truths ensured by perfect coherence in the behaviour of the group'.[78] Multiple studies conducted since the 1990s illustrated this dual phenomenon, particularly among the youth.[79] Farhad Khosrokhavar's analysis illustrates how the quest for social recognition leads young western Muslims to redefine the role that Islam can play for them in society. In this perspective, to become a 'real' Muslim is a way to boost their self-esteem and to acquire a clear social identity. Khosrokhavar suggests that religious integration takes place in different ways, depending on the socio-economic situation of the individuals.[80] He notes that there is an 'Islam of integration', endorsed by young lower-middle class Muslims, that enables them to support individual claims to equality by placating a clear communal identity. By contrast, those who are the most economically and socially excluded generate what he calls an 'Islam of exclusion', which turns their marginality into a religious requirement to separate themselves from the rest of a decadent western society. As in similarly positioned minorities, the dissolution of inherited cultural identities can directly lead to the re-formation of closed communal identities, and to the strengthening of ultra-conservative

---

[77] See Mandaville, *Transnational Muslim Politics*; Gary Bunt, *Islam in the Digital Age: E-Jihad, Online Fatwas and Cyber Islamic Environments* (London: Pluto Press, 2003).

[78] Hervieu-Léger, 'Islam and the Republic', pp. 216–7.

[79] See Leïla Babès, *L'islam positif: la religion des jeunes musulmans en France* (Paris: L'Atelier, 1997); Jocelyne Cesari, *Musulmans et républicains: les jeunes, l'islam et la France* (Paris: Complexe, 1997).

[80] Farhad Khosrokhavar, *L'islam des jeunes* (Paris: Flammarion, 1997).

trends that validate a very particular faith regimen. This is not a typical communitarian reflex in the sense that the community has to be reinvented first in order to provide protection for its members. In the last few years, it has been noted how some of the most successful movements in multicultural settings, like the Tablighi Jamaat, have facilitated such exclusionary values and practices in order to sustain a pure (or refuge) identity in the face of an overbearing modernity.[81]

This process of building exclusive identities and communities is heavily emphasised by Roy who estimates that many second-generation Muslim migrants in western settings go first through a process of 'deculturation', and then recast Islam as pure religion. Roy observes that in this 'neo-fundamentalist' trend, what matters most is the sacralization of the believer's life rather than the Islamization of society as a whole.[82] In his view, these new forms of religiosity are characterised more by reconstruction and break from the past than by references to a specific cultural tradition. This is to say that the 'deculturation' of Islam does not correspond to the transportation into western settings of a 'fundamentalist' Islamic culture (e.g. Wahhabism) that subsequently clashes with secular modernity. For Roy, 'neo-fundamentalists do not articulate an antimodernist reaction from among traditional sectors of society. They are actors of deculturation and change inside traditional societies'.[83] This transformation implies that the various multiculturalist models trying to accommodate traditional cultural and religious preferences are effectively inadequate. Roy concludes that since their premise is that religion is embedded into culture, 'the model of multiculturalism failed not because of the "multi" but because of the "culturalism".'[84] He directs this critique

---

[81] See Barbara Metcalf, 'New Medinas: The Tablighi Jama'at in America and Europe', in Metcalf, *Making Muslim Space*, pp. 110–27. The contributors to Metcalf's collection illustrate nonetheless, that this trend is only one among many in the Muslim diasporas. See also M.K. Masud (ed.), *Travellers in Faith: Studies of the Tablighi Jammat as a Transnational Islamic Movement for Faith Renewal* (Leiden: Brill, 2000).

[82] Roy, *Secularism Confronts Islam*.

[83] Roy, *Globalized Islam*, p. 262.

[84] In a nutshell, Roy argues that, 'immigration models have failed because they have been unable to acknowledge and deal with what is at the root of the present forms of religious revivalism: the disconnect between religion and culture'. Olivier Roy, 'Islam in the West or Western Islam? The disconnect of

at both French-style läcité systems aiming to assimilate the migrants and Anglo-American models enabling more communitarian forms of national integration.

This severe diagnosis of the flawed interaction between multicultural-ism and Islamism is not shared by all analysts, many of whom find such a reading of the religiosity of political Islam in western settings too rigid and unidirectional. They argue that there is a possibility that contempo-rary multiculturalism and identity politics could be modified to better take into account the religious foundations of 'groupness'. Ethno-nation-alist (or gendered) referents can be as loose—or strict—as religious ones; and if moderately effective policies could be devised for the former, why not for the latter. Even if 'neo-fundamentalist' or 'de-traditionalized' forms of Islamism develop well in multicultural settings, it does not imply that a dialogue with the secular liberal tradition and new forms of accommo-dation are impossible. The contemporary trends in the re-construction of religiosity indicate that the cultural tropes and traditional institutions that used to govern authority in Islamic settings are not likely to provide a solid politico-legal framework for most contemporary Muslim communi-ties. No longer are European states in a position where they can rely durably and effectively on Islamic religious leaders being imported from the Middle East, South Asia and so on, under the supervision of their state of origin. At the same time, the formation of new religious leaders through the educational institutions devised and vetted by European governments, has had very limited success thus far.[85] That old methods of religious institutionalization geared towards dialogue with state institu-tions should not work when different modes of religiosity are on the ascendancy, is not altogether surprising. Yet, these conceptual and practi-cal difficulties do not necessarily signify the end of multiculturalism as we know it—even if the cultural referents in the debates may have to be re-thought.

John Bowen deploys a notion of public reasoning, borrowed from Rawls, to emphasise 'generally accepted principles of fairness and equality that diverse groups in a country can agree upon, what [Rawls] calls the overlapping consensus. In a similar fashion, many legal analysts of Islam

---

religion and culture', *The Hedgehog Review* 8 (1–2) 2006, pp. 127–33, at pp. 128–9

[85] See Frégosi, *La formation des cadres religieux musulmans en France.*

in Europe, at normative moments in their writings, have drawn a line between those elements of Islamic law that do overlap with European norms, which themselves are taken as the standard, and those that do not, and therefore cannot be tolerated'.[86] In this context, the issue is less to define a recognizably liberal Islam then to articulate new forms of Islamism that would not be antithetical to it. Rawls' own attempts at integrating an abstract Muslim/Islamic polity ('Kazanistan') in the international system underpinned by his *Law of Peoples*, serve to illustrate that non-liberal polities could be 'reasonably' accommodated alongside liberal ones.[87] Undoubtedly, such an accommodation is more easily conceived in an international order composed of sovereign units, within which the entire gamut of democratic and liberal practices is not expected to be relevant for all in the same way. In a national context, the demands for the ideological convergence of Islamism and liberalism are unmistakably informed by a different kind of 'reasonableness', especially after 9/11. Yet, there remains the possibility of creating greater synergies between the two than what is currently being debated. Undoubtedly to date, there is a paucity of, and a need for, more in-depth studies exploring the potential for more institutionalised interactions between these discourses and practices in concrete institutional systems.[88]

---

[86] Bowen, 'Shari'a, state and social norms', p. 3

[87] Rawls, *The Law of Peoples*.

[88] See for example Andrew F. March, 'Islamic foundations for a social contract in non-Muslim liberal democracies', *American Political Science Review* 101 (2) 2007, pp. 235–52; 'Liberal citizenship and the search for an overlapping consensus: the case of Muslim minorities', *Philosophy & Public Affairs*, 34 (4) 2006, pp. 373–421; and from different angle, An-Naim, *Islam and the Secular State*.

7

ISLAMISM IN TERRORISM
AND SECURITY STUDIES

Signalling the boundaries of political Islam in security debates

Until the end of the Cold War, security studies formed a rather well structured field of expertise concerned primarily with military-centric constructions of the national interest. For better and for worse, this focus was somewhat lost in the post-Cold War context as wider notions of security were proposed that stretched this mainly 'realist' framework of analysis. Terrorism studies, by contrast, never were a very neatly defined disciplinary field, but the events of 9/11 helped to structure the priorities of the discipline. In the post-9/11 context, the wider literature on security met a reinvigorated scholarship on terrorism that had become a central consideration of the security debates in these new international circumstances. In analyses produced post-9/11, there is an intense focus on the specificities of 'radical Islam', which is deemed to be the main engine of contemporary international and domestic terrorist activities. The al-Qaeda organization and its spin-offs have been at the centre of this rapidly growing cottage industry. Beside a new contingent of self-proclaimed 'security experts', more seasoned terrorism scholars have contributed to the growing debate on the nature of so-called 'Islamic terrorism' or 'jihadi terrorism'. In those debates, there has been little detailed analysis of how the broader phenomenon of political Islam is developing, and at most analysts point to rather weak correlations. It is also noticeable that specialists of both Islamism and terrorism have been divided on issues of terminology. The myriad labels in use include: political Islam, radical

Islam, militant Islam, Islamic fundamentalism, Islamic extremism, Islam-ism, jihadism, salafist jihadism, jihadi terrorism among others. It is not uncommon for these terms to be used interchangeably depending on the context. This diversity reflects not only the multiple attributes that are thought to characterize political Islam, but also the difficulties of finding a suitable overarching concept.

These difficulties pre-date 9/11; they came to prominence in the 1980s in connection to the Iranian revolution and the rise of Hizbollah in Leba-non.[1] Since then, the various ways in which political Islam has been labelled and identified in security studies illustrate a continuing lack of conceptual development in these methodologies. The different defini-tional approaches are not merely about finding a coherent analytical posi-tion but also (and for some analysts primarily) an exercise in expediency. Security studies, and even more so terrorism studies, have a keen interest in demonstrating the policy relevance of their analyses. As such, defini-tional debates are tightly connected to the production of a set of policy recommendations; and therefore constrained by the need to underpin practical policy options. As noted earlier in the debate about international studies, security and terrorism perspectives on political Islam are clearly intended to be 'problem solving' approaches. They are therefore heavily dependent upon prevailing theoretical paradigms in other disciplines to make their case.

There is some agreement that the notion of international terrorism has been evolving and that in the so-called 'new terrorism' that prevails since the collapse of the Soviet Union (and even more so since 9/11), the reli-gious—and particularly 'Islamic'—dimension of violence has been notice-able. For many analysts, this evolution does not create a qualitatively different phenomenon, but they note that there are analytically important distinctions to make as one form of political violence takes precedence over earlier ones.[2] The issue of whether this difference is substantive or

---

[1] See Bruce Hoffman, "'Holy terror": The implications of terrorism motivated by a religious imperative', *Studies in Conflict & Terrorism* 18 (4) 1995, pp. 271–84; Magnus Ranstorp, 'Terrorism in the name of religion', *Journal of International Affairs* 50 (1) 1996, pp. 41–62.

[2] The significant difference is the proposition that standard political goals and negotiating practices applies less to religious actors whose goals, in this world and in the next, are more encompassing than that of nationalist actors. See for

analytical remains nonetheless a side issue in the face of pressing demands for concrete explanations of, and predictions about, the phenomenon. Regardless of how much emphasis one places on the 'newness' of these security dilemmas, it is noticeable that increasingly analysts have turned to Islamic specialists to understand better the key trends in the transformation of religious doctrines and practices. Particularly, there has been a proliferation of arguments linking contemporary security issues to the emergence of a revolutionary political ideology that emphasise 'Holy War' (military 'jihad') as the main engine of 'radical Islam'.[3] In some of the literature produced after 9/11 there is a heavy emphasis on how much political Islam (very loosely defined) creates completely new types of violence and security contexts.[4]

Three broad trends can be readily identified in this context. The first is a political science approach to the formation and internationalization of conflicts involving Muslim polities that is most commonly associated with international security scholarship. It explains how a particular socio-political context can lead to the emergence and entrenchment of political violence, which in these circumstances is framed by the discourses and practices of Islamism. The second perspective is that of behavioural psychology, which is usually associated with terrorism studies. It analyses how a specific socio-psychological context can lead to the emergence of

---

example David Rapoport, 'The four waves of modern terrorism', pp. 46–73, in A.K. Cronin and J.M. Ludes (eds.), *Attacking Terrorism: Elements of a Grand Strategy* (Washington DC: Georgetown University Press, 2004); Martha Crenshaw, '"New" versus "old" terrorism: a critical appraisal', pp. 25–37, in R. Coolsaet (ed.), *Jihadi Terrorism and the Radicalisation Challenge in Europe* (Aldershot: Ashgate, 2008).

[3] See Emmanuel Sivan, *Radical Islam: Medieval Theology and Modern Politics* (New Haven: Yale University Press, 1985); Quintan Wiktorowicz, 'A genealogy of radical Islam', *Studies in Conflict and Terrorism* 28 (2) 2005, pp. 75–97.

[4] Commonly, Islamism is seen to be merging modern concepts of revolutionary politics with the Salafist and Wahhabist traditions. It is perceived to emphasize armed jihad to overthrow postcolonial regimes and repel their western backers, as well as to impose an order based on the Islamic law (shari'a). For some typical security views see John C. Zimmerman, 'Sayyid Qutb's influence on the 11 September attacks', *Terrorism and Political Violence* 16 (2) 2004, pp. 222–54; David A. Charter, 'Something old, something new…? Al-Qaeda, jihadism, and fascism', *Terrorism and Political Violence* 19 (1) 2007, pp. 65–93.

violent individuals whose activities can be rationalized through references to a particular ideology, which may be Islamism. The final approach is more diffuse—it used to be linked to areas studies but its appeal has expanded in recent years—and it highlights the role of ideology (or theology) in political violence. This third trend introduces the notion of a 'viral' Islamist ideology that can radicalize otherwise docile polities, communities or individuals and is the main single cause and driver of the spread of Islamist violence worldwide.

Political causes of political Islam

This first corpus of literature focuses on the political antecedents to violence legitimized though political Islam. This starting point is generally favoured more by security studies than by terrorism studies, as it points directly to the issue of political bargaining and military action as the most adequate means of understanding and engaging with opposition. As such it requires only a limited input from Islamic or terrorism specialists, except when the logic of the conflict appears to be fundamentally at odds with experience. Proximate explanations of terrorism and political violence as 'rational choice' processes in situations of socio-economic and political tensions characterized by a lack of option between violent and non-violent protest, have been emphasised by many analysts.[5] Mohammed Hafez's *Why Muslims Rebel* strongly suggests that there is nothing particularly unique or significantly different in Islamic motivated or phrased insurgencies. More precisely, he indicates that Islamist activism can be analysed using the same theoretical tools that are being used for other forms of militant activism. Hafez concludes that 'Muslims' rebel when they are excluded from the political system and at the same time subjected to heavy repression by the powers that be. The conjunction of these two factors is presented as the key to understanding the political violence that ensues.[6]

---

[5] See for example Tariq Ali, *The Clash of Fundamentalisms: Crusades, Jihads and Modernity* (London: Verso, 2002); Jessica Stern, *Terror in the Name of God: Why Religious Militants Kill* (New York: HarperCollins, 2003).

[6] Mohammed M Hafez, *Why Muslims Rebel: Repression and Resistance in the Islamic World* (Boulder: Lynne Rienner Publishers, 2003). Hafez is developing in this context the much older behaviouralist argument set out in Ted Gurr's *Why Men Rebel* (Princeton: Princeton University Press. 1970).

Assessing the recent literature on the development of radical Islamism in Southeast Asia, Natasha Hamilton-Hart notes that 'global religious ideology dominates as the source of the problem in most terrorism studies, while the particularities of locality end up overriding global political conflicts in most politics-driven accounts'.[7] In contradistinction to the accounts focusing on local dynamics, there are analysts who argue for the uniqueness of the al-Qaeda phenomenon and the associated global 'War on Terror'. Empirically, these assessments face greater difficulties to explain the causal mechanisms of Islamist violence due to the paucity of reliable data available in relation to this 'new' global phenomenon. Unlike more mainstream conflict studies or international security approaches with a large body of historical evidence regarding the dynamics of violence, 'War on Terror' focused studies have to emphasize the present, and frame the past in light of the contemporary processes of radicalization. Whatever available data there may be, these have usually only been collected systematically post-9/11, and with the clear intention of establishing an argument about the emergence of a new form of international violence or threat. In some regional contexts, such as Southeast Asia, some analysts have had a reasonably clear agenda in building a narrative that presents the region as the 'second front' of the 'War on Terror', not least because it suited their primary field of expertise.[8] This tendency is also noticeable in the case of the republics of Central Asia and the Caucasus, as well as within Russia itself, where international jihadist movements have supposedly made progress in coopting local movements to the al-Qaeda cause.[9]

---

[7] Natasha Hamilton-Hart, 'Terrorism in Southeast Asia: expert analysis, myopia and fantasy', *The Pacific Review* 18 (3) 2005, pp. 303–25, at p. 320.

[8] See Amitav Acharya and Arabinda Acharya, 'The myth of the second front: localizing the 'War on Terror' in Southeast Asia', *Washington Quarterly* 30 (4) 2007, pp. 75–90; and compare for example, Zachary Abuza, *Militant Islam in Southeast Asia: Crucible of Terror* (Boulder: Lynne Rienner Publisher, 2003); Rohan Gunaratna, *Inside Al Qaeda: Global Network of Terror* (New York: Columbia University Press, 2002), particularly chapter four.

[9] See Anna Zelkina, 'Islam and security in the new states of Central Asia: how genuine is the Islamic threat?', *Religion, State & Society* 27 (3–4) 1999, pp. 355–72; Shirin Akiner, 'The politicisation of Islam in postsoviet Central Asia', *Religion, State & Society* 31 (2) 2003, pp. 97–122; and compare Gordon Hahn, *Russia's Islamic Threat* (New Haven: Yale University Press, 2007).

In these situations, the specificity of the 'Islamist terror network' explanation appears to be a fairly trivial component of the process of production of violence as well as one with a very changeable definitional basis. As Andrew Tan notes in the Southeast Asian context, the threat of 'terrorism' predates 9/11, as Islamist guerrilla groups have been working toward establishing a separate Islamic state, and actively confronting various regimes in the region in long-running insurgencies.[10] These local processes are also relevant to understand the leadership structure of the al-Qaeda network in the Afghan-Pakistani context. As Mariam Abou Zahab and Olivier Roy indicate, the local structure of the organization that we now know as al-Qaeda was interpenetrated by Islamist guerrilla organizations in Afghanistan and Pakistan with a long history of struggle for independence or autonomy.[11] These political explanations of violence always tell a tale of historically framed local grievances, struggle for socio-economic power, localized forms of repression and disempowerment, and the framing of local agendas in the production of political demands. All these aspects of the Islamist challenge undermine the relevance of the global religious dimension of these conflicts and question the relevance of an international security framework primarily defined in term of its global Islamist character.[12]

Some of the more sophisticated security experts endeavour to link up political and terrorism frameworks of analysis. In the Southeast Asia context, David Wright-Neville proposes such an integrated narrative by emphazising a notion of 'radicalization' that explains how ordinary military and political struggles produce an abnormal process of terror and violence that challenges the very basis of societal and political order. For

---

[10] Andrew Tan, 'Southeast Asia as the "second front" in the war against terrorism: evaluating the threat and responses', *Terrorism and Political Violence* 15 (2) 2003, pp. 112–38, at p. 112. See also John Gershman, 'Is Southeast Asia the second front?', *Foreign Affairs* 81(4) 2002, pp. 60–74.

[11] Mariam Abou Zahab and Olivier Roy, *Islamist Networks: The Afghan–Pakistan Connection* (London: Hurst & Co, 2004).

[12] It is nonetheless possible to present the local religious dimension either as a case of instrumental manipulation of the disenfranchised, as in Jessica Stern's account, or as a case of reframing the boundaries of the licit and illicit, as in Mark Juergensmeyer's narrative. Stern, *Terror in the Name of God*; Mark Juergensmeyer, *Terror in the Mind of God: The Global Rise of Religious Violence* (Berkeley: University of California Press, 2003).

Wright-Neville, 'terrorism is a tactic that appeals to individuals only after a prolonged period of alienation, marginalization and brutalization. It is the manner in which these characteristics collide with different psychological impulses which generates in some individuals the urge to murder for a political cause.'[13] This and many other accounts of how a 'terroristic abnormality' grows out of more traditional resistance movements, rely heavily on psychological notions of radicalization. These narratives rarely explain these notions in much detail, often assuming that commonsense will suffice, as this appears to be, on the face of it, a rather straight-forward process to envision. The 'common sense' approaches which support the 'global Islamist terror networks' explanation are commonly deployed in relation to 'hotbeds' of Islamism. Countless reports by security analysts on the evolution of Islamist terror networks in the Muslim world point toward some elusive socio-economic and political 'root causes' of radicalization and terrorism. Commonly, the growing influence of violent forms of Islamism is perceived to be buttressed by failures in governance and political development, as poor and disaffected communities look to Islamist networks for support and self-realization. The argument regarding the failures of the state institutions applies equally well to the case of secularized regimes (e.g. Syria) as it applies to those promoting their Islamic credentials (e.g. Saudi Arabia).[14]

The inquiries into the role of failing state institutions and, at the extreme of state failure, rose again to prominence in international security debates in the post-9/11 context. Then, state weaknesses rather than its military strength became a key problem for the international system.[15] In

---

[13] David Wright-Neville, 'Losing the democratic moment? Southeast Asia and the War on Terror', Working Paper no. 110, Global Terrorism Research Project, Asia Research Centre, Monash University, 2004, pp. 3–4; 'Dangerous dynamics: activists, militants and terrorists in Southeast Asia', *The Pacific Review* 17 (1) 2004, pp. 27–46.

[14] See Guy Sands-Pingot, *The Sources of Radical Islamic Conduct: Understanding and Neutralizing a Transnational Ideological Threat* (Ft. Belvoir; Defense Technical Information Center, 2003); Sherifa Zuhur, *Egypt: security, political, and Islamist challenges* (Carlisle: Strategic Studies Institute of the U.S. Army War College, 2007).

[15] See Robert I. Rotberg, 'Failed states in a world of terror', *Foreign Affairs* 81 (4) 2002, pp. 127–40; Stephen D. Krasner and Carlos Pascual, 'Addressing state failure', *Foreign Affairs* 84 (4) 2005, pp. 153–63.

particular, concerns regarding international terrorism have shifted from the fear of relatively strong states sponsoring terrorist organizations to that of relatively weak states unable to control the transnational activities of non-states actors. As Ray Takeyh and Nikolas Gvosdev have emphasized, 'today's terrorist does not need a strong state to provide funding and supplies. Rather, it seeks a weak state that cannot impede a group's freedom of action but which has the veneer of state sovereignty that prevents other, stronger states from taking effective counter-measures'.[16] Although Takeyh and Gvosdev note that 'these groups also seek to utilize "brown zones" in Western societies, whether specific neighborhoods or particular types of organizations, where state governments are reluctant to intervene', typically in that literature this aspect of partial failure in established western democracies is not deemed to be particularly relevant to the discussion.[17] The alternative to analyzing the structural failures of weak statehood has been to develop a political motivation approach. One consequence of this change in focus is that analysts of state-sponsored terrorism now concentrate on 'passive terrorism' that involves a range of permissive state attitudes toward actual or potential terrorist networks and/or their supporters.[18] Partial state failure—whether wilful or accidental—is deemed to be more significant than complete collapse.

In extreme cases of failure, the arguments regarding how socio-economic deprivation and political lawlessness increase the risks of terror networks taking root, lose their primacy in the face of other factors. Regional experts have repeatedly pointed out that a country like Somalia may not be an attractive base for al-Qaeda and other Islamist networks despite the seemingly fertile ground for violent activism, due to local political dynamics. For Ken Menkhaus:

the case of Somalia suggests that we may have been partially mistaken in our assumptions about the relationship between terrorism and collapsed states. In

[16] Ray Takeyh and Nikolas Gvosdev, 'Do terrorist networks need a home?', *Washington Quarterly* 25 (3) 2002, pp. 97–108, at p. 98.

[17] Takeyh and Gvosdev, 'Do terrorist networks need a home?', p. 98. For some considerations on these areas in western democracies see, Dan Bulley, '"Foreign" terror? London bombings, resistance and the failing state', *British Journal of Politics and International Relations* 10 (3) 2008, pp. 379–94.

[18] Daniel Byman, *Deadly Connections: States That Sponsor Terrorism* (Cambridge: Cambridge University Press, 2005); 'Passive sponsors of terrorism', *Survival*, 47 (4) 2005, pp. 117–44.

fact, transnational criminals and terrorists have found zones of complete state collapse like Somalia to be relatively inhospitable territory out of which to operate (...) Terrorist networks, like mafias, appear to flourish were states are governed badly, rather than not at all.[19]

Like Takeyh and Gvosdev, Menkhaus outlines how areas of complete collapse are more exposed to international counter-terrorist actions, as sovereignty matters less. In addition, he stresses that foreign operatives are less likely to blend into the population because of the general lack of foreigners living in those areas, and that the networks are also likely to fall victim to the chaos that surrounds them—including becoming a target for local factions or being betrayed for financial rewards. Such analyses dovetail nicely with observations regarding the situation of al-Qaeda during the first part of the 1990s, when Afghanistan was in the midst of a violent civil conflict and the network had to relocate elsewhere.[20]

As discussed earlier in the context of international studies, the security studies approach to the issue of 'failed' states is in itself quite problematic. In the footsteps of international relations approaches that emphasize overarching Westphalian-Weberian models of sovereignty, contemporary analyses focus more on what an ideal type of international security should be like than on the mechanisms of construction/deconstruction of political violence.[21] Yet, as Mark Duffield observes, 'there is a distinction between seeing conflict in terms of having causes that lead mechanically to forms of breakdown, as opposed to sites of innovation and reordering resulting in the creation of new types of legitimacy and authority'.[22] Security specialists tend to see the violence emanating from Islamist groups as univocally destructive and not part of a meaningful reorganization of

---

[19] Ken Menkhaus, 'Somalia: State collapse and the threat of terrorism', Adelphi Papers no. 364, London: International Institute for Strategic Studies, 2004, p. 71. See also Ken Menkhaus, 'Political Islam in Somalia', *Middle East Policy* 9 (1) 2002, pp. 109–23; 'Quasi-states, nation-building, and terrorist safe havens', *Journal of Conflict Studies* vol. 22 (2) 2003, pp. 7–23; 'Governance without government in Somalia: spoilers, state building, and the politics of coping', *International Security* 31 (3) 2006/07, pp. 74–106.

[20] See Zahab and Roy, *Islamist Networks*.

[21] See H. Bull and A. Watson (eds.) *The Expansion of International Society* (Oxford: Clarendon Press, 1984).

[22] Mark Duffield, *Global Governance and the New Wars: The Merging of Development and Security* (London: Zed Books, 2001), p. 6.

political order. At the margins, however, there is recognition, particularly by those analysts focusing on well-organized Islamists movements (having both military and social wings) that the ordering function of these movements in society is non-negligible.[23] Some sociological accounts, suggest that there can be an inter-generational stabilizing function; even in the case of extreme forms of violence like suicide bombing.[24] Such arguments from security specialists feed into a larger narrative proposed by social scientists, areas specialists and even development experts. The political strength of Islamist movements, including violent ones, is related to the failures of authoritarian regimes in the Muslim world and the propensity of the state to use violent techniques of governance in dealing with citizens. But while other scholars can content themselves with analyzing past trajectories of violence and pointing to the range of possible causes, terrorism and security analysts are engaged in a far more ambitious task. They seek to explain these processes prospectively and to identify not only likely roots but specific pathways into terrorism. On this issue, they part with analysts in other disciplines who do not primarily seek (or find) this type of direct causal relationship.[25]

From psychological to ideological explanations of political Islam

Psychological explanations of the involvement of Islamists in terrorism have been particularly fashionable in the post-9/11 context. In particular, pseudo-psychological narratives provide easy ammunition for media and

---

[23] See Augustus Richard Norton, *Hezbollah: A Short History* (Princeton: Princeton University Press, 2007).

[24] See Jean-Paul Azam, 'Suicide-bombing as inter-generational investment', *Public Choice* 122 (1–2) 2005.

[25] The issue of the relationship between socio-economic deprivation and terrorism is one common connection invoked, even though direct causation is difficult to prove except in the case of particular individual pathways. Nonetheless, these arguments are still used in policy formulation applied to the level of entire communities/countries. See for example Kim Cragin and Peter Chalk, *Terrorism and Development: Using Social and Economic Development to Inhibit a Resurgence of Terrorism* (Santa Monica: RAND, 2003); and compare Alan B. Krueger and Jitka Maleckova, 'Education, poverty, political violence and terrorism: is there a causal connection?', *Journal of Economic Perspectives* 17 (4) 2003, pp. 119–44.

policy accounts that present Islamist terror networks, particularly those involved in suicide operations, as a motley crew of insane and evil people.[26] As scholars specializing in the psychology of terrorism have indicated, however, the trajectories of the individuals that become involved in extreme violence, be it of the suicide variety or not, be it Islamist or not, show very few signs of pathological deviance.[27] (As for the 'evil' nature of the persons involved, again there appears to be very few if any distinctive characteristics prior to the actions that are considered to be 'evil'.) Yet, psychological and behavioural processes are clearly relevant and useful to problem solving approaches that dominate the security field. If 'insanity' can be understood and managed, then surely the processes underpinning the unprecedented growth (or perceived growth) of international violence by Islamist networks can equally be better understood. The psychological and behavioural approaches to Islamism used in security studies face nonetheless a difficult task in reconciling security inquiries about a specifically religious form of violence, and a scientific methodology that is not structured specifically, to make generic statements about the faith-dimension of a community—let alone to address one specific religious faith. Hence while religious studies specialists emphasize that the ideas of violent Islamic activists are undeniably constructed in a religious framework, they stress that the specificity of their religiousness, as opposed to other ideological or material factors, is difficult to pin down.[28] In addition, from a psychological approach to violence, it can well be that instead of providing new insights, the focus on religion becomes a hindrance if analysts take it for something mystical beyond rational analysis.[29]

Unsurprisingly, psychological-behaviouralist perspectives have been most usefully put to work when detailing the mechanisms through which specific frameworks of interpretation and of behaviour are produced in given social circumstances. Two initially popular types of narrative have focused on the individual's tendency to engage in Islamist violence and

---

[26] For a critique see Scott Atran, 'Mishandling suicide terrorism', *The Washington Quarterly* 27 (3) 2004, pp. 67–90.

[27] See for example John Horgan, *The Psychology of Terrorism* (London: Routledge, 2005).

[28] See Juergensmeyer, *Terror in the Mind of God*.

[29] See Horgan, *The Psychology of Terrorism*.

terrorism. The first accounts have centred on key leaders and ideologues in Islamist movements and detailed their organizational contribution to contemporary strategies of violence.[30] The second narratives are composed of micro-analyses of personal life stories that are used to develop a classification of factors leading to Islamist violence. In effect, the latter has become increasingly trivialized in the literature because, as Max Taylor and John Horgan point out, 'analyses of this form overemphasize the *inevitability* of particular circumstances, giving a false sense of predictability and inevitability'.[31] To overcome some of these difficulties, there has been in recent years a renewed focus on the role of group socialization into violent/terroristic behaviour. From this perspective, it is argued that the socialization of individuals within groups promoting specific worldviews and practices contributes to the strengthening of particular mechanisms of behaviour validation. Mark Sageman's *Understanding Terror Networks* makes a strong case for group dynamics at the expense of the individuals' personal characteristics in this account of the al-Qaeda phenomenon.[32] Admittedly the data that Sageman relies on to make his case—there are no direct interviews—as well as the fact that he investigates the behaviour of the upper echelons of the al-Qaeda network, may skew the conclusions in that direction. However, this framework highlights some network dynamics that are compatible with, and complementary to many studies of cost-benefits analyses organizations using political violence—be they Islamic-minded or otherwise.

In the case of Islamist actors, however, there is an additional emphasis placed on the role of religious indoctrination, which is deemed stronger than the ideological factors influencing other actors. Robert Pape notes that 'the small number of studies addressed explicitly to suicide terrorism tend to focus on the irrationality of the act of suicide from the perspective of the individual attacker. As a result, they focus on individual motives—either religious indoctrination (especially Islamic Fundamentalism) or psychological predispositions that might drive individual

---

[30] See for example Brynjar Lia, *Architect of Global Jihad: The Life of Al Qaeda Strategist Abu Mus'ab Al-Suri* (New York: Columbia University Press, 2008)

[31] Max Taylor and John Horgan, 'The psychological and behavioural bases of Islamic fundamentalism', *Terrorism and Political Violence* 13 (4) 2001, pp. 37–71, at p. 52.

[32] Marc Sageman, *Understanding Terror Networks* (Philadelphia: University of Pennsylvania Press, 2004).

suicide bombers'.[33] Yet, Pape's study leads him to conclude that 'the data show that there is little connection between suicide terrorism and Islamic fundamentalism'; a conclusion endorsed by other leading analysts in this field.[34] Although these studies indicate that the rationale behind the choice of suicide terrorism has much to do with cost-benefit analyses by groups engaged in specific conflicts and that there is very little difference between Islamists and non-Islamist organizations, the emphasis on psychological deviance and religious indoctrination remains a commonplace in security narratives about Islamism.[35] The alleged specificity of the 'Islamist' case in this literature frames the argument that this religious character gives political violence a very specific tenor and shape. These views are well developed in some of the more sensationalist analyses in terrorism and security studies—as well as being fashionable in media and policy accounts. The sources of this Islamist exceptionalism are deemed to be multiple but some common themes are easily identifiable. Some argue that radical Islamists are able to mobilize supporters regardless of the odds by drawing on apocalyptic/millenarian interpretations of Islamic history. Others emphasize the fact that Islamism generates hatred of Jews and Christians and induces Muslims to view their relations with non-Muslims through the prism of a brutal and ongoing clash between their civilization and (western) barbarians.[36] On the more scholarly side of the

[33] Robert A. Pape, 'The strategic logic of suicide terrorism', *American Political Science Review* 97 (3) 2003, pp. 343–61, at p. 343.

[34] Robert A Pape, *Dying to Win: The Strategic Logic of Suicide Terrorism* (New York: Random House, 2005), p. 4. See also Mia Bloom, *Dying to Kill: The Allure of Suicide Terror* (New York: Columbia University Press, 2005); D. Gambetta (ed.), *Making Sense of Suicide Missions* (Oxford: Oxford University Press, 2005); Farhad Khosrokhavar, *Suicide Bombers: Allah's New Martyrs* (London: Pluto Press, 2005).

[35] For example, Jerrold Post et al. suggest on the basis of a limited numbers of interviews with imprisoned 'Middle Eastern terrorists' in the particular context of the Palestinian-Israeli conflict, and with limited direct evidence, that 'the type posing greatest danger are religious fundamentalist terrorists'. Jerrold M. Post, Ehud Sprinzak, and Laurita M. Denny, 'The terrorists in their own words: Interviews with thirty-five incarcerated Middle Eastern terrorists', *Terrorism and Political Violence* 15 (1) 2003, pp. 171–84, at p. 172.

[36] See for example the contributors to E. Brown, H. Fradkin and H. Haqqani (eds.), *Current Trends in Islamist Ideology, Vol. 1* (Washington: Hudson Institute,

analysis, from both security experts and specialists of religion, there is a more sophisticated debate about the role of religion in modifying some common cost-benefit criteria of political analysis. Bruce Hoffman suggests that 'the restraints on violence that are imposed on secular terrorists by their desire to appeal to a tacitly supportive or uncommitted constituency are not relevant to the religious terrorist'—and he remarks that Islamist groups are most noticeable in this respect.[37] Mark Juergensmayer also emphasizes how the transcendental aspect of religion is invoked in the most spectacular aspects of activist violence, while acts of 'religious terrorism' become devices for symbolic empowerment in conflicts that may not be winnable in this world.[38]

It is noticeable that those accounts insisting that there is something specific to Islamism in contemporary security dilemmas remain very unspecific when they detail the mechanisms of this ideology-induced violence. Analytically, they face difficulties in pinning down exactly what the 'threat' consists of and how to assess it—especially beyond references to the usual correlations regarding anti-western and anti-liberal views. Attitudes towards US foreign policy are one such symbolic indicator of whether an Islamist movement is 'moderate' or 'radical'. If movements are somewhat supportive or at least grudgingly quiescent, then they are perceived to be moderate and a stabilizing force. By contrast, if they voice their opposition to it then they are perceived to be antagonistic to the US and therefore directly or indirectly responsible for the climate of terrorist violence against the 'West'.[39] As recent studies of 'anti-americanism' indi-

---

2005); Raphael Israeli, Islamikaze: *Manifestations of Islamic Martyrology* (London: Routledge, 2003); Douglas J. MacDonald, *The New Totalitarians: Social Identities and Radical Islamist Political Grand Strategy*, (Carlisle: Strategic Studies Institute of the U.S. Army War College, 2007); David Cook, 'The recovery of radical Islam in the wake of the defeat of the Taliban', *Terrorism and Political Violence* 15 (1) 2003, pp. 31–56.

[37] Bruce Hoffman, *Inside Terrorism* (New York: Columbia University Press, 1998), p. 92.

[38] Juergensmeyer, *Terror in the Mind of God*.

[39] See François Burgat, *Islamism in the Shadow of al-Qaeda*, trans. P. Huntchison (Austin: University of Texas Press, 2008); Hamilton-Hart, 'Terrorism in Southeast Asia'; Jillian Schwedler, 'Islamic identity: myth, menace, or mobilizer?' *SAIS Review* 21 (2) 2001, pp. 1–17.

cate, this argument is deployed more forcefully today regarding the responses from the Muslim world than it is for those from other constituencies, even though the political rationale for these reactions is similar.[40] Regarding the contemporary Muslim world however, such western-centric discourses imply that there is more than mere disagreement regarding policy objectives. Scholars engaged in discourse analysis have shown on multiple occasions that the construction of an image of the United States or the 'West' analogous to that of the civilized world, ensures that it is easier to cast anyone disagreeing with US policies as someone opposing civilization and, therefore, as a pathologically deviant case.[41] Importantly, in the context of the debate over the liberal nature of western governance, what is being produced is a category of the 'radical Islamist' using loosely related criteria (views on social mores, women, justice, theology, etc.). The multiplication of these discourses ensure that large sections of the Muslim population can be described as threatening in some way because 'radical', quite independently of their actual political actions.[42] As Hakan Yavuz notes from a Turkish perspective, in such a context, 'any issue can be securitized if it is regarded as anti-secular'.[43] Such a trend is also increasingly noticeable in the behaviour of security agencies' dealings with Muslim diasporas in western democracies, as suddenly the danger posed by the citizens or residents appears to increase exponentially.[44]

[40] See Marc Lynch, 'Anti-Americanisms in the Arab world', pp. 196–225; John R. Bowen 'anti-Americanism as schemas and diacritics in France and Indonesia', pp. 227–50, both in P.J. Katzenstein and R.O. Keohane (eds.), *Anti-Americanisms in World Politics* (Ithaca: Cornell University Press, 2006).

[41] See David *Campbell, Writing Security: United States Foreign Policy and the Politics of Identity* (Minneapolis: University of Minnesota Press, 1992).

[42] For a critical reading see Michael S. Kimmel, 'Globalization and its mal(e) contents: the gendered moral and political economy of terrorism', *International Sociology* 18 (3) 2003, pp. 603–20. For an illustration of this policy trend see Cheryl Benard, *Civil Democratic Islam: Partners, Resources, and Strategies* (Santa Monica: RAND, 2004)

[43] M. Hakan Yavuz, *Islamic Political Identity in Turkey* (New York: Oxford University Press, 2003), p. 245.

[44] See Robert S. *Leiken, Bearers of Global Jihad? Immigration and National Security after 9/11* (Washington: The Nixon Center, 2004).

Securitizing a viral Islamist ideology

Security narratives tend to emphasize how the growth of a radical Islamist discourse dramatically transforms the views and behaviour of previously moderate Muslims—a move that usually corresponds to a politization of what was previously private. Today, this argument is particularly developed in connection to Muslim diasporas where the issue of an understanding of the 'pathways to radicalization' is high on the political agenda.[45] The insights regarding how a specific socio-psychological context leads to the emergence of violent individuals whose activities are rationalized with references to an Islamist ideology produce a new type of explanation. This explanation describes a 'viral' Islamist ideology that radicalizes otherwise docile communities or individuals and causes the spread of political violence. This approach draws explicitly or implicitly on orientalist approaches to Islam insisting that the Scriptures are key to understanding Muslim behaviour throughout history.[46] In the contemporary context, it is the acquaintance with specific theological and political discourses that allows the analyst to understand and to some degree predict the behaviour of Muslims. Emanuel Sivan's works provide a useful reference point for this type of analysis. Sivan suggests that since the Islamic 'radicals' have achieved 'cultural hegemony' in the Muslim world and since all the remaining 'conservatives' will eventually be won over, ultimately 'jihadism' can be seen to underpin all contemporary forms of Islamism. For Sivan this hegemony explains the continuing vitality of Islamism, especially as many regimes in Muslim-majority countries have had to buy into this religious discourse to prop up their flagging claims to legitimacy. In those states, Sivan diagnoses, 'they infuse the school sys-

---

[45] See Quintan Wiktorowicz, *Radical Islam Rising: Muslim Extremism in the West*, (Lanham: Rowman & Littlefield, 2005). And compare Tahir Abbas (ed.), *Islamic Political Radicalism: A European Perspective* (Edinburgh: Edinburgh University Press, 2007). See also Alison Pargeter, 'North African immigrants in Europe and political violence', *Studies in Conflict and Terrorism* 29 (8) 2006, pp. 731–47; David J Kilcullen, 'Subversion and countersubversion in the campaign against terrorism in Europe', *Studies in Conflict and Terrorism* 30 (8) 2007, pp. 647–66.

[46] Since orientalist readings of history emphasise stasis rather than change, this argument is (partially) grounded on a reading of military jihad throughout history. For a useful historical contextualisation of this phenomenon see, David Cook, *Understanding Jihad* (Berkeley: University of California Press, 2005).

tem with heavy doses of Islamic contents so that many children thus educated are later amenable to accept the radicals' worldview, transmitted in what is for them a familiar discourse. Because schooling is predicated upon learning by rote (talqin), the young are conditioned to accept a dogmatic message with no sense of critical inquiry, just the mindset in which radicalism thrives'.[47]

This radical discourse is usually presented as a variant of the Wahhabi-Salafi tradition with a jihadi rationale at its core. On the political science side of the debate, there are some detailed analyses of how ideological variants of jihadism have come to the fore in conflict zones over time. This process has been well studied in the cases of polities of the Muslim world where insurrections grew in the context of resistance to an occupying foreign power. Yet, as the case of suicide operations in Chechnya illustrate, analysts still have difficulty in isolating the specific causal contribution of (neo)Wahhabi ideology in that case, in the organization of violence.[48] They note that pragmatic considerations regarding external financial and military resources often were crucial in ensuring the Chechen warlords' endorsement of 'Wahhabism' as their main ideology; which was then deployed to justify and legitimate political violence.[49] Similar trends (and grey areas) regarding the causal role of 'Wahhabi' ideology in shaping political violence and facilitating suicide attacks have also been noted in Iraq.[50] This 'Wahhabi-Salafi' phenomenon has also been observed

---

[47] Emmanuel Sivan, 'Why radical Muslims aren't taking over governments', *Middle East Review of International Affairs* 2 (2) 1998, pp. 9–16., at p. 12. See also Emmanuel Sivan 'The holy war tradition in Islam', *Orbis* 42 (2) 1998, pp. 171–94; 'The Clash within Islam', *Survival* 45 (1) 2003, pp. 25–44; *Radical Islam.*

[48] See Anne Speckhard, and Khapta Ahkmedova, 'The making of a martyr: Chechen suicide terrorism', *Studies in Conflict and Terrorism* 29 (5) 2006, pp. 429–92; Anne Nivat, 'The Black Widows: Chechen women join the fight for independence—and Allah', *Studies in Conflict and Terrorism* 28 (5) 2005, pp. 413–19.

[49] See Julie Wilhelmsen, 'Between a rock and a hard place: the Islamisation of the Chechen ceparatist movement', *Europe-Asia Studies*, 57 (1) 2005, pp. 35–59.

[50] See Mohammed M. Hafez, *Suicide Bombers in Iraq: The Strategy and Ideology of Martyrdom* (Washington: United States Institute of Peace Press, 2007); Ahmed Hashim, *Insurgency and Counter-insurgency in Iraq* (London: Hurst & Co., 2006).

in zones of latent conflict. In Lebanon, the historical factors that contributed to a climate of political violence in the country have deep and multiple roots, but recently violence took a more 'Salafist' slant when local and foreign jihadist leaders began to promote their views in Lebanese society.[51] The observation of such an evolution in a context of relative peace leads to more speculative debates about the reach and implications of the spread of Salafi/Wahhabi ideology.

Commonly it is argued that this radical message is spread in Muslims community primarily via Saudi-funded mosques and the *madrasa* schooling system, as well as the more ad hoc activities of various preachers and websites. In recent years, this argument has been made most forcefully in the case of Muslim communities that were previously deemed to have a 'moderate' or even 'liberal' set of Islamic practices. In the Southeast Asian case, analysts paint a picture of tolerant Muslim communities in vulnerable socio-economic circumstances slowly being radicalized by Wahhabi propaganda.[52] More than active terror networks they argue, it is this groundswell in radicalized views that constitute the real security threat in the region and beyond. As a once fashionable study of al-Qaeda argued, 'the real danger to Indonesia's long-term stability stems not from al-Qaeda—which only has a few cells in place—but from other Islamist parties and groups that continue to campaign aggressively for the enforcement of Islamic law—shariah. Many of these are directly and indirectly radicalizing Indonesian Muslims to support al-Qaeda's aims and objectives'.[53] In these contexts, analysts posit a simple linear progression from moderate to radical, from apolitical religiosity to violent activism, and from ideological fundamentalism to supporting terrorism. As Kumar Ramakrishna's account of Jemaah Islamiyah illustrates, the main driver behind this drift is ideological indoctrination supported by pathological

---

[51] See Bilal Y. Saab and Magnus. Ranstorp, 'Securing Lebanon from the threat of Salafist Jihadism' *Studies in Conflict and Terrorism* 30 (10) 2007, pp. 825–55.

[52] See for example Abuza, *Militant Islam in Southeast Asia*; Angel Rabasa, 'Political Islam in Southeast Asia: Moderates, Radicals and Terrorists', Adelphi Papers no. 358, London: International Institute for Strategic Studies, 2003; Wayne A Larsen, 'Beyond al Qaeda Islamic terror in Southeast Asia', Washington: Georgetown University, Institute for the Study of Diplomacy, 2005; Barry Desker, 'Islam and society in Southeast Asia after September 11', Working Paper no. 33, Singapore: Institute of Defence and Strategic Studies, 2002.

[53] Gunaratna, *Inside Al Qaeda*, p. 268.

rejection of modern life and obsession with the West.[54] Similar arguments are developed in other regional contexts, such as Central Asia or Europe, where movements ranging from the Tablighi Jamaat to Hizb-ut-Tahir are seen as potential Trojan horses for future violent Islamist networks.[55]

The mechanisms enabling a radical Islamist ideology to act as a catalyst for the recruitment and activation of violent activism are not often examined in much depth and assumed to be a matter of commonsense. Not only the complex (and at times contradictory) nature of the Islamist views is not taken into account, but also the dynamics of their political enactment are not well understood. Taylor and Horgan note that commonly there is a 'failure in analyses of the psychological effects of ideology to make a fundamental distinction between ideology as a *process* (structuring and influencing behaviour) and the content of *particular* ideologies'.[56] In the abovementioned cases, 'radical Islam', 'Wahhabism', 'Salafism' and any other term performing a similar function, are less an explanatory factor applied to specific circumstances than a cause *sui generi* of violence. This flippancy makes it difficult to obtain a meaningful behavioural explanation of how the exposure to militant ideology is connected to particular militant activities. These difficulties are particularly evident when arguments about the social learning of the acceptability of violence are used reversibly by the analysts. As Jeff Victoroff stresses, 'the social learning/cognitive restructuring model fails to explain why only a small minority among the hundreds of thousands of students educated for jihad in

---

[54] Kumar Ramakrishna, '"Constructing" the Jemaah Islamiyah terrorist: a preliminary enquiry', Working Paper no. 71, Singapore: Institute of Defence and Strategic Studies, 2004. And compare, for a more comprehensive and carefully constructed argument, Greg Barton, *Indonesia's Struggle: Jemaah Islamiyah and the Soul of Islam* (Sidney: University of New South Wales, 2005)

[55] Compare, on the securitarian side of the debate, Zeyno Baran, 'Fighting the war of ideas', *Foreign Affairs* 84 (6) 2005, pp. 68–78; and Jessica Stern, 'The protean enemy' *Foreign Affairs* 82 (4) 2003, pp. 27–40; with, on the critical side, Emmanuel Karagiannis and Clark McCauley, 'Hizb ut-Tahrir al-Islami: evaluating the Threat posed by a radical Islamic group that remains nonviolent', *Terrorism and Political Violence* 18 (2) 2006, pp. 315–34; and Yoginder Sikand, 'The Tablighi Jama'at and politics: a critical re-appraisal', *The Muslim World* 96 (1) 2006, pp. 175–95.

[56] Taylor and Horgan, 'The psychological and behavioural bases of islamic fundamentalism', p. 48.

madrasas, the millions exposed to extremist publications, and the tens of millions exposed to public glorification of terrorists have become terrorists. [...] while social learning probably helps animate the small minority who turns to political violence, this theory fails to explain why *these* particular individuals become terrorists.'[57] At best these narratives provide a post-hoc understanding of specific ideological trajectories and behavioural responses. They do not and cannot amount to a prospective model for explaining jihadist violence.

Ideology-based security narratives commonly lack the fine-grained tools of analysis that would enable them to differentiate between relevant (e.g. violent) and irrelevant (e.g. isolationist) modes of enactment of political Islam. Over-generalization regarding the impact of online propaganda, the role of madrasas, increased migration and so on, are commonly underpinned by orientalist readings of Islamism that present militant Salafism as the dominant discursive trend in the contemporary revival.[58] By seeing the roots of radical Islamism everywhere, some accounts contribute in themselves to creating dilemmas for policy making, as they imply that since the threat is nowhere in particular, it is potentially everywhere. Thus, there appear to be few manageable answers to the 'Threat', short of an exponential increase in the capabilities of security agencies and the securitization of most aspects of life. This exponential securitization has been particularly noticed and analyzed in the context of the possible violent radicalization of Muslim groups in liberal democracies. Security analysts commonly point to an overall rise in Islamic activism among these communities, which then provides the foundations for direct action by Islamists. The solution to this process of radicalization is therefore portrayed as a combination of tighter migratory policies, more pro-active governmental policies of integration and, crucially, a toughening up of the police action targeting any would be Islamist leader, as well their sites of radicalization (e.g. internet, mosques, prisons, and so on).[59] Unsurprisingly, there is a concomitant increase in

---

[57] Jeff Victoroff, 'The mind of the terrorist: a review and critique of psychological approaches', *Journal of Conflict Resolution* 49 (3) 2005, pp. 3–42, at p. 18.

[58] As analyses of the *madrasa* system point out, however, these accounts often make large and unwarranted generalizations about the role of Islamic education. See R.W. Hefner and M.Q. Zaman (eds.), *Schooling Islam: Modern Muslim Education* (Princeton: Princeton University Press, 2006).

[59] See for example, Thomas J. Donalds, *Radical Islam in Britain: Implications for*

the perception among Muslim communities that what is being waged is a war against all things Islamic, even the more anodyne as they can always become potential pathways to radicalization.[60]

This partial disconnection of the ideological contents from their social context has been criticized for mishandling the tension between the 'conservative' and 'radical' trends in contemporary Islamism. Recent analyses of the spread of Salafism indicate that, far from directly inciting radical violence and political activism, this world view could do just the opposite; with conservative trends promoting a withdrawal from political activism and a focus on individual betterment and the creation of pure social groupings.[61] Quintan Wiktorowicz stresses that:

among salafis, the most prevalent intramovement conflict is a debate about the use of violence as a tactic for religious transformation, and this debate has fragmented the salafist community into two major groupings. Jihadis, such as Bin

---

the war on terrorism (Carlisle: U.S. Army War College, 2007); Javier Jordan and Nicola Horsburgh, 'Mapping jihadist terrorism in Spain', *Studies in Conflict and Terrorism* 28 (3) 2005, pp. 169–91; Paul Gallis, Kristin Archick, Francis Miko, and Steven Woehrel, *Muslims in Europe: Integration Policies in Selected Countries*, Congressional Research Service Report, 18 November, 2005, Washington: Library of Congress.

[60] The tension between a securitarian logic and the political implications of securitization is palpable in connection to terrorism financing and the charity function of Islamic networks. As Matthew Levitt candidly notes, 'terrorist financing through charitable organizations is not unique to Islamic charities, per se, but the fact is that the majority of terrorist groups operating in the world today and targeting the United States are of the radical Islamic variety, and it therefore stands to reason that the majority of charitable organizations engaged in terrorist financing are Islamic organizations. Matthew A. Levitt, 'The political economy of Middle East terrorism', *Middle East Review of International Affairs* 6 (4) 2002, pp. 49–65, at p. 60. For further considerations of a similar nature, see J. Millard Burr, and Robert O. Collins, *Alms for Jihad: Charity and Terrorism in the Islamic World* (Cambridge: Cambridge University Press, 2006).

[61] See Quintan Wiktorowicz, 'Anatomy of the Salafi Movement', *Studies in Conflict & Terrorism* 29 (3) 2006, pp. 207–39; International Crisis Group, 'Indonesia backgrounder: why salafism and terrorism mostly don't mix' Asia Report no. 83, Brussels, September 2004; Samir Amghar, 'Salafism and radicalisation of young European Muslims', in S. Amghar, A. Boubekeur and M. Emerson

Laden, believe in waging a jihad against the United States (as well as Muslim governments viewed as "un-Islamic") [...]In contrast, reformist Salafis prioritize less violent tactics of reform such as preaching, publication, and lessons.[62]

In security approaches to political Islam, instead of viewing all groups connected with Salafism as so many 'conveyor belts' for terrorists, it could be possible to make a useful distinction between activist and isolationist expressions of this worldview.[63] This distinction would not only enable policy-makers and security agencies better to manage their resources, but it would also diminish the likelihood of pushing toward more radical positions those communities and organisations that feel persecuted for merely holding certain beliefs. For Wiktorowicz, this analytical distinction is mainly relevant for tactical purposes, as in relation to ideology his conclusions go in the same direction as those of Sivan. He stresses that 'the difference between the jihadi and the reformist factions of the transnational salafi movement is not due to a disagreement over whether jihad is needed but rather to a disagreement about appropriate timing for any struggle'.[64] This would tend to confirm the overarching negative impact for security of developments in Islamist ideology, understood as a core influence that drives and sustains the increase in contemporary forms of political violence. In terms of ideology, this assessment does not negate the evolution of Islamic scholarship in other directions, but it suggests a significant shift in the contemporary readings of the Islamic doctrine in the direction of jihadism. In particular, pointing to the evolution of jihadi thought in recent decades, Wiktorowicz argues that there has been an 'erosion of critical constraints used to limit warfare and violence in classical Islam'.[65] From this perspective, there is a causal connection between

---

(eds.), *European Islam: Challenges for Public Policy and Society*, Brussels: Centre For European Policy Studies, 2007, pp. 38–51.

[62] Quintan Wiktorowicz, 'The salafi movement: violence and the fragmentation of community', in M. Cooke and B.B. Lawrence (eds.), *Muslim Networks from Hajj to Hip Hop* (Chapel Hill: The University of North Carolina Press, 2005), pp. 208–34, at p. 215.

[63] In the case of Hizb-ut-Tahir, compare Baran, 'Fighting the war of ideas', with Karagiannis, and McCauley, 'Hizb ut-Tahrir al-Islami'.

[64] Wiktorowicz, 'The salafi movement', p. 231.

[65] Wiktorowicz, 'A genealogy of radical Islam', p. 75; see also Quintan Wiktorowicz, 'The new global threat: transnational salafis and jihad', *Middle East Policy* 8 (4) 2001, pp. 18–38.

the development of the discourse on apostasy (*takfir*) and the practice of military jihad, at home and abroad.

This type of assessment rests nonetheless largely on the assumption that these ideological factors are causes for action and not merely post-facto justifications. Other perspectives on jihadism have questioned the notion of a coherent ideological evolution and pointed to the rather haphazard development of jihadi rhetoric. Faisal Devji's study of al-Qaeda emphasizes the rather eclectic approach to ideological and theological sources of the al-Qaeda leadership; an approach induced by the heterogeneous ideological make up of the organization itself.[66] This issue of ideological direction is also placed in a different light by the literature on organized criminality. Particularly in relation to converts and to Muslims 'rediscovering' their faith, it is unclear how far jihadist ideology turns ordinary citizens into violent Islamists, and how far violence-minded individuals seek out a radical version of Islamism to justify their behaviour. Detailed studies of conflicts have also noted repeatedly that it is not uncommon for organized criminality to acquire a political role during times of civil violence, only to lose it again when the situation reverts to normal.[67] Regarding post-facto justification, many accounts of the 'War on Terror' grounded on discourse analysis have also indicated how the increased visibility of Islamic discourses about jihad is linked to the increased invocation in liberal discourses of the notion of 'just war' (which also contain explicitly and implicitly religious referents).[68] Alongside the

---

[66] Faisal Devji, *Landscapes of the Jihad: Militancy, Morality, Modernity* (London: Hurst & Co., 2005).

[67] See Loretta Napoleoni, *Modern Jihad: Tracing the Dollars Behind the Terror Networks* (London: Pluto Press, 2003); Thomas M. Sanderson, 'Transnational terror and organized crime: blurring the lines', *SAIS Review* 24 (1) 2004, pp. 49–61; Louise Shelley, 'The unholy trinity: transnational crime, corruption, and terrorism,' *Brown Journal of World Affairs* XI (2) 2005, pp. 101–11; Chester Oehme III, 'Terrorists, insurgents, and criminals—growing nexus?', *Studies in Conflict & Terrorism* 31 (1) 2008, pp. 80–93. For specific examples from the Algerian Islamist revolt see, Luis Martinez, *The Algerian Civil War, 1990–98,* trans. J. Derrick (London: Hurst & Co, 2000).

[68] See Bruce Lincoln, *Holy Terrors: Thinking About Religion After September 11,* 2nd ed. (Chicago: University of Chicago Press, 2006); Ali, *The Clash of Fundamentalisms*; Juergensmeyer, *Terror in the Mind of God.*

issue of distinguishing between correlation and causation—usually a moot point in policy discourses—there is a great difficulty in assessing the relevance of various ideological innovations. Security narratives, by their very nature tend to focus on the threatening aspects of Islamist discourse, not on its contribution to peace and order. Although security and terrorism experts may find relevant the views of some of the most violent military leaders of Islamist movements—e.g. Zarkawi in Iraq during the most intense periods of the inter-confessional conflict, or some of the leaders of the Algerian GIA in the closing stages of the civil conflict—even radical Islamist ideologues are not usually advocating a total war of annihilation. There is a risk in these debates of having 'the tail wagging the dog' as it were. As more critically-minded analysts readily point out, such explanations of a pernicious religious ideology underpinning the activities of terrorist networks are usually very specific in their choice of authors and texts. This criticism may be partly deflected by the argument that it is precisely the function of security accounts to concentrate on security threats. Yet, that accounts focusing primarily on security issues should become the dominant reading for a socio-political and religious phenomenon creates in its turn new security dilemmas.[69]

Ultimately it is far from clear how much the recent developments of jihadi ideology are in fact shaping the much larger Salafist debate regarding the issue of violence in politics. More holistic assessments of trends in contemporary Islamic thinking show that more liberal versions of Islam have also emerged concomitantly to the jihadist tendency.[70] These

---

[69] As Beck summarises, the terrorism threat means that: '(bad) intention replaces accident, active trust becomes active mistrust, the context of individual risk is replaced by the context of systemic risks, private insurance is (partly) replaced by state insurance, the power of definition of experts has been replaced by that of states and intelligence agencies; and the pluralization of expert rationalities has turned into the simplification of enemy images'. Ulrich Beck, 'The terrorist threat: world risk society revisited', *Theory, Culture & Society* 19 (4) 2002, pp. 39–55, at p. 45. See also Didier Bigo, 'Security, exception, ban and surveillance', in D. Lyon (ed.), *Theorizing Surveillance: The Panopticon and Beyond* (Cullompton: Willan Publishing, 2006), pp. 46–68; Jef Huysmans, 'Minding exceptions: the politics of insecurity and liberal democracy', *Contemporary Political Theory* 3 (3) 2004, pp. 321–41.

[70] See the perspectives presented in C. Kurzman (ed.), *Liberal Islam: A Source-Book* (New York: Oxford University Press, 1988). See also for a more contemporary

insights do not in themselves allow us to identify a clear direction for a general shift in political theology, let alone a clear causal relation for the implementation of practices in political Islam. Even when the focus remains on those contexts in which the actual endorsement of jihadi tactics is well documented, there are still serious difficulties in moving beyond either a political explanation or a collection of psychological profiles—and most commonly a combination of the two. In these situations, security and terrorism studies, especially those focusing on radicalization, usually frame their arguments as if they were dealing with 'why' questions when they are effectively dealing mostly with 'how' issues. Yet, in doing so, they contribute to the diffusion of putative answers to the 'why' of Islamist violence, thereby acting as self-fulfilling prophecies.

---

focus, O. Safi (ed.), *Progressive Muslims: On Justice, Gender and Pluralism* (Oxford: Oneworld, 2003).

8

ISLAMISM AND GLOBALIZATION

Locating political Islam in a globalized modernity

The discourse and debates on globalization can often be more confusing than those on Islamism, and to outline the connections between the two phenomena is by no means a straightforward matter. Both phenomena suffer from the same tendency to conflate and merge *explanan* and *explanandum*—i.e. what these processes explain, and what are they explained by. Commonly the roots of globalization are located in the diffusion of a western modernity organized by states through the international political and economic system. Globalization is also commonly presented as a circular process, whereby the resulting global phenomenon eventually gains a life of its own and causally influences the very roots of its emergence. In the recent literature, globalization—like Islamism—is presented fashionably as an *explanan* that enables us understand better the changing character of the world politics. Still, many of the perspectives proposed in this context resemble more a reification of specific issues than comprehensive explanations.[1] Alternatively, globalization can be likened to an 'empty signifier' whose meaning can extend in different directions, so long as it is posited in contradistinction to state-centric models of development. In all these perspectives, Islamism like other forms of religious revivalism is affected by globalization. Yet, religious specialists are keen to stress that even in the age of globalization, 'when it comes to religion,

---

[1] For a sharp critique of these trends in the globalization literature see, Justin Rosenberg, *The Follies of Globalisation Theory* (London: Verso, 2000).

there is no global rule'.[2] Although all religious traditions are being transformed by globalization, they are so in different ways as globalization is
not homogeneous. In relation to political Islam, probably the most relevant point to make is that globalization processes always require to be
articulated in (and are in turn influenced by) local social, political, and
cultural settings. Resistance to the dominant templates for global order
contribute to the formation of heterogeneity in the concrete formations
of globalization.[3] One of the sociological pioneers of globalization,
Roland Robertson, chose to rename this particular aspect of globalization
processes 'glocalization' in order to stress the tension between the homogeneous nature of these global trends and the heterogeneous character of
their local embodiments.[4] This rephrasing also distinguishes the globalization perspective from cosmopolitan views relying on the notion of
a global homogeneity underpinned by the normative construction of a
world community.[5]

From the perspective of western social sciences, two main approaches
to the processes of globalization are easily recognizable. Globalization
from an economic perspective refers to the increased economic opening
of national economies and intensification of international integration via
policies like privatization, trade liberalization, and financial deregulation—with the so-called 'Washington consensus' principles underpinning
this policy drive by international institutions. By contrast, globalization
from a cultural perspective is grounded on the importance of cultural flows
reshaping the parameters of the global, social and political debate. These
two trends are meshing into one another, not least when it comes to the
study of the Muslim world (or the 'Islamic world', as it is often loosely
identified in that literature). Some of the popular works on globalization

---

[2] José Casanova, 'Rethinking secularization: a global comparative perspective',
The Hedgehog Review 8 (1–2) 2006, pp. 7–22, at p. 17.

[3] For a useful overview of the main perspectives on globalization see, R. Robertson and J.A. Scholte (eds.) *Encyclopedia of Globalization* (London: Routledge,
2006).

[4] Roland Robertson, *Globalization: Social Theory and Global Culture* (London:
Sage, 1992).

[5] For considerations on this issue in the Middle Eastern context see, R. Meijer
(ed.), *Cosmopolitanism, Identity and Authenticity in the Middle East* (London:
RoutlegeCurzon, 2003).

and Muslim polities in the 1990s explicitly emphasized the connection between socio-economics and cultural politics. Benjamin Barber's *Jihad vs. McWorld* and Thomas Friedman's *The Lexus and the Olive Tree* are good representatives of this trend. In their well-publicized books they stressed that the Middle East was economically backward and culturally resistant to the kind of globalization promoted by western democracies, and constituted therefore an exceptional region of the world. Barber paints a colourful picture of local communitarian reflexes (tribalism) trying to oppose a hectic economic and cultural opening of the region to the rest of the world. Though not without problems, this process is one in which, according to Barber (western) globalization could and should eventually vanquish (Islamic) tribalization.[6] The work by Friedman runs along very similar lines, but while Barber views the democratic culture promoted by (good) globalization threatened as much from above by global consumerism as from below by identity-based reactions, Friedman places a heavier emphasis on local fundamentalist resistance. Considering the eventual long-term success of western-style democracy in the face of these local resistances, Friedman notes that globalization made in America can rely on its own version of Adam Smith's Hidden Hand, namely the 'hidden fist' of the US military.[7] The direct role played by the US in the region has been hotly debated in the literature on new (American) empires recently; but in the early 1990s it was still perceived to be relatively marginal to the shaping of this globalized order.[8] In many ways, these accounts correspond to a take on western-induced globalization that reflect traditional realist views of an international order centred on key military and economic powers, as discussed in chapter three.

These accounts of globalization portraying a progressive western political and economic tradition in which liberal democracy and free market capitalism go hand in hand for the benefit of all have already received their fair share of criticism in the academic and policy literature, as well as in the media. There are two political issues of importance that need to

---

[6] Benjamin R. Barber, *Jihad vs. McWorld: How Globalism and Tribalism are Re-Shaping the World* (New York: Ballantine, 1996).

[7] Thomas Friedman, *The Lexus and the Olive Tree: Understanding Globalization* (New York: Farrar, Strauss and Giroux, 1999), p. 373.

[8] See for example John G. Ikenberry, 'Illusions of empire: defining the new American order', *Foreign Affairs* 83 (2) 2004, pp. 144–54.

be stressed in connection to the contemporary positioning of Islamism in these debates. First, it is noticeable that the purported emancipatory dimensions of western-spurred globalization do not always apply in practice, mainly due to particular local and geopolitical factors (e.g. security, energy, etc.). Second, political and economic liberalization are not necessarily two sides of the same coin. As Hamed El-Said and Jane Harrigan highlight, there are several important caveats for economic globalization in Middle Eastern and North African settings.[9] One such caveat is that the flow of international finance is partly determined by geopolitical factors—i.e. regimes having a pro-western stance. Another is that the terms of these financial transactions have commonly resulted in a decline in state provision of social welfare and increased inequalities. Finally, this model of economic globalization has been challenged by Islamist groups that have moved in to fill the welfare gap created by the withdrawal of the state; a rollback that simultaneously strengthened the Islamists' hand and undermined the regimes' legitimacy.[10] This last aspect has been used by many analysts to explain the relatively weak integration in many globalization processes of the states of the Muslim world, particular in the Middle East, as local regimes only advance on this road with extreme caution and even reluctance. Clement Henry and Robert Springborg's detailed studies of general trends in the Middle East and North Africa emphasize how these socio-political dimensions of globalization underpin resistance to change at the state level.[11] The case of the Egyptian economic opening of the 1980s provides an illustration of how Islamic-minded actors can take advantage of the structural space afforded by the shrinking role of the state in society. As many area specialists noted, the impact of neo-liberal globalization modified the political opportunity structures in many Muslim-majority country in ways that enabled Isla-

[9] Hamed El-Said and Jane Harrigan, 'Globalization, international finance, and political Islam in the Arab world', *The Middle East Journal* 60 (3) 2006, pp. 444–67.

[10] For an illustration of how new statist developmental policies attempt to deal with this issue see, Sami Zemni and Koenraad Bogaert, 'Trade, security and neoliberal politics: whither Arab reform? Evidence from the Moroccan case', *The Journal of North African Studies* 14 (1) 2009, pp. 91–107.

[11] Clement Henry and Robert Springborg, *Globalization and the Politics of Development in the Middle East* (Cambridge: Cambridge University Press, 2001).

mist movements to better provide both a counter-discourse and welfare options to the population.[12] Although in many cases—such as the Egyptian 'opening'—the rolling back of the state was quickly followed by a security clampdown designed to curtail the activities of the Islamists, the more progressive and in-depth process of opening to global liberal markets in Turkey showed the potential for a reciprocal transformation of state and Islamist actors over a number of years.[13]

Regarding the socio-economic dimension of globalization, it is also noticeable that new forms of integration in the global economy increasingly bypass the model of the 'developmental state' that was posited as a first step towards integration in the global markets.[14] Regarding these new globalization trends in the African context, James Ferguson expand the scope of earlier arguments about the fragmented nature of the state to show that the piecemeal conditions of sovereignty in many states can also operate as an instrument of integration in global socio-economic networks.[15] He outlines how differently globalization is constructed discursively and practically in situation of patchwork sovereignty. For

[12] As Clark stresses, however, participation in the welfare structures of various Islamist movements does not necessarily entails adherence to the overall political discourse of the Islamists. Janine Clark, *Islam, Charity, and Activism: Middle-Class Networks and Social Welfare in Egypt, Jordan, and Yemen* (Bloomington: Indiana University Press, 2003).

[13] See Bjorn Olav Utvik, *The Pious Road to Development: Islamist Economics in Egypt* (London: Hurst & Co., 2006); Cihan Tugal, *Passive Revolution: Absorbing the Islamic Challenge to Capitalism* (Stanford: Stanford University Press, 2009). For a more global perspective see, Charles Tripp, *Islam and the Moral Economy: The Challenge of Capitalism* (Cambridge: Cambridge University Press, 2006).

[14] This process has been studied most usefully in recent years by scholars with a background in anthropology. In the case of Africa see, James Ferguson, *Global Shadows: Africa in the Neoliberal World Order* (Durham NC: Duke University Press, 2006). For a focus on Asia see, A. Ong and S.J. Collier (eds.), *Global Assemblages: Technology, Politics, and Ethics as Anthropological Problems* (Malden: Blackwell, 2005).

[15] Ferguson, *Global Shadows*. See also William Reno, 'How sovereignty matters: international markets and the political economy of local politics in weak states', in T. Callaghy, R. Kassimir and R. Latham (eds.), *Intervention and Transnationalism in Africa: Global-Local Networks of Powers* (Cambridge: Cambridge University Press, 2001).

Ferguson, while the state system provides a standard of legal recognition for these frameworks, on the ground, networks develop that facilitate socio-economic flows and avoid specific governmental nodes. Thus, security is privatized, economic development and in some case social and educational projects are devolved to transnational actors, thereby creating a patchwork of enclaves that have varied levels and dynamics of interaction with the global system. In a more Foucauldian vein, Aihwa Ong argues that these trends characterize 'sites that resulted from post-developmental strategies of reconfiguring space and reregulating populations and their flows'.[16] Rather than using the old imagery of a neoliberal capitalist order backed by military strength spreading gradually over the entire globe, she stresses how forms of 'graduated sovereignty' are emerging. For Ong, 'neoliberalism is conceptualized not as a fixed set of attributes with predetermined outcomes, but as a logic of governing that migrates and is selectively taken up in diverse political contexts'. In addition, she notes 'the restless nature of the neoliberal logic and its promiscuous capacity to become entangled with diverse assemblages, thereby crystallizing political conditions and solutions that confound liberal expectations'.[17] This process is not only taking place in relatively unstable African states but also in relatively well-policed countries, from Malaysia to the Gulf States.[18] Regarding socio-economic globalization, if there remain few serious defenders of a specifically Islamic economy today, there are valuable scholarly analyses of the growing Islamization of the financial system (e.g. Islamic banking) and of its associated moral economy.[19] More often than

---

[16] Aihwa Ong, *Neoliberalism as Exception: Mutations in Citizenship and Sovereignty* (Durham: Duke University Press, 2006), p. 91.

[17] Aihwa Ong, 'Neoliberalism as a mobile technology', *Transactions of the Institute of British Geographers* 32 (1) 2007, pp. 3–8, at pp. 3, 7.

[18] See the contributors to J.W. Fox, N. Mourtada-Sabbah and M. Al-Mutawa (eds.), *Globalization and the Gulf* (London: Routledge, 2006); Aihwa Ong, 'Graduated sovereignty in South East Asia', in J.X. Inda (ed.), *Anthropologies of Modernity: Foucault, Governmentality, and Life Politics* (Oxford: Blackwell Publishing, 2005), pp. 83–104.

[19] For a more economic focus see the contributors to C.M. Henry and R. Wilson (eds.), *The Politics of Islamic Finance* (Edinburgh: Edinburgh University Press, 2004). For a greater emphasis on the moral economy see, Ibrahim Warde, *Islamic Finance in the Global Economy* (Edinburgh: Edinburgh University Press, 2000); Tripp, *Islam and the Moral Economy*.

not such evolutions, especially when connected to Islamic movements have been presented by mainstream analyses of globalization as cases of deviance or regression. These negative assessments are feeding back into globalization accounts that portray Muslim societies in general and the Middle East in particular as providing a closed-minded, fundamentalism response to contemporary global transformations.[20]

The aforementioned studies into new forms of globalization provide additional support for what many critical assessments of mainstream globalization had long claimed. As Ahmed Akbar and Donnan Hasting indicate, the 'economic content of international contacts has thus been emphasized at the expense of the cultural flows that were obviously also taking place alongside the material exchanges'.[21] From this perspective, though economic globalization may facilitate the atomization of previously traditional social systems, the emergence and multiplication of global or transnational communication networks can also help cementing new identities.[22] In the Muslim context, many have emphasized the role played by the rise of the internet and satellite television on the re-formation of Islamic communities. Similarly, commenting on the 'al-Jazeera Effect', Marc Lynch suggested that 'the rise of a new kind of Arab public sphere in the second half of the 1990s, driven primarily though not exclusively by the emergence of satellite television stations such as al-Jazeera, provided a potent forum for Arabs and Muslims publicly to debate these questions'.[23] Jon Anderson also stressed the benefits of the new media for the articulation of plurality in Muslim societies, not least in relation to Islamism.[24] However, one should not overstate the impact of the media, since it remains tightly controlled by the state in most of the region. As

---

[20] For a useful critique see, Christopher D. Merrett, 'Understanding local responses to globalization: the production of geographical scale and political identity', *National Identities* 3 (1) 2001, pp. 69–87.

[21] Akbar S. Ahmed and Hastings Donnan, 'Islam in the age of postmodernity', in A.S. Akbar and H. Donnan (eds.), *Islam, Globalization, and Postmodernity* (London: Routledge, 1994), p. 3.

[22] See for example the contributors to M. Al-Rasheed (ed.), *Transnational Connections and the Arab Gulf* (London: Routledge, 2005).

[23] Marc Lynch, *Voices of the New Arab Public: Iraq, Al-Jazeera and Middle East Politics Today* (New York: Columbia University Press, 2006).

[24] Jon W. Anderson, 'New media, new publics: reconfiguring the public sphere of Islam', *Social Research* 70 (3) 2003, pp. 887–906.

Lynch recognized, 'for all its newfound prominence, the Arab public sphere remains almost completely detached from any formal political institution'.[25] Emma Murphy noted in particular that not uncommonly we witness the formation of vacuous public networks, particularly online, more concerned with global pretence that with acting up locally.[26]

For these authors, it is precisely the disconnection between the growing significance of this public sphere and the reform of political institutions that remains crucial and yet under-investigated in contemporary accounts of globalization in the Muslim world. Optimistically, Anderson suggests nonetheless that even if in the short term there emerges an anarchic diversity 'in the longer term, this diversity partly resolves against a background of increased access to the texts of Islam with two generations of mass public education, and in a still longer term against a background of elevating texts as sources over personal and official mediations of religion'.[27] It seems indeed credible to suggest, looking at the evolution of the newspaper ventures of Mohammed Abduh or Rashid Rida at the turn of the previous century to the current Internet globalization of neo-scripturalism, that these media have facilitated and sustained a shift in the organization of Islamic 'authorities' and 'legitimate knowledge'. As Hakan Yavuz indicates in the contemporary Turkish context, this transformation ensures that new debates operate in 'a discursive space outside the hegemony of both the state and the traditional hierarchy of Islam'.[28] These Islamic voices are then able to articulate counter-propositions regarding the form that globalization should take, both in cultural and in economic terms. There remain nonetheless tensions between the formation of new substantive discourses about the public good (*mashala*) in debates not controlled by authoritarian regimes or conservative religious authorities, and the mere proliferation of consumerist forms of Islamic activism, like the 'cool' or 'light' Islam of various television star preachers.[29]

---

[25] Lynch, *Voices of the New Arab Public*, p. 25.

[26] Emma C Murphy, 'Agency and space: the political impact of information technologies in the Gulf Arab states', *Third World Quarterly* 27 (6) 2006, pp. 1059–83.

[27] Anderson, 'New media, new publics', p. 902.

[28] M. Hakan Yavuz, *Islamic Political Identity in Turkey* (New York: Oxford University Press, 2003), p. 108.

[29] Compare the assessments of substantive changes contained in A. Salvatore and

According to Akbar and Hasting, there also remains an important tension between a postmodern form of cultural globalization characterized by 'noise, movement and speed' and conservative religious world views that emphasize 'quiet, balance, and discourage change'.[30] There are voices of Islamic modernity—even those who claim to be genuinely ancient voices, like the neoscripturalist trend—that may benefit disproportionately from the information overload created by the new media.[31] Movement and speed may facilitate the move from closed to open social relations, from communal interactions involving dense reciprocities to more impersonal and contractual associational relations. Yet, there are different ways of reconceiving and reconstructing social cohesion. As Bryan Turner suggests, 'the image of the world as a global system may be represented in terms of a global supermarket (open-associational space) or as a super-church (open-communal) or as a global village (closed-communal)'.[32] A good practical illustration of these alternatives is given by the complex global reconfigurations of Islamic teaching institutions, from traditional madrasas to new self-help evening schools set up to reintroduce a meaningful religious message into an educational field dominated by secular institutions.[33] Anderson suggests that the threat of

---

M. LeVine (eds.), *Religion, Social Practice, and Contested Hegemonies: Reconstructing the Public Sphere in Muslim Majority Societies* (Palgrave Macmillan, 2005), and in B. Gräf and J. Skovgaard-Petersen (eds.), The *Global Mufti: The Phenomenon of Yusuf al-Qaradawi* (New York: Columbia University Press, 2008); with that of their potential shallowness in Patrick Haenni, *L'islam de marché, l'autre révolution conservatrice* (Paris: Le Seuil, 2005). For a tentative synthesis see, Peter Mandaville, *Global Political Islam* (London: Routledge, 2007), chapter nine.

[30] Akbar and Donnan, 'Islam in the age of postmodernity', p. 13.

[31] In this context it may well be that, as Volpi and Turner suggest, 'too much information produces too little knowledge'. Frédéric Volpi and Bryan S. Turner, 'Making Islamic authority matter', *Theory, Culture and Society* 24 (2) 2007, pp. 1–20, at p. 13.

[32] Bryan S. Turner, *Orientalism, Postmodernism and Globalism* (London: Routledge, 1994), p. 80.

[33] See the contributions to R. W. Hefner and M. Q. Zaman (eds.), *Schooling Islam: The Culture and Politics of Modern Muslim Education* (Princeton: Princeton University Press, 2006).

anarchical development should be contained by the fact that in the in later stages of mediatization, this shared knowledge loses authorship as it gains readership.[34]

Positively, global cultural flows could thus be presented as a version of McLuhan's notion that the medium is the message; and the open nature of the new media contributes to produce a more open Islamic public sphere. If this expectation of incremental openness is detached from its liberal moorings, however, it is also possible to envision a non western-centric, non Enlightenment-centric new social sphere. For Tariq Ramadan, the very notion of 'Western Muslim' is based on the principle that 'the assertion of the Muslim universal is not achieved here through the negation of the Western universe, but rather through acknowledgment of plurality'.[35] In this context Ramadan insists that such a conceptual opening and practical dialogue implies remaining 'faithful to the Message of Islam'. This dialogic approach would imply discarding many of the current 'disciplinarian' rationales put forward by Islamic ideologues in the face of (alleged) wilful disobedience of Muslims to Islamic principles. As other scholars have also suggested, this opening would also imply a greater emphasis on the feasibility of implementing religious principles according to a historicized notion of the common good (*maslaha*).[36] These debates are not primarily about a classical 'East/West' divide in relation to the reconstruction of Islamic authority and normativity. It is not a matter of evaluating claims about whether the intellectual leadership and the new orthopraxis of the Muslim community will be shaped in European or Middle Eastern countries, as mentioned in chapter six. Rather, it is to note that this situation creates more than the two options which are commonly said to be available for the global reconfiguration of Islamic authority—i.e. either an increased hermeneutic engagement with other religious and political authorities, or a withdrawal into closed communities that use new technologies to selectively insulate their worldview

---

[34] Anderson, 'New media, new publics'.

[35] Tariq Ramadan, *Islam, the West, and the Challenges of Modernity* (Leicester: The Islamic Foundation, 2001), p. 76.

[36] See for example Muhammad Qasim Zaman, 'The ulama of contemporary Islam and their conceptions of the common good', in A. Salvatore and D.F. Eickelman (eds.), *Public Islam and the Common Good* (Leiden: Brill, 2004), pp. 129–56.

against westernization. This creates hybridity and creolization, and the possibility of a not-as-we-know-it liberal and Islamic modernity.[37]

A new global structure for the ummah?

One of the most common forms of inclusion of political Islam in debates and theories of globalization remains via an analysis of transnational Islamist networks of the al-Qaeda type. Arjun Appadurai assessed that in connection to Muslim communities, this trend illustrates nowadays what he calls the 'fear of small numbers'—in contradistinction to the fear of the masses that traditionally characterized the formation of modern nation-states. In this perspective, Muslims are not seen to be a global threat because they are involved in mass movements that can topple the state—they have failed to do so in most Muslim-majority countries for most of the twentieth century. Instead, they are seen as a global threat because they are a minority that can operate unnoticed in society and that can strike unexpectedly from within. Appadurai suggests that 'the history of Muslim minorities in the twenty-first century surely is the dominant tale of this kind of fearful symmetry between the fear of small numbers and the power of small numbers'.[38] These global challenges posed by political Islam appear credible not only because of their immediate visibility in security studies, but also because they neatly fit into the time-space compression narratives that underpin most contemporary globalization theories. One illustration is Ulrich Beck's post-9/11 rephrasing of his 'world-risk society' argument, in which Islamism is only mentioned in the context of global terrorism, and therefore reduced to the notion of 'jihadi terrorism' proposed by terrorism studies. Beck merely sees this phenomenon as another illustration of his argument about the uncontrollable effects of reflexive modernity that 'pushed us into a new

---

[37] See for example Salman Sayyid, 'Beyond Westphalia: nations and diasporas—the case of the Muslim *umma*', in B. Hesse (ed.), *Un/settled Multiculturalisms: Diasporas, Entanglements, Transruptions* (London: Zed Books, 2000), pp. 33–50; Armando Salvatore, 'The exit from a Westphalian framing of political space and the emergence of a transnational Islamic public', *Theory, Culture & Society* 24 (4) 2007, pp. 45–52.

[38] Arjun Appadurai, *Fear of Small Numbers: an Essay on the Geography of Anger* (Durham: Duke University Press, 2006), p. 113.

phase of globalization, the globalization of politics, the moulding of states into transnational cooperative networks. Once more, the rule has been confirmed that resistance to globalization only accelerates it'.[39] Beck's perspective on 'jihadi terrorism' is not based on new research insights but fits well into his earlier argument about the irony of reflexive modernity. He sees in the increased sophistication and dangerousness of these movements an illustration of his argument that 'science, the state and the military are becoming part of the problem they are supposed to solve'.[40] Thus instead of enlarging the western-centric scope of the risk society model by considering the case of global Islamism, this type of argument effectively reduces the relevance of political Islam to that of yet another violent by-product of modernity.[41]

The focus on al-Qaeda as a byword for the new global dynamics of political Islam is also that of Manuel Castells. In the revised edition of *The Power of Identity* he devotes much of his analysis of the Islamist phenomenon to that of this particular network, while other, larger trends across the Muslim world are quickly explained away by an argument about worsening patterns of socio-economic exclusion.[42] The activities of al-Qaeda, by contrast, are for Castells directly the product of the Information Age (and of its deficiencies), which enables and structures the conditions of possibility of global jihadist networks. It is these global jihadi organizations that mostly contribute in their turn to the rise of

---

[39] Ulrich Beck, 'The terrorist threat: world risk society revisited', *Theory, Culture and Society* 19 (4) 2002, pp. 39–55, at p. 46. See also *passim* Ulrich Beck, *World Risk Society* (Cambridge: Polity Press, 1998).

[40] Ulrich Beck, 'Living in the world risk society', *Economy and Society* 35 (3) 2006, pp. 329–45, at p. 338.

[41] This type of explanation tends to downplay the agency of these movements. However, specialists of political Islam have noted that there are clear indications of agent-led causality, particularly as Islamist ideologues recognized that drawing the United States into a conflict in the Muslim world would encourage mobilization and resistance. Gerges makes this point well in relation to the strategic evolution of al-Qaeda, and the shift in focus from the 'near enemy' to the 'far enemy'. Fawaz A. Gerges, *The Far Enemy: Why Jihad Went Global* (Cambridge: Cambridge University Press, 2005), p. 271.

[42] Manuel Castells, *The Power of Identity: The Information Age—Economy, Society and Culture vol. II*, 2nd edition (Oxford: Blackwell, 2004), at pp. 12–22.

what Castells calls the 'network state', thereby durably transforming the international order (in ways which are not too dissimilar to those highlighted by Beck). For Castells too, the very nature of the strengths of our network society ensures the resilience and growth of those radical organizations that have gained recognition using the tools and models of networking utilized in the most networked parts of the world.[43] These views are endorsed and reinforced by security specialists and even specialists of political Islam who suggest that particularly in 'western' contexts, the al-Qaeda network resembles more a virtual network than an actual organization. Olivier Roy also finds this situation indicative of the fact such movements are 'perfectly adapted to a basic dimension of contemporary globalization: that of turning human behaviour into codes, and patterns of consumption and communication, delinked from any specific culture'.[44] For these scholars, such developments in political Islam indicate that it is less an anti-modern religious phenomenon undermining western modernity than an embodiment of post-modern/reflexive modernity, which only appears to oppose the existing practices and institutions of modernity because it goes much further than them.

The spatio-temporal redistribution of risk and violence by terror networks may be the most postmodern aspect of this global reconfiguration of Islamism, but there is a danger of missing the wood for the tree if this is uncritically taken to be the paradigmatic form of Islamic globalism. Turner's earlier account of 'traditional' global fundamentalist responses provides a useful counterweight to these network narratives. In the early 1990s, he proposed that 'fundamentalism in both Islam and Christianity can [...] be analysed as a value-system which actually promoted modernization, because modernization was an attack on magical beliefs, local culture, traditionalism, and hedonism. Fundamentalism is therefore the cultural defence of modernity against postmodernity'.[45] Writing at the same period, Bikhu Parekh made a similar point when he noted that 'fundamentalism does, no doubt, revolt against parts of modernity, but it does so with modernist weapons, in a modernist spirit and in the interest of a

---

[43] Castells, *The Power of Identity*, at pp. 108–44.

[44] Olivier Roy, *Globalized Islam: The Search for a New Ummah* (London: Hurst & Co., 2004), p. 258. See also Gilles Kepel, *The War for Muslim Minds: Islam and the West*, trans. P. Ghazaleh (Cambridge: Belknap Press, 2004).

[45] Turner, *Orientalism, Postmodernism and Globalism*, p. 78.

modernist view of religion'.[46] The transformations affecting these modern Muslim communities have led to generic yet multiple reformulations of religiosity, from the more traditionalist trend illustrated by the Taliban to the more post-modern Islamists of al-Qaeda.[47] Perspectives emphasizing differently the role played by modern and post-modern forms of Islamic globalization estimate differently the causal relevance of each set of mechanisms that regulate social order in a globalized system. Unmistakably, those movements trying to have a direct impact on state power (e.g. the military activities of al-Qaeda) are more noticeable than those using more social forms of influence (e.g. the educational activities of the Fethullah Gülen's movement) or those advocating personal piety (e.g. the proselytism of the Tablighi Jamaat). Yet, the visibility of political activism is not in itself a sufficient factor to estimate the longer-term significance of different types of transnationalism and globalism in the modern ummah.[48]

One of the most sophisticated recent efforts at presenting an exhaustive account of the global dynamics of political Islam can be found in Roy's *Globalized Islam*. In this work, Roy revises the framework of analysis that he proposed in the 1990s with a view to downplay the role played by national-based revolutionary Islamist movements and to emphasize the role of democratic-inclined Islamic parties and above all of globalized 'neo-fundamentalists'. While his earlier work was mostly focusing on the domestic and international aspects of the state in the Muslim world, his latest effort is clearly placing the emphasis on the global and transnational dynamics of the formation of a 'new *ummah*' (as the subtitle of his book

---

[46] Bikhu Parekh, 'The concept of fundamentalism', in A. Shtromas (ed.), *The End of 'Isms'? Reflections on the Fate of Ideological Politics after Communisms Collapse* (Oxford: Blackwell, 1994), p. 116. See also for the parallel with a new 'protestant ethics', Ellis Goldberg, 'Smashing idols and the state: the Protestant ethic and Egyptian Sunni radicalism', *Comparative Studies in Society and History* 33 (1) 1991, pp. 3–35.

[47] See Charles Kurzman, 'Bin Laden and other thoroughly modern Muslims', *Contexts* 4 (1) 2002, pp. 13–20.

[48] Regarding these last two trends see, M.K. Masud (ed.), *Travellers in Faith: Studies of the Tablighi Jama'at as a Transnational Islamic Movement for Faith Renewal* (Leiden: Brill, 2000); M.H. Yavuz and J.L. Esposito (eds.), *Turkish Islam and the Secular State: The Gulen Movement* (Syracuse: Syracuse University Press, 2003).

indicates). Overall Roy's argument concerning the globalization of Islam and reconfiguration of the *ummah* uses the traditional tropes of globalization narratives regarding deterritorialization to undermine 'realist' accounts of international politics. Roy insists that 'there is no geostrategy of Islam because Islam is not a territorial factor. Instead of a land of Islam or of an Islamic community, there is simply a religion that disembodies itself painfully from the ghosts of the past; there are simply Muslims who are negotiating new identities by conflicting means, usually peacefully, sometimes violently'.[49] In that context, he suggests that 'international Islamic terrorism is a pathological consequence of the globalization of the Muslim world rather than a spillover of the Middle Eastern conflicts'.[50]

Although part of his analysis looks at the radical jihadist networks, Roy is careful not to make it the key component of his account, nor does he take it to be the central *explanan* for the contemporary transformation of the Muslim world. For him the engine of this global transformation is the rise to prominence of a neo-fundamentalist tendency, which, through its quest for an untainted universally applicable Islam, disconnects religion from its cultural context. In its turn, Roy argues, 'neo-fundamentalism contributes to the collapse (or the adaptation) of traditional societies and pave the way for other forms of westernization and globalization, including in the economic sphere'.[51] The strength of Roy's account is that it details the multiple mechanisms that enable a new community and identity to be inscribed in social norms and institutional frameworks. The weakness of his argument is the flipside of this strength. By focusing so much on the transformation of the Muslim community in the context of globalization, he leaves out a more general account of the modern/postmodern condition that influences all forms of contemporary social reconstruction. While Beck and Castells may be criticized for squeezing an analysis of political Islam into their pre-existing globalization narrative

---

[49] Roy, *Globalized Islam*, p. 340.

[50] Roy, *Globalized Islam*, p. 337. See also Olivier Roy, *The Politics of Chaos in the Middle East* (New York: Columbia University Press, 2008).

[51] Roy, *Globalized Islam*, p. 262. Yet, the current success of neo-fundamentalist thinking is also sewing the seeds of its future downfall, as Roy notes, in an argument reminiscent of Gellner's account of 'High Islam'. Ultimately, for Roy, creating 'an artificial social order that deliberately ignores the gap between explicit rules and practical conduct' is self-defeating since 'no human behaviour can be reduced to explicit norms'. Ibid, p. 267.

(via the portrayal of the al-Qaeda phenomenon, Roy's argument may be faulted for displaying the opposite tendency. It tends to overstate the collective agency of the 'neo-fundamentalists' as the driving force behind all the articulations of contemporary Islamism in global modernity.

What is concretely new in Islamic globalism?

At one level of analysis, globalization can be linked to various stages of the history of Muslim societies and rather than being viewed as an element of disruption, it can instead provide a sense of ideological unity and structural continuity. Historically, there is a strong tradition within Islam defining the factors of social cohesion throughout the *ummah*, in particular through the conception of the common good, as codified for example by the four canonical schools of Law (Maliki, Shafi, Hanbali, Hanafi).[52] Though globalization could be described in such an Islamic perspective, this viewpoint is commonly missing, or remains extremely underdeveloped in mainstream social science literature. Some of the most noticeable efforts at including an Islamic perspective on globalization hark back to the ambitious reworking of orientalist accounts by Marshall Hodgson in the 1970s.[53] Similar notions have been reinterpreted more recently by scholars in the so-called 'world history' literature. Due to their historical nature, these accounts unavoidably place much emphasis on the classical and early modern period of Islamic history in their presentation of Islamic identity as a proto-global communicative glue. They emphasize the ability of the Islamic community to absorb, rephrase, and spread ideas and practices that then became identified and identifiable as Islamic culture. From this perspective, in spite of methodological differences, it is possible to view the forces driving 'archaic globalization' in the medieval world primarily associated with Islam; while in early modern times during the age of 'proto-globalization', there was a tri-polar world, in which Islamic and East Asian empires were also serious contenders for global hegemony.[54] Yet, as historical sociology indicates, these Islamic civiliza-

---

[52] See John O. Voll, *Islam: Continuity and Change in the Modern World.* (Syracuse: Syracuse University Press, 1994); Armando Salvatore, *Islam and the Political Discourse of Modernity* (Reading: Ithaca, 1997).

[53] Marshall G.S. Hodgson, *The Venture of Islam; Conscience and History in a World Civilization,* (Chicago: University of Chicago Press, 1974).

[54] See Amira K. Bennison, 'Muslim universalism and Western globalization', in

tional constructs have now become objects of historical research rather than functioning political entities. Currently, Islamic globalization can no longer take the form of these earlier developments in which an Islamic modernity was created simply through the expansion of polities and societies that happened to be Muslim dominated.

In the modern period and particularly during the age of the European empires in the nineteenth century, these dynamics were transformed and gave way to a situation in which many Islamic scholars and political leaders argued that one had to modernize Islam in order to ensure its continuing relevance for Muslim states and societies.[55] This situation was again transformed in the second half on the twentieth century, when Islamists movements refocused their efforts in order to 'Islamize modernity' rather than to 'modernize Islam'. In particular, as Gilles Kepel notes, this new globalized attempt at re-Islamization was designed to cut off the connection between western-produced modern technology and the liberal and secular normativity that underpinned it.[56] Thus, the active endorsement of technologies that facilitate the formation of a global *ummah* is tied to a critique and/or rejection of the social and political order that these technologies currently empower. Turner characterizes this articulation of modern fundamentalism as 'a two-pronged movement to secure control within the global system and also to maintain a local regulation of the life-world'.[57] However, while social scientists contributing to the debate about globalization have easily assimilated in their argument the notion of modernization of Islam and the process of appropriation of technical expertise by Islamic groups, there is still little study and under-

---

A.G. Hopkins (ed.), *Globalization in World History* (New York: W.W. Norton, 2002), pp. 73–98; Richard M. Eaton, 'Islamic history as global history', pp. 1–36, and Janet Lippman Abu-Lughod, 'The world system in the thirteenth century: dead-end or precursor?', pp. 75–102, both in M. Adas (ed.), *Islamic and European Expansion; The Forging of a Global Order* (Philadelphia: Temple University Press, 1993).

[55] See Albert Hourani, *Arabic Thought in the Liberal Age 1798–1939* (Cambridge: Cambridge University Press, 1983).

[56] Gilles Kepel, *The Revenge of God: The Resurgence of Islam, Christianity and Judaism in the Modern World*, trans. A. Braley (University Park: Pennsylvania State University Press, 1994).

[57] Turner, *Orientalism, Postmodernism and Globalism*, p. 78.

standing of the social alternative presented as Islamized modernity. Only at the margins are scholars of transnationalism able to propose some novel insights into how these trends operate in, and shape the processes of globalization.[58]

As many scholars of transnationalism have long pointed out, in so far as one can identify a fairly well demarcated Islamic set of ideas and practices in various geographical regions of the globe, transnational networks of migration, pilgrimage and scholarly exchange have always been key to creating these communities.[59] The substantial global issues for Muslim communities have to do not only with the interaction between the 'Islamic' and the 'Western' world, but also with the internal reconstruction of an effective Islamic signifier in a globally changing social system. In the contemporary debates, scholars examining the multiple dimensions of 'south-south' globalization usefully highlight the mechanisms that ensure the continuing relevance (or disruption) of globalized networks set up and developed between Muslim communities.[60] Mona Abaza's account of the interaction between the Middle East and South East Asia is helpful to create a more complex narrative on contemporary forms of globalization. In particular, it helps dissipate misplaced assumptions about a power-laden North-South mode of globalization being potentially replaced by a more interactive form of South-South globalism.[61] Abaza shows how the attempts at replacing 'western' by 'Islamic' globalization are also characterized by power-laden hierarchies in cultural and economic exchanges between various parts of the Muslim world—in this

---

[58] See Peter Mandaville, *Transnational Muslim Politics: Reimagining the Umma* (London: Routledge 2003); Mona Abaza, *Debates on Islam and Knowledge in Malaysia and Egypt: Shifting Worlds* (London: Routledge, 2002).

[59] See for example D.F. Eickelman and J. Piscatori (eds.), *Muslim Travellers: Pilgrimage, Migration, and the Religious Imagination* (Berkeley: University of California Press, 1990); Richard W. Bulliet, *Islam: The View from the Edge* (New York: Columbia University Press, 1994); Robert R. Bianchi, *Guests of God: Pilgrimage and Politics in the Islamic World* (New York: Oxford University Press, 2004).

[60] See the contributors to J. Meuleman (ed.), *Islam in the Era of Globalization: Muslim Attitudes towards Modernity and Identity* (London: Routledge, 2002).

[61] Mona Abaza, 'More on the shifting worlds of Islam: the Middle East and Southeast Asia: a troubled relationship?', *The Muslim World* 97 (3) 2007, pp. 419–36; *Debates on Islam and Knowledge in Malaysia and Egypt.*

case from the 'core' regions of the Middle East to the Southeast Asian 'periphery'. In the South-South context, the same acceleration of the global interactions that are occurring in western types of globalization is also apparent. The Tablighi Jamaat is commonly mentioned as a powerful illustration of these trends in South-South (as well as South-North) globalization.[62] The relatively ancient (by modern standards) nature of this movement serves to illustrate that there is more to what Roy calls the neo-fundamentalist trend than a tactical adaptation to the failure of revolutionist Islamic movements. Certainly, because the Tablighi Jamaat remains focused on personal piety and does not espouse a political agenda, it can better operate in unsympathetic political environments. Their practices give nonetheless credence and substance on a global level to the kind of alternative social and ethical order that Mahmood or Ismail depicted at the local level in Egypt, as indicated in chapter four. Such movements give concreteness to the perception that it is possible to meet the needs and aspirations of ordinary Muslims even in the midst of western global modernity.

This South-South perspective is a useful way to approach the issue of where to locate political Islam in the overall process of globalization, as it avoids over-simplistic assumptions regarding the dominance of particular aspects of the phenomenon that are given greater visibility in western narratives. In this perspective, Islamic movements can be compared to anti-globalization movements that are not against the idea of globalization—after all Islam is a universal religion—but against the architecture of global relations that is currently proposed by the main international institutions. To achieve their goals, Islamic movements attempt to recreate an alternative public sphere and solidarity community that can challenge currently dominant (state-centric) notions of globalization.[63] Here, the social movement approaches to globalization dovetail with the cultural-based accounts mentioned earlier, as they stress that not only technologies carry culture across state boundaries but also people.[64] As critical studies of the anti-globalization phenomenon indicate vis-à-vis the notion of 'alter-globalization', not only do activists construct their role via global (material and ideological) markets and networks, but also they

---

[62] See Masud, *Travellers in Faith*.

[63] See Mandaville, *Transnational Muslim Politics*; Roy, *Globalized Islam*.

[64] See Akbar and Donnan, 'Islam in the age of postmodernity'.

consciously frame their protest and project their ideology onto a global stage in order to awaken and elicit a response from a globalized audience.[65] In this context the term 'anti-globalization' is misleading since they fight for an alternative globalization rather than no globalization.

Analysts approaching this issue from the angle of the world system literature propose that transnational Islamic activism can also be seen as a fairly ordinary representative of these antisystemic movements.[66] Paul Lubeck notes that Islamist networks too can be viewed as both a product of, and a reaction against neo-liberal models of globalization. He notes that by invoking the Islamic obligation to provide alms to the poor (*zakat*) they propose alternatives to structural-adjustment programs that are in their view 'usury-driven, foreign controlled and mired in a dependency that merely reproduce a corrupt, illegitimate, secular state'.[67] As noted earlier, from Egypt to Turkey, these Islamic-minded alternatives to the dominant views of global free-markets need not be revolutionary to gain momentum among the masses.[68] More detailed examinations indicate that in relation to key 'global themes' (poverty, women, rights, etc.) there is a genuine diversity of responses, not only in terms of the usual splits between the Islamic left and the conservatives but also between various intellectual currents within political Islam.[69] These convergences (as well as the divergences) between Islamic and alter-globalization movements,

---

[65] See Timothy Peace, 'L'impact de la "participation musulmane" sur le mouvement altermondialiste en Grande-Bretagne et en France', *Cultures & Conflits*, no. 70, 2008.

[66] See Paul M. Lubeck and Thomas E. Reifer, 'The politics of global Islam: U.S. hegemony, globalization and Islamist social movements', in T.E. Reifer (ed.), *Globalization, Hegemony, and Power: Antisystemic Movements and the Global System* (Boulder: Paradigm Publishers, 2004), pp. 162–80.

[67] Paul M. Lubeck, 'The Islamic revival: antinomies of Islamic movements under Globalization', in R. Cohen and S.M. Rai (eds.), *Global Social Movements* (New Brunswick: Athlone Press, 2000), pp. 146–64, at p. 161.

[68] See Utvik, *The Pious Road to Development*; Tuğal, *Passive Revolution*; Tripp, *Islam and the Moral Economy*.

[69] See Muhammad Khalid Masud, 'Muslim perspectives on global ethics', in W.M. Sullivan and W. Kymlicka (eds.), *The Globalization of Ethics: Religious and Secular Perspectives* (Cambridge: Cambridge University Press, 2007), pp. 93–116; Ahmad Shboul, 'Islam and globalization: Arab world perspectives', in V. Hooker and A. Saikal (eds.), *Islamic Perspectives on the New Millennium* (Singapore: Institute of Southeast Asian Studies, 2004).

which are only beginning to be analyzed in detail, provide much needed additional resources and frames of reference to position meaningfully political Islam in the debate about globalization, and to cut down to size the narratives based on transnational Islamist terror networks.

9

CONCLUSION

REFRAMING POLITICAL ISLAM

Back to a social anthropology of Islamism?

I started this book using perspectives and concepts most readily connected to the field of social anthropology. It is probably appropriate now
to return to these perspectives in order to begin to reframe what such
studies of political Islam are bringing to the debate, both conceptually
and empirically. Taking micro-political approaches and contextualizing
their findings in larger socio-historical frameworks provides new perspectives on what Saba Mahmood calls 'politics in unusual places'.[1] Both in
the core regions of the Muslim world and among Muslim minorities living on its edges, these perspectives contribute to an understanding of the
contemporary dynamics of what may be called politics-in-religion contexts, to draw a parallel with Joseph Migdal's state-in-society approach.
Moving past the rigid textual-based historicism of analyses influenced by
orientalism, these analyses emphasize the importance of phenomenology,
while being critical of the secularist bias of the social sciences frameworks. Yet, the greatest strength of these approaches, their focus on practices of the self is also their main weakness, particularly when it comes to
packaging these insights into a grander narrative that can be 'sold' to
policy makers. By challenging the assumptions and generalities that are
common among 'western' social science narratives about political Islam,

[1] Saba Mahmood, *Politics of Piety: The Islamic Revival and the Feminist Subject*
(Princeton: Princeton University Press, 2004).

197

they provide opportunities to move beyond the clichés and pseudo-dilemmas that currently characterize contemporary Muslim communities. Yet, by the same token, they face greater difficulties of reinsertion into the main disciplinary paradigms of other social sciences, as well as into the common perspectives of policy makers and the mass media.

Across the board, in asking how can the notion of political Islam be more or less usefully constructed, it is helpful first to stop trying to answer so many 'why' questions about political Islam. The chapters of this book have outlined how no one in particular is responsible for creating a particular set of 'truths' about Islamism. These are produced by a combination of incremental but unconnected efforts at capturing the essence of a phenomenon that remains at the margins of each disciplinary field and paradigm. In a Foucauldian vein, it could be said that social science narratives about 'political Islam' do not so much produce a knowledge of the subject as illustrate the epistemic power of various disciplines to shape the academic, policy and media framings of social phenomena. Importantly, a power/knowledge reading of current representations of political Islam does not imply that alternative readings, especially by 'indigenous' actors evade these dilemmas or necessarily provide more useful perspectives. It has not been the purpose of this book to examine the interconnections between different theological and ideological trends within the Islamic and Muslim intelligentsia regarding the nature and dynamics of political Islam. Clearly this is a field of investigation that deserves much more scrutiny. In particular, it seems obvious that these dynamics are not altogether well encapsulated by the numerous collections of writings from 'leading' Islamist thinkers that are now commonly translated and published on the subject. (Usually, the rationale for bringing specific thinkers and ideologues together remains very elusive, or polemical.) Nonetheless, even if such investigations might bring useful insights, their 'truth' status would be no different from the views from the western social sciences that were under scrutiny in this book.

Such a deflationary view of 'knowledge' is more usefully deployed at a practical level to understand a specific evolution of perceptions about political Islam. It contextualizes the reasons why analysts chose to defend or endorse specific positions in order to make their case regarding a phenomenon deemed to be happening 'out there', since their own disciplinary paradigms are seldom re-considered in the process. Developing further the more conceptual implications of a power/knowledge perspective to generate a self-standing post-modernist field of post-orientalism remains nonetheless problematic, as the abrasiveness of the argument can undermine the entire debate; thereby making it difficult to show policy relevance. Mapping out this plurality across and within disciplines constitutes a conceptually worthy exercise because it ensures that the dynamics of epistemic power—the power to name what 'is'—are not predictably monopolized by one set of views. This applies as much to the Islamic-led as to the politics-led dynamics of political Islam, even though this book mainly focused on the latter. From this perspective, meta-theoretical questions about the 'why' of politics that underpin the conditions of possibility of Islamism are clearly worth studying in more details. However, the more pragmatic focus of the book was on the politics of representations of political Islam according to pre-existing paradigms.

The present narrative began with an account of orientalist historiography, or more precisely a political sketch of the evolution of modern orientalist scholarship. In this discipline political Islam, as a subset of the 'Islam' category, has a recognized place near the centre of the explanatory paradigms of this field of expertise. This set of approaches, with its well rehearsed *explanan* and *explanandum*, with its specific claims to explain and understand Islam and Muslims, has at least readily identifiable paradigms that can be if not verified or falsified, at least shifted or subverted. As indicated in chapter two, the positioning of a 'master explanation' of everything Islamic so centrally in the discipline has ensured the enduring appeal of orientalist narratives about Islamism, as well as been the cause of its intellectual weakening and partial collapse in recent decades. Other disciplinary fields, regardless of the quantity and quality of their borrowings from orientalist narratives, do not face the same challenges regarding their 'raison d'etre'. In their case, the question becomes that of knowing what function Islamism performs in different disciplines, and how it is integrated in their own explanatory paradigms. These disciplines' relation to orientalism is nonetheless important to identify in order to map out accurately the opportunities and constraints they have in addressing the issue of political Islam. The strength of the orientalist position in its engagement with other social science disciplines rests squarely on the claim to know better the particularism of the oriental 'Other' and the Islamic subject. This claim to fame is particularly effective when an Islamic phenomenon appears to be an exception to what is otherwise the norm in processes described by various disciplinary paradigms.

These notions of 'norm' and 'exception' are important aspects of the explanation of political Islam in the social sciences today. The view that the exception can have more explanatory power than the norm is particularly relevant to the study of Islamism. It has also been made quite central to the analysis of the political, at least from Carl Schmitt onwards; with Georgio Abamgen's analysis of the state of exception being particularly relevant in relation to the post 9/11 situation.[2] It is because political Islam is presented as an exception to routine politics and religiosity that a specific *explanan* can be developed. Disciplines devise their own cohesive frameworks by connecting and prioritizing the multiple observations available about what is deemed to constitute Islamism. The problem remains that they are less concerned with explaining political Islam per se than with specifying what is normal and what is not in their disciplinary perspective. Peter Berger's identification of the aspects of political Islam that are deemed most consequential for sociology, as opposed to politics, is illustrative of this tension. Berger notes that:

to be sure, it is interesting to ask, for example, why and how militant Islam came to power in the Iranian revolution at a particular time. But the phenomenon as such, in this or that form, has always been around. It is the exception, not the norm, that invites critical scrutiny. In other words, sociologists of religion should pay less attention to Iranian mullahs, and more to Harvard professors and to ordinary people in London or Paris.[3]

Indirectly, Berger evokes an orientalist mindset by implying that after all, the behaviour of Shi'a clerics in the Islamic Republic of Iran is quite unexceptional, and not worthy of much sociological scrutiny. In this perspective, although this may be a politically challenging situation, the social processes that it brings to light are nothing 'new', and better insights could be obtained by understanding why 'ordinary', secularized individuals in the 'West' should be interested in Islam(ism).

This tension is indicative of at least two predicaments for any interdisciplinary approach to Islamism. First, it points to difficulties of prioritization between disciplines that are investigating political Islam for different purposes, as they have different sets of priorities and interests. In this

---

[2] Giorgio Agamben, *State of Exception*, trans. K. Attell (Chicago: University of Chicago Press, 2005).

[3] Peter L. Berger, 'Reflections on the sociology of religion today', *Sociology of Religion* 62 (4) 2001, pp. 443–54., at p. 446.

case, as critical analysts have noted, sociologists look at how religion structures routine communal and individual social practices, while political analysts concentrate their gaze on decision-making in state institutions and on the institutionalization of religious authorities.[4] These difficulties of harmonization between explanations are replicated across the board, in other disciplinary fields. Second, and more importantly, it shows how these disciplinary accounts construct political Islam as an 'unexceptional exception'—i.e. a phenomenon with a bounded exceptionalism. In some cases, as with socio-economic approaches to Islamist mobilization or rational-choice approaches to Islamist violence, analysts may be concerned primarily with explaining the 'Islamic' away. More commonly, however, political Islam is deemed to require specific explanations that account for its presence; but these explanations are bounded within each discipline and do not challenge other paradigmatic assumptions. Very much like those terrorism studies concerned with ideology, Islamist dynamics are presented as being somewhat insulated from the wider conceptual environment and as having implications only for those who fall under their remit. Multiple disciplinary approaches are used to peer into these dynamics, but whatever insights might be gained from the study of political Islam itself are hardly deemed to be relevant for the processes lying outside this domain of 'exception'. Even though they may be constructed differently in the six disciplinary fields evoked in the book, these two sets of predicaments appear to remain relatively constant.

Interlocking disciplines or misguided nominalism?

Orientalism positioned Islam centrally in its disciplinary field and engaged with other academic disciplines on the ground that it knew something about knowing the Orient and the Islamic world that no one else knew quite so well. At heart, these positions reflected the perspectives predating the linguistic turn in the philosophy of knowledge regarding the nature of Truth—in this case of the Truth of the Orient/Islam.[5] In

---

[4] See Maia Carter Hallward, 'Situating the "secular": negotiating the boundary between religion and politics' *International Political Sociology* 2 (1) 2008, pp. 1–16.

[5] See Richard Rorty, *Philosophy and the Mirror of Nature* (Princeton: Princeton University Press, 1979).

orientalism this foundational knowledge had to do with the fusion of historical and textual continuities, as well as the connection between the normative and the descriptive—i.e. it explains how Muslim society is constructed because of what is required by the Scriptures. From this perspective, the impact and rationale of political Islam in the contemporary societal context can be seen as an outcome of performative injunctions contained in the Scriptures, which are more or less well interpreted, and by a greater or lesser number of individuals. The causal mechanisms identified in these explanations operate primarily in one direction, from the text to the social world, from abstract/formal thinking to practice. In this way, the internal dynamics of the process of textual exegesis are one step removed from their social context and firmly located in the domain of moral or legal philosophy—fields that are said to be accessible only through a firm grasp of the natives' language. These characteristics of orientalist approaches to Islam ensure the ability of this scholarship to continuously produce some 'truths', or at least 'insights' about Islamism while at the same time being insulated from the debates and challenges from other disciplines.

In recent decades, it is precisely on these issues of the unidirectionality of change and the insulation of theology from society that post-orientalist critiques have challenged these orientalist interpretations and outlined more hermeneutic processes of practical reinvention of the Islamic tradition(s). These post-orientalist accounts have had nonetheless difficulties in disseminating their alternative explanations of political Islam, particularly since their analysis removed the sense of unavoidability and inalterability that characterized orientalist views. This difficulty is even more pronounced in accounts focusing on the micro-politics of Islamist practice, as they are further away from grand narratives about an Islamic civilization. Post-orientalist accounts presenting political Islam as a distinctively modern phenomenon in more familiar path-dependent frameworks have been more successful at linking up their insights with other disciplinary readings of the phenomenon. By emphasizing a direct link between Islamism and the politics of the state across the Muslim world, they avoided being perceived as dealing with obscure socio-political processes and conceptual worldviews. Yet, they obtained recognition this time at the cost of resurrecting some form of grand narrative regarding a specifically 'revolutionary' political Islam; a narrative that was then incorporated in a piecemeal fashion into other disciplines.

During much of the Cold War the dominant paradigms for the international politics of the Muslim world were primarily framed by (neo) realist and (neo)liberal institutionalist approaches that forced the religious dimension of international interactions out of mainstream explanations. International order in the second half of the twentieth century was primarily depicted in terms of state interactions, while 'civilizational' narratives only received attention at the margins of the discipline. International relations theory was comforted by the views propounded in international sociology that upheld a modernization-secularization thesis as the main *explanan* of social continuity and change. Tentatively after the Iranian revolution, more assertively after the collapse of the Soviet Union, and most vividly after 9/11 there have been events-induced attempts at reintroducing religious factors in international studies. Generally, however, the lingering influence of realist and orientalist narratives meant that religiously-phrased phenomena were made a dependent variable within state-centric explanatory frameworks. In this perspective, political Islam became mainly a strategy or tactic of the Iranian state, the Saudi state, and so on. However, the attempts at re-centring religion in IR indirectly received support from more central challenges to the neo-realist and neo-liberal paradigms mounted by constructivist scholars emphasizing the intersubjective construction of international understandings, actors and practices.

Constructivist challenges to traditional notions of national interest and perceptions of power relations induced analysts to better contextualize their utilization of dependent and independent variables. Still, religious norms, practices and organizations did not feature prominently in constructivist analyses which, due to their critical lineage, tended not to focus on this particular subset of normative behaviour. In this context, political Islam remained an under-theorized category because the causal mechanisms emphasized in international studies were still only partially able to frame a non state-centric religious *explanan*. Commonly today, political Islam is being 'naturalized' in analyses, as a phenomenon defined by the attempt to establish an Islamic state and to implement an Islamic legal system (shari'a). The debates on the evolution of international norms and international society that consider the politico-legal role of Islamism from this perspective have therefore retained a rather narrow focus. In these debates, the insights borrowed from comparative studies of religion and area studies hardly provide more open-ended frameworks of analysis than those of earlier orientalist narratives; even though they are better socially and politically grounded. Political Islam remains mostly static and reactive, and it is therefore not perceived to indicate a significant (non-western) rephrasing of international interactions. In its turn, this situation feeds a lack of theoretical interest in the political significance of the transnational evolution of Islamic thought and practice, except in relation to security issues.[6]

Importantly, in the last two decades, studies in the sociology of religion (as well as in development studies) have also laboriously but significantly moved away from the universalist positions of the secularization-modernization narratives. This transformation has been spurred by two kinds of reconsiderations. First, it has been detailed how the complex transformation of religiosity in western societies cannot be encapsulated by one overarching set of propositions regarding secularization and modernization. Second, it has become increasingly evident that generalizations about the developing world had been made on the basis of insufficient information—a paucity of data that ensured that analyses were unable to frame meaningfully the manifestations of secularization and modernization in those societies. Regarding Muslim-majority countries in particular, this induced a reassessment of the expectation that political and economic modernization would ensure a privatization of the role of Islam in the face of new forms of institutionalized legitimacy and of more individualistic modes of social interaction. The secularization-modernization debate became decidedly more sophisticated at the end of the Cold War and took a new turn with a growing interest in the notion of Islamic 'Reformation'. Though much attention has been paid to reformist thinkers and movements in the last twenty years, the notion of a unitary Reformation that would bring Muslim polities in line with 'western' views and practices regarding the separation of the religious and the secular (or the public in the private) has not shed as much light on the Islamist phenomena as some had hoped. The complexity and multiplicity of the reformist discourses (as opposed to a single Reformation) ensured that the insights obtained from such analyses remained quite modest.

In contemporary debates there is now a broad consensus that the expectation that the role played by a public religion would simply grind

---

[6] At the margins there are exceptions to this trend. See Peter Mandaville, *Transnational Muslim Politics: Reimagining the Umma* (London: Routledge 2001).

to a halt in the face of an increase in rational-scientific methods in politics and society, was over-sanguine from the start. At best empirical research can establish the institutional differentiation that is taking place; less as a result of a retreat of the religious than as the outcome of the expansion of the modern nation-state. The apparent 'politicization' of Islamic actors in response to this situation and the dynamics of their 'political' behaviour in relation to state politics became the object of much investigation by sociologists of religion and area specialists. The evolution of Islamism viewed in terms of revolutionary or party politics was used to explain the dynamics of political Islam in its entirety. Initially, far less attention was paid to the process of Islamization from below and far less energy was spent considering the viability of their non secular-based, non modernization-based efforts at social organization.[7] Only at the turn of this century did scholars genuinely take notice of the insights coming from studies of the micro-practices of Islamism. These micro-social approaches are at the polar opposite of the grand narratives generated by orientalism. They are also at odds with the narratives proposed by many post-orientalist scholars of Islamist political movements that dominate the study of Islamism today. Importantly, the debate now increasingly centres on the issue of whether new grassroots developments in Islamism represent a de facto retreat from the political sphere (as defined by western standards), or whether they constitute a continuation of Islamism by other means.

Democratization studies, as a relatively new field of expertise initially borrowed heavily from the abovementioned disciplines to frame the role of political Islam in the transformation of Muslim-majority polities. The historical perspectives on Islam deployed by orientalism as well as the sociological views on modernization and secularization influenced early positions regarding the trajectory of political development in these polities. In particular, they helped shaping, at least until the end of the Cold War, quite over-deterministic socio-economic and cultural narratives about the possibility of reconciling an immovable Islamic tradition with a modern liberal democratic institutional order. In this perspective, the aggressive modernization and secularization of these polities appeared to

---

[7] There are some exceptions to this trend. See Talal Asad, *Genealogies of Religion: Discipline and Reasons of Power in Christianity and Islam* (Baltimore: Johns Hopkins University Press, 1993).

be a 'natural' political pathway for a subsequent turn to democracy—a view that persisted after the Cold War in various civilizational narratives. In addition, the realist views borrowed from international studies regarding the role of state power and national interests in a conflict-ridden regional context contributed to reinforce these narratives of state domination of society. In such a context, while political Islam was initially a marginal factor in narratives concerned primarily with state capabilities and *realpolitik*, it was subsequently repositioned as a key *explanan* in the post-Cold War context; albeit only as a destabilizing influence. Critically, however, studies of democratization in Latin America and Eastern Europe brought new insights and perspectives into the debates about Muslim polities in the 1990s, particularly in relation to the role of civil society and civic activism.

Increased attention paid to civil society initially reinforced some orientalist views about political Islam, as the liberal trends that were on the rise in other polities did not appear with similar clarity in Muslim contexts. While civic activism was generally viewed positively, the Islamic dimension of civil society was perceived to be directly or indirectly contributing to the lack of 'progress' towards the models of electoral democracy that had emerged in other regions. Analyses borrowing from orientalist scholarship framed this predicament in the context of a culturalist or ideological tension between the essence of Islam and Democracy. More socio-economic minded and institutionalist perspectives avoided these essentialist assertions, but often at the expense of an actual explanation of political Islam as a dynamic phenomenon—rather than a by-product of other structural factors. In the last decade, the apparently growing impact of pro-democratic Islamist movements in the region led analysts to concentrate more on the mechanisms of social and political activism rather than on formal discourses and institutions. Many of these new studies of the evolution of Islamist democratic trends in pseudo-democratic or semi-authoritarian contexts focused on how Islamist parties contributed, alongside authoritarian regimes, to the formation of 'grey areas' of democracy. In those areas, some but not all of the basic principles of liberal democracies were implemented; and the expectation was that over time these hybrid regimes would fully conform to these norms. More promisingly, other analyses are beginning to bypass this liberal teleology and to document the demotic-based alternatives to these common democratic models. These studies focus primarily on movements promoting Islamization at grassroots level rather than on formal party politics. They propose new perspectives on democratization in relation to non liberal-based views of the institutionalization of popular decision-making processes. Both approaches note however that the dynamics of democratization face an unfavourable regional and international context shaped by the demands for stability of both local autocracies and international actors particularly after 9/11.

For 'western actors', the increased visibility of political Islam in debates about multiculturalism reflects the growing visibility of Muslims, as Muslims, in countries where they constitute a minority (and especially a new minority). The relative newness of this phenomenon ensures that the scholarship on political Islam informed by studies of multiculturalism remains quite distinct from the analyses proposed by area studies specialists in Muslim-majority countries. However, these new studies are well attuned to the evolution of the debates on race and gender, two driving forces in the study of multiculturalism. In this perspective, socio-economic disparities and the lack of recognition of formal rights have been identified as key inequality-generating factors that had to be redressed. The specificity of the religious dimension of community building has stimulated the debate further by encouraging a reconceptualization of the boundaries of a fair liberal democratic political system; as well as spurred anti-multiculturalist backlashes. As with the debate on democratization, the argument over what might constitute successful multicultural models and policies highlighted the need for governments and publics to look beyond the certainties of liberalism and established public-private distinctions. Yet, these suggestions have been received with much scepticism in policy circles, especially after 9/11. Conceptually, there remain important disagreements regarding the cohesiveness of the social groups that are identified by multicultural theorists. Practically, there is also uneasiness toward what are perceived to be dangerous concessions made to a community that does not appear to endorse the core values of liberal multiculturalism.

In those contexts, the boundaries and meanings of the 'Muslim community' have evolved rapidly, especially in western settings where there previously only existed limited Islamic repertoires and organization. This evolution has also been shaped by greater access to new media that linked these minorities to other Muslim diasporas and communities in the core regions of the Muslim world. More individualized and reconstructed forms of religious practice and of transmission of a common religious ethos became a crucial aspect of the situation. Despite the internal and external efforts at enshrining a unitary 'Muslim community', fragmentation and contradictions characterize the interactions between Islamism and multiculturalism. In this context, the attempts by secular states to establish institutional structures to manage the growth of political Islam have directly contributed to the recasting of power politics inside these communities. In policy terms, the institutionalization of Islamic leadership by western governments has itself produced specific dilemmas for multicultural interactions, especially as it framed the debate as a zero-sum game between organizations within each community, and between the communities themselves. In addition to these state-centric processes, the construction of a global discourse and practice of Islamism has had an important impact on these reconstituted Muslim communities. In their turn, these communities have themselves given a new impetus for the construction of new forms of political Islam. A central query in the debates regarding the development of the interaction between political Islam and multiculturalism is the direction that Islamism is taking in these new circumstances. There are disagreements between those who view such interactions as enabling critical and novel voices in the Islamist discourse, and those who estimate that they reinforce neo-fundamentalist and neo-scripturalist tendencies. These two perspectives in their turn inform the policy debates on the modification of the legal and political tools of liberal-democratic institutions to address new Islamic views and practices. Hence, the debate that oscillates between offering a greater flexibility of social contracts, and proposing a more forceful imposition of a national ethos in public life.

In the aforementioned debates, security remains a crucial policy consideration. Until the 1980s, political Islam was integrated in the broad field of security and terrorism studies via analyses of conflicts in which Islamist guerrilla movements were involved. As such, the specifically Islamic character of the violence produced by these movements was not analytically distinguished from that of other actors, both secular and religious. Both in the case of domestic insurrections and international struggles, the methodologies of conflict analyses based on rational choice and cost-benefit estimates subsumed Islamism under generic models of political rebellions. Only after the Iranian revolution did security studies began to address directly Islamism in relation to geopolitical calculations; whilst terrorism studies turned their attention to Iranian-inspired phenomena such as the rise of Hizbollah in Lebanon. This interest grew unabated in the 1990s, as in the post-Cold War context ethno-religious violence appeared to be spreading. At that time the repercussions of the successful Mujahidin fight against the Soviet Union in Afghanistan were becoming increasingly visible throughout the Muslim world. Typically, since the Iranian Revolution and the growth of suicide terrorism spearheaded by Hizbollah in the Middle East, many in terrorism studies have repeatedly suggested that there is a specifically 'Islamic' character to this violence. This religious violence is viewed as creating new challenges for the domestic and international systems; an argument that has been particularly fashionable in relation to the global threat associated with transnational Islamist terror networks after 9/11. Some of the earlier conflict studies perspectives have also been rearticulated in relation to the role played by weak states in the post-Cold War situation; states that (unwittingly) facilitate the operation of transnational non-state actors in the globalized economy of violence. More conspicuously after 9/11, there has been a growing emphasis placed on psychological and behavioural explanations of the violence generated by 'radical Islam'. Psychological approaches to violent activism across traditional national boundaries emphasized both the continuing rational-choice dimension of the phenomenon, as well as the importance of group socialization, be it political or informal via kin and social networking.

The quest for a grand narrative of the growth of Islamist violence has led many security specialists to pay attention to Islamist ideology as a main causal factor. In particular, drawing selectively from the Islamic and area studies literature, it has been suggested that behind the current spread of violence waged in the name of Islam is a specific evolution of the dogma and practice of Holy War (jihad). This narrative depicts the global diffusion of a mainly Wahhabi-Salafi interpretation of the Islamic Scriptures that is transforming the understanding and practices of Muslim communities worldwide. Although mapping out these doctrinal transformations has provided some new insights, the connection between these ideological trends and the evolution of political Islam throughout the Muslim world remains largely under-examined. The actual relevance of jihadist interpretations in the contemporary formation of political Islam is however far more difficult to estimate than security analyses may suggest since non-violent (and even liberal) doctrinal evolutions are occurring simultaneously. These transformations are also happening at a time when 'western' state actors are invoking preventative military and security options underpinned by arguments from 'just war' theory. Hence, the contemporary ideological landscape as a whole is moving towards more securitarian moral and practical philosophies of state and society. By extracting Islamism from the general context of securitization that has developed after 9/11, these security narratives ensure that political Islam appears only as abnormal and threatening for a national, international and societal system that remains taken for granted.

Similar 'taken for granted' processes are usually evoked in the globalization studies literature to portray the Muslim world as economically and politically lagging behind developments taking place on a global scale. In the closing decades of the twentieth century, globalization was mainly presented as a unidirectional process with communities in the core regions of the Muslim world being passive recipients of this western-led phenomenon. Only recently have studies began to detail the heterogeneity of the region and showing that in the Muslim context as well there are various levels of connectivity with globalized processes. Still, mainstream globalization literature commonly assessed the adaptations produced from an Islamic perspective negatively, as devious rearticulations of global processes by religious actors perceived to be 'fundamentalist' and isolationist. The non-isolationist stance of transnational Muslim constituencies has been nonetheless highlighted by analysts focusing on the media and cultural dimensions of these processes. From this perspective, the formation of more globalized Muslim and Islamic public spheres ensure that these communities are increasingly fine-tuning their social interactions to those of other communities worldwide. Positively, this is seen as a process undercutting the formation of closed-minded Islamist practices. More sceptical voices have nonetheless noted both the relative lack of impact of these new publics on the religious and political institutions prevailing in most Muslim-majority countries, as well as the ambiguity of this public sphere vis-à-vis more liberalized forms of Islamism. Unsurprisingly, the potential pitfalls of these processes of globalization in Muslim communities have been particularly emphasized by those analyses that have taken transnational networks of the al-Qaeda type to be the best illustration of Islamist globalization.

The inclusion of the transnational Islamist terror networks into pre-existing explanations of globalized modernity has been commonly used as a generic *explanan* in this literature for the emergence of an abnormal post-modernity in Islamic contexts. In this perspective, these networks provide a good illustration of the argument regarding the reflexivity of a modernity that is turning upon itself. However, not unlike what happened previously in the sociology of religion, these analyses commonly lack detailed examinations of these processes. They tend to present globalization primarily as a North-South phenomenon that can only produce reactions or subversions from the individuals and communities at the receiving end. Yet, the South-South dimension of globalization in Muslim communities has also changed dramatically since the early days of the formation of a proto-global ummah. These interactions between different parts of the Muslim world remain highly relevant today for the re-imagining and reorganization of a reasonably unified globalized ummah. New technologies and resources enable new forms of integration between communities, especially in relation to a global Islamic normativity. Beyond the spectaculars of al-Qaeda, it is clear that a powerful global wave of Islamization is taking place at the grassroots level, led by 'alter mondialist'-type Islamic movements. These movements that choose either not to engage with what is identified as the 'political' or that operate at the infra-political level provide the mass resources for a global reconfiguration of contemporary Muslim communities.

'So fascinating a chameleon as political Islam', or the non-future of Islamism

As James Piscatori's turn of phrase indicates, the Islamist phenomenon's ever-changing appearance is unmistakably part of the reason why it generates so much interest in contemporary social science debates.[8] Not only is political Islam apparently continuously changing but it is also evolving in ways that seem to defy prediction and at times even explanation. The arguments developed in this book showed that the puzzling nature of Islamism has much to do with the evolution of key debates in the social sciences. Not only is political Islam changing, but scholarly accounts of what is relevant and important to understand about Islamism are also reframed as disciplinary paradigms are revised. The slippery character of Islamism is therefore not only a function of what Islamists are doing and

---

[8] James P. Piscatori, 'Introduction', in J.P. Piscatori (ed.), *Islam in the Political Process* (Cambridge: Cambridge University Press, 1983), p. 2.

saying, but also a consequence of unreflective nominalism in many aca-demic, policy and media discourses that make the label 'political Islam' apply to different objects and processes. Hence to better frame contem-porary debates about Islamism it is crucial not only to observe Islamist activism in detail, but also to observe how the notion of political Islam is being pieced together in the western social sciences. Each of the chapters in this book mapped out the specificities of these constructions and inter-actions in several key disciplinary approaches. Overall, two tendencies remain dominant in all these cases. The first is that functional and/or instrumental notions underpin the positioning of the Islamist phenom-enon in explanations of both continuity and change. Political Islam is commonly viewed as a marginal phenomenon in contemporary social processes, and is used to support or invalidate aspects of the paradigms that structure each discipline, without generating a critique of these frameworks. This trend is evidently strongest in those approaches that position themselves in the 'problem solving' category in order to inform policy making. The second observation applying across the board concerns the legacies of orientalism, as a heritage that introduced a particular path-dependency in the analyses proposed by other disciplinary fields. Although orientalism itself is no longer a dynamic scholarly tradition, post-orientalist analyses of Muslim politics have yet to create the kind of narrative about Islamism that can meaningfully inform other disciplines without pre-determining the content of the explanation.

In all likelihood, there is not much future for 'political Islam' in western social sciences. There is no future in the sense that the notion of Islamism does not fit neatly within pre-existing disciplinary paradigms, nor does it advance them as a distinctive explanatory category.[9] In this respect, nominalism is misleading as it only wraps together ever-changing sets of Islamic practices without identifying which structuring principles of the phenomenon are shared between different disciplinary approaches. In the main, the function that orientalism performed to sustain this nominalism in relation to Islam can no longer be performed by post-orientalist nar-ratives about political Islam. Post-orientalist narratives do point to the

[9] I am using the notion of western social sciences as a placeholder for the domi-nant global scientific paradigm in the contemporary context in much the same way as Appadurai outlines this process of paradigm construction in Arjun Ap-padurai, 'Grassroots globalization and the research imagination', *Public Culture* 12 (1) 2000, pp. 1–19.

crucial and multifaceted agency of Islamist movements in re-shaping social and political practices, as well as normativity, in Muslim communities. We may not yet have an account that encapsulates the implications of this transformation as neatly as *The Protestant Ethic and the Spirit of Capitalism* did at the turn of the previous century, but they are clear indications that the significance of Islamism can be as far reaching at that of this earlier remodelling of views and practices. In these circumstances, and despite the extreme difficulty of doing so in the present international context, it is more likely that such a transformative narrative will be produced by the 'subaltern voices' that the post-colonial studies are so keen to stress than by mainstream western social sciences. That would be so, not because of any intrinsic truth that an indigenous account would hit upon, but because such a perspective would be less hindered by the dominant paradigms that currently block our view. How far such an account could then be noticed and taken up by mainstream social sciences remains to be seen. Thus far, the feedback loop in the social construction of Islamism has been mainly described in terms of the impact of social sciences observations regarding Muslims' observance of their faith and on the views that Muslim have of themselves. Clearly, as the research on multiculturalism probably indicates best, this unidirectionality cannot last forever.

Practice-induced reinterpretations of the mechanism of political Islam are bringing, in a piecemeal fashion, new insights into the construction of better explanatory frameworks. Such trends are beginning to be noticeable from studies of the formal influence of the shari'a in constitutionalism and finance, to investigations of the informal workings of Islamic pietist movements, and from social movement theory. Yet, for a new subject-centric view of Islamism to be integrated fully into pre-existing social science paradigms it is probably necessary that the old, non-reflective explanations of political Islam that are still lingering in these disciplinary fields, lose their appeal. Islamism as we know it, as it is framed in these disciplinary explanations, has to be put aside (at least temporarily) for political Islam to be framed more meaningfully and reflectively in terms of the 'norm' rather than the 'exception'. This implies that such analyses could be framed to make sense not only of Islamism as we know it but also of common western notions of the political and the religious.[10]

---

[10] See Talal Asad, *Formations of the Secular: Christianity, Islam, Modernity* (Stanford: Stanford University Press, 2003); Mahmood, *Politics of Piety*.

The recent debates on 'post-Islamism' are clearly addressing some of these issues, but thus far remain too focused on explaining Islamism back into western normality and normativity. Clearly, one cannot question everything at once. Yet, as the conditions of possibility of these 'post-Islamist' movements are beginning to be investigated, so too should the conditions of western post-modernity be detailed with the same dedication, and without prejudging that the latter necessarily frames the former. In this perspective, political Islam may not be merely indicative of the reframing of the relation between religion and politics in quaint Muslim communities it may be an 'ideal-type' for new forms of religion and politics in a globalized post-modernity. Whether it is so remains to be seen; but to be seen, it has to be considered first. And to be so considered, Islamism has to stop being seen as an exceptional Other against the backdrop of Western normality. Each disciplinary approach considered in this book has some way to go before making this type of reconsideration an everyday occurrence.

Political Islam and policy making

In the policy world, current stereotypes regarding political Islam are reinforced by a situation in which conflict in the Muslim world (Iraq, Afghanistan, Palestine, etc.) and the fear of al-Qaeda shape the policy makers' short-term perspectives. As Mahmood Mamdani evoked, this is a context propitious to binary distinctions—'good' versus 'bad' Islamists— that are made to correspond to specific foreign and domestic policy objectives.[11] Good Islamists are the ones willing to cooperate with the foreign military forces in Iraq or Afghanistan, bad Islamists are the others. Good Islamists are the ones who accept the framework for peace put forward by the Quartet in the Palestinian-Israeli conflict, bad Islamists are those who do not (even if they happen to receive a popular mandate in electoral contests). Such an instrumental categorization and instrumentalization of Islamist movements is evidently nothing new; the US support for the Mujahidin in Afghanistan in the 1980s is an older illustration of this trend.[12] However, as the longer-term implications of the Islamists' resist-

---

[11] Mahmood Mamdani, *Good Muslim, Bad Muslim* (New York: Three Leaves Press, 2004).

[12] See Fawaz A. Gerges, *America and Political Islam: Clash of Cultures or Clash of Interests?* (Cambridge: Cambridge University Press, 1999).

ance against the Soviet occupation indicated, such a tactical approach to Islamism can create more problems than it solves. Hence today, the inclusion of various Taliban groups in a pro-governmental coalition in order to increase support for the Afghan regime and ease the pressure on foreign military forces in the country has ill-defined long-term costs. In a different context, but with a similar rationale, the western-sanctioned 2006 Ethiopian intervention in Somalia against the Union of Islamic Courts, which was perceived to play a 'bad' Islamist role in the region, came with a higher than expected long-term cost not only for the Somali population but also for regional (maritime) security. In all those cases, short-term tactical considerations prevent the elaboration of policies seeking to address the substance of these problems and the prerequisites for a long-term solution.

The prioritization of short-term objectives in foreign policy has its pendant in security fixes for domestic politics. In this context, the securitization drive designed to contain an elusive al-Qaeda threat discount potential long-term negative consequences in order to make immediate political and security gains. Not only is there the much debated issue of potential erosion of civil liberties induced by the 'exceptional' measures devised to counter the activities of would-be al-Qaeda activists, but there is an equally serious communitarian reflex towards national stereotypes. The French policy of forbidding 'ostentatious' Islamic clothing in public schools, the various European debates about the Islamic veil and the creation of state-sponsored national Islamic councils are all indicative of governmental attempts to control the development of Islamism in the name of pre-defined national identities (to which Muslims should conform). When security issues are raised, old assumptions about the political loyalties of citizens, migrants and foreigners come once more to the fore and shape the policy debates about political Islam. These debates in their turn generate dissonance with practices and strategies developed in the context of a greater globalization of political, cultural and socio-economic interactions. Such attempts at putting Islamism back into boxes—an external threat that needs to be neutralized via collaboration with ruling autocrats in Muslim-majority countries; a domestic threat that needs to be contained via a mixture of repression and cooptation of religious leaders in the western Muslim communities—are driven by convenience and expediency rather than by a longer-term strategic vision.

The policy tendencies towards compartmentalizing political Islam in separate issues that can be dealt with independently of one another is underpinned and reinforced by the perspectives provide by the experts that are called upon to inform policy makers. As indicated in this book, various academic disciplines carve out their own version of political Islam from the mass of data available on Islamism, and describe the dynamics and the evolution of the phenomenon using their preferred analytical tools and paradigms. Policy makers are thus presented with a bounded explanation of Islamism that describes the phenomenon within the specific boundaries created by each discipline. It is then up to them to realize and fathom the possible implications and ramifications that particular manifestations of political Islam can have in other social and political domains; a task in which many policy analysts have failed to perform well in recent years. This failure to comprehend the ramifications of political Islam has evidently much to do with a reliance on simplistic narratives about Islamism—the parsimony of orientalist-inspired explanations being particularly appreciated by politicians and the media. After 9/11, it has also much to do with the rise of an all-encompassing security discourse that makes it easier to fall back on a traditional imagery of 'good' and 'bad', 'us' and 'them' than to explore the grey areas of social and political change create by a renewed globalization of Islamic religiosity.

What can be done today to improve policy assessments and responses to political Islam has become quite restricted, not least due to the developments that have taken place in the last decade. From terrorism studies to studies of multiculturalism, and from foreign policy analysis to democratization studies, we now have well established cottage industries dealing with Islamism. Each field of expertise proposes its own refined set of 'truths' and solutions about how to deal with political Islam; usually quite independently of what the others argue. In such a context, academic or policy attempts at producing a multidisciplinary perspective commonly amount to little more than bringing together established experts from each discipline in order to compile a catalogue of perspectives on political Islam, without querying much about the compatibility of these different views. As the present book sought to indicate, these different 'nuggets' of expertise are not additive. Collating multiple perspectives on Islamism does not mean necessarily having a better comprehension of the phenomenon as a whole. What may be sound policy recommendations regarding how best to ensure that a particular faction of the Taliban joins a progovernmental alliance in Afghanistan, or a particular chapter of the Tablighi Jamaat recognises the formal authority of a government-sponsored national Islamic council, have implications for political Islam that exceed the security or multicultural parameters of the analyses used to produce such recommendations. Policy making is evidently very concerned with ensuring that governments and administrations can win specific battles but, to continue with a military metaphor, one can win many battles and still lose the war. In the decade since 9/11, governmental policies have had some clear success in dealing with particular Islamist challenges; but these policies have also contributed to displace the problem, or to create a problem where there were none before—the rise of jihadism in Iraq is a good illustration of this point. Policy makers and policy analysts should be careful not to mistake the insights about Islamism provided by experts in specific fields for a comprehensive picture of political Islam. What is still thoroughly missing today from policy circles is a more integrated longer-term understanding of what political Islam is (and is not), of what it is likely to become (and what is wishful thinking). This book sought to outline the strengths and weaknesses of the contemporary expertise on Islamism, particularly in connection to their ability to link up with each other and to produce more accurate global accounts of the phenomenon. Ultimately, however, such a research direction remains tributary to the recognition by the policy community that what is now required to respond to the challenges as well as the opportunities presented by political Islam, is a more comprehensive and longer term approach to this phenomenon.

SELECTED BIBLIOGRAPHY

Ahmed, Akbar S., *Postmodernism and Islam: Predicament and Promise*, revised edition (London: Routledge, 2004).

—— and Hastings Donnan (eds.), *Islam, Globalization, and Postmodernity* (London: Routledge, 1994).

Al-Azmeh, Aziz, *Islams and Modernities* (London: Verso, 1993).

An-Naim, Abdullahi Ahmed, *Toward an Islamic Reformation: Civil Liberties, Human Rights, and International Law* (Syracuse: Syracuse University Press, 1990).

Arkoun, Mohammed, *Rethinking Islam: Common Questions, Uncommon Answers*, trans. R.D. Lee (Boulder: Westview Press, 1994).

Asad, Talal, *Genealogies of Religion: Discipline and Reasons of Power in Christianity and Islam* (Baltimore: Johns Hopkins University Press, 1993).

—— *Formations of the Secular: Christianity, Islam, Modernity* (Stanford: Stanford University Press, 2003).

Ayoob, Mohammed, *The Many Faces of Political Islam: Religion and Politics in the Muslim World* (Ann Arbor: The University of Michigan Press, 2007).

Ayubi, Nazih N., *Political Islam: Religion and Politics in the Arab World* (New York: Routledge, 1992).

Bayat, Assef, *Making Islam Democratic: Social Movements and the Post-Islamist Turn* (Stanford: Stanford University Press, 2007).

Bowen, John R., *Why the French Don't Like Headscarves: Islam, the State, and Public Space* (Princeton: Princeton University Press, 2007).

Browers, Michaelle, *Political Ideology in the Arab World: Accommodation and Transformation* (Cambridge: Cambridge University Press, 2009).

—— and Charles Kurzman (eds.), *An Islamic Reformation?* (Lanham: Lexington Books, 2004).

Burgat, François, *Islamism in the Shadow of al-Qaeda*, trans. P. Huntchison (Austin: University of Texas Press, 2008).

Cesari, Jocelyne, *When Islam and Democracy Meet: Muslims in Europe and in the United States* (New York: Palgrave, 2006).

219

Devji, Faisal, *Landscapes of the Jihad: Militancy, Morality, Modernity* (London: Hurst & Co., 2005).

Eickelman, Dale F. (ed.), *Russia's Muslim Frontiers: New Directions in Cross-cultural Analysis* (Indianapolis: Indiana University Press, 1993).

—— James Piscatori, *Muslim Politics* (Princeton: Princeton University Press, 1996).

—— and Jon W. Anderson (eds.), *New Media in the Muslim World: The Emerging Public Sphere* (Bloomington: Indiana University Press, 1999).

Esposito John L. and John O. Voll, *Islam and Democracy* (Oxford: Oxford University Press, 1996).

—— and François Burgat (eds.), *Modernising Islam: Religion in the Public Sphere in Europe and the Middle East* (London: Hurst, 2002).

Euben, Roxanne L., *Enemy within the Mirror: Islamic Fundamentalism and the Limits of Modern Rationalism: A Work of Comparative Political Theory* (Princeton: Princeton University Press, 1999).

Fuller, Graham, *The Future of Political Islam* (London: Palgrave Macmillan, 2003).

Geertz, Clifford, *Islam Observed: Religious Development in Morocco and. Indonesia* (Chicago: University of Chicago Press, 1968).

Gellner, Ernest, *Postmodernism, Reason and Religion* (London: Routledge, 1992).

Gerges, Fawaz A., *America and Political Islam: Clash of Cultures or Clash of Interests?* (Cambridge: Cambridge University Press, 1999).

Hafez Mohammed M., *Why Muslims Rebel: Repression and Resistance in the Islamic World* (Boulder: Lynne Rienner Publishers, 2003).

Halliday, Fred, *Islam and the Myth of Confrontation: Religion and Politics in the Middle East*, revised edition (London: I B Tauris, 2003).

Hefner, Robert W., *Civil Islam: Muslims and Democratization in Indonesia* (Princeton: Princeton University Press, 2000).

Ismail, Salwa, *Rethinking Islamist Politics: Culture, the State and Islamism* (London: I. B. Tauris, 2003).

—— *Political Life in Cairo's New Quarters: Encountering the Everyday State* (Minneapolis: University of Minnesota Press, 2006).

Kepel, Gilles, *The Revenge of God: The Resurgence of Islam, Christianity and Judaism in the Modern World*, trans. A. Braley (Pennsylvania State University Press, 1994).

—— *Jihad: The Trail of Political Islam*, trans. A. Roberts (London: I B Tauris, 2002).

Khosrokhavar, Farhad, *Suicide Bombers: Allah's New Martyrs* (London: Pluto Press, 2005).

Lockman, Zachary, *Contending Visions of the Middle East: The history and Politics of Orientalism* (Cambridge: Cambridge University Press, 2004).

Mahmood, Saba, *Politics of Piety: The Islamic Revival and the Feminist Subject* (Princeton: Princeton University Press, 2005).

Mamdani, Mahmood, *Good Muslim, Bad Muslim* (New York: Three Leaves Press, 2004).

Mandaville, Peter, *Transnational Muslim Politics: Reimagining the Umma* (London: Routledge, 2001).

Metcalf, Barbara (ed.), *Making Muslim Space in North America and Europe*, Berkeley (Berkeley: University of Berkeley Press, 1996).

Mitchell, Timothy, *Colonising Egypt* (Berkeley: University of California Press, 1991).

Modood, Tariq, *Multicultural Politics: Racism, Ethnicity and Muslims in Britain*, (Edinburgh: Edinburgh University Press, 2005).

Norton, Augustus Richard (ed.), *Civil Society in the Middle East* (Leiden: EJ Brill, 1995).

Ramadan, Tariq, *Western Muslims and the Future of Islam* (New York: Oxford University Press, 2003).

Roy, Olivier, *The Failure of Political Islam*, trans. C. Volk (Cambridge: Harvard University Press, 1996).

—— *Globalized Islam: The Search for a New Ummah* (London: Hurst & Co., 2004).

Sageman, Mark, *Understanding Terror Networks* (Philadelphia: University of Pennsylvania Press, 2004).

Said, Edward, *Orientalism: Western Conceptions of the Orient* (London: Penguin Classics, 2003).

Salvatore, Armando, *Islam and the Political Discourse of Modernity* (Reading: Ithaca Press, 1997).

—— and Dale F. Eickelman (eds.), *Public Islam and the Common Good* (Leiden: Brill, 2004).

Sayyid, Salman, *A Fundamental Fear: Eurocentrism and the Emergence of Islamism*, revised edition (London: Zed Books, 2003).

Thomas, Scott M., *The Global Resurgence of Religion and the Transformation of International Relations: the Struggle for the Soul of the Twenty-first Century* (London: Palgrave, 2005).

Tripp, Charles, *Islam and the Moral Economy: The Challenge of Capitalism* (Cambridge: Cambridge University Press, 2006).

Turner, Bryan S., *Orientalism, Postmodernism and Globalism* (London: Routledge, 1994).

Volpi, Frédéric, *Islam and Democracy: The Failure of Dialogue in Algeria* (London: Pluto Press, 2003).

White, Jenny, *Islamist Mobilization in Turkey: A Study in Vernacular Politics* (Seattle: University of Washington Press, 2002).

Wickham, Carrie Rosefsky, *Mobilizing Islam: Religion, Activism, and Political Change in Egypt* (New York: Columbia University Press, 2002).

Wiktorowicz, Quintan (ed.), *Islamic Activism: A Social Movement Theory Approach* (Bloomington: Indiana University Press, 2004).

Yavuz, M. Hakan, *Islamic Political Identity in Turkey* (New York: Oxford University Press, 2003).

Zubaida, Sami, *Islam, the People and the State: Political Ideas and Movements in the Middle East* (London: I. B. Tauris, 1993).

—— *Law and Power in the Islamic World* (London: I. B. Tauris, 2005).

INDEX